Maine at 200

An Anecdotal History Celebrating
Two Centuries of Statehood

TOM HUNTINGTON

Down East Books
Camden, Maine

Down East Books

Published by Down East Books
An imprint of Globe Pequot
Trade division of The Rowman & Littlefield Publishing Group, Inc.
4501 Forbes Blvd., Ste. 200
Lanham, MD 20706
www.rowman.com
www.downeastbooks.com

Distributed by NATIONAL BOOK NETWORK

British Library Cataloguing in Publication Information available

Library of Congress Cataloging-in-Publication Data available

ISBN 978-1-60893-716-5 (hardcover)
ISBN 978-1-60893-717-2 (e-book)

∞™ The paper used in this publication meets the minimum requirements of American National Standard for Information Sciences—Permanent of Paper for Printed Library Materials, ANSI/NISO Z39.48-1992.

Contents

CONTENTS

Introduction

As the saying goes, you get only one chance to celebrate your 200th birthday.

Come to think of it, maybe that's not a saying. But if it were, it would apply to the state of Maine, which entered the Union on March 15, 1820. That's not to say the area we now call Maine didn't exist before then. Its history, of course, stretches back much more than two centuries. Paleoindians inhabited the land at least 10,000 years before the first Europeans set foot on its rocky shores. At that time, an estimated 20,000 Native Americans lived in what is now Maine. They were known as the Wabanaki.

And then Europeans arrived. John Cabot, born in Italy as Giovanni Caboto and sailing under a commission from England's Henry VII, may have reached the Maine coast in 1497; Giovanni da Verrazano, an Italian sailing for France, definitely did in 1524. The arrival of these people from across the sea proved disastrous for the original inhabitants. They lacked resistance to the diseases the Europeans brought with them, which ended up wiping out at least 75 percent of the native populations. Then the chain of events echoed the history in North America generally—increasing encroachment by Europeans, heightening tensions, wars, treaties, broken treaties, more wars, more treaties and, eventually, near-total dominance by the European powers.

The Massachusetts Bay Colony had its eye on Maine and began to consolidate its control in the 1650s. In 1665 a British royal commission directed Massachusetts to leave Maine alone, but almost as soon as the last commissioner sailed back to England in 1668, Massachusetts declared its annexation of Maine. In 1677 the Bay Colony's General Court purchased the Maine land belonging to the Gorges family, which had earlier tried and failed to establish its own proprietary colony. Massachusetts's domain over Maine was legalized formally with a royal charter in 1691. Maine residents would remain Massholes for more than a century, until Maine became the nation's 23rd state.

Two centuries later, Maine remains unique. It's the only state in the Union with a single-syllable name, and the only one that borders just one other state. Maybe those facts have some bearing on Mainers' reputation for being taciturn and independent. We enjoy being by ourselves in our monosyllabic corner of the nation, with our only neighbor, three-syllable New Hampshire, providing a buffer between us and the rest of the country.

When Louis Clinton Hatch oversaw a history of Maine a century ago, he and his editors filled up four fat volumes. If you're looking for a similarly comprehensive history of the state's 200 years, look elsewhere. This isn't even *Maine's Greatest Hits*. Instead, look at it as more like a box set with a few hit songs, but also B-sides, demos, and rarities. My goal here was to tell some interesting stories from each decade of Maine's two centuries of statehood. Some of the stories are about native Mainers. Some are about people who came to Maine. Some are about people who affected the state; others are about people the state affected. All are like threads in a much larger and very colorful tapestry of Maine history.

It reminds me of the fable about the blind men and the elephant. Each man examined a different part of the beast. "An elephant is like a tree trunk," says the man examining a leg. "No, an elephant is like a large snake," says the man feeling the trunk. "Not all," says the man rubbing the animal's side. "An elephant is rough like the side of a barn."

Well, this book is like that elephant. There are even elephants!

1820s

Maine Achieves Statehood: Peter Brawn Fights a Bear

THE RELATIONSHIP BETWEEN MAINE AND MASSACHUSETTS PROMISED to be a difficult one, especially with New Hampshire blocking any real intimacy. Taxes, as they often do, provided one bone of contention. So did Maine's underrepresentation in the Massachusetts General Court (the legislature), and its distance from the seat of government in Boston. Settlers in Maine's interior bristled over the vast tracts of land owned by rich proprietors in Massachusetts. By 1785 all these factors prompted some Mainers to contemplate splitting off from Massachusetts and forming a new state. On September 17 of that year an announcement appeared in the first issue of the Falmouth *Gazette*—Maine's first newspaper—calling for a meeting to discuss the question. Thirty-three people showed up the next month and they sent out a notice calling for a convention in January to discuss the matter further. Despite several meetings, response to the idea of separation remained lukewarm at best.

The question came up again in 1791 and the next year the state representatives from the Maine district requested that public opinion be sounded on the subject. The vote took place in March, and while 2,074 voted in favor of separation, 2,525 voted against it. "This result, so unexpected to the sanguine advocates of separation, suspended for a short time any further attempts on their part," wrote William Wills in an 1865 history of Portland. People offered more resolutions and convened more meetings over the next few years, but nothing came of them until after the War of 1812. Massachusetts had refused to lend military assistance to Maine when the British occupied Down East territory during the war, and this only helped strengthen the sentiment for statehood.

The growing movement benefitted from the efforts of several talented and ambitious men who remained determined to see Maine become a state. Chief among them was William King, "the father of Maine." Born in Scarborough in 1768, King became a successful merchant in Topsham before moving to Bath and doing even better there. "In his person, he was tall and of a striking figure," wrote Louis Clinton Hatch in his multi-volume history of Maine, "and with a finely formed head, strongly-marked features, high forehead, and black, impending brows, he had a natural and majestic air of command." Because King had served as a major general in the Massachusetts militia, people referred to him as General King. He was also known as "the sultan of Bath." "King was an able, vigorous, downright man," wrote Hatch. "He never shunned a contest, and strove to bend all around him to his will; he was loved and admired by his friends and followers; feared, perhaps hated, by his opponents." King had initially been a Federalist—the party of George Washington, John Adams, and Alexander Hamilton—but later shifted to the Democratic-Republican party of Thomas Jefferson. With King's financial backing, the *Eastern Argus* newspaper in Portland became a prominent voice for separation.

King had allies in a "junto" that worked for statehood. John Holmes was a successful lawyer who had been born in Massachusetts but moved to the district of Maine in 1799 after graduating from Rhode Island College (later Brown University). "His chief characteristic was his ready wit," wrote Hatch in his history. "He had few equals in keenness of repartee and power of ridicule. Indeed, his sense of humor was at times injurious to him. He could not resist an opportunity to tell a good story, and he would interrupt a legal argument to relate an anecdote, thereby weakening, or at least appearing to weaken, the closeness of his reasoning." Holmes was also a heavy drinker with a reputation for arrogance. When he defected from the Federalist Party to become a Democratic Republican, many suspected the change "was wholly of a mercenary character."

4

William Preble was a difficult man with a sharp tongue. Born in York, he graduated from Harvard and became an accomplished mathematician, but he was not a natural politician. "Preble's nature was such as to repel rather than attract men," Hatch said, which was probably why he found it better to work behind the scenes instead of as an elected representative.

Albion Parris, a future Maine governor, was born in Hebron and graduated from Dartmouth. A lawyer, he served in the Massachusetts General Court and later as a U.S. congressman. He tended to shy away from the hardball politics that others in the junto practiced, which perhaps explained his personal popularity. In his history of the statehood movement, Ronald F. Banks points out that many baby boys were named after Albion Parris.

John Chandler was born in New Hampshire in 1762 and joined the army when he was 14 to fight in the American Revolution. Captured by the British while serving on a privateer, he managed to escape from prison in Savannah and make his way home. He later moved to Monmouth and became a protégé of Henry Dearborn, Thomas Jefferson's secretary of war and a major landowner in Maine. With Dearborn's backing, Chandler eventually became a Massachusetts congressman and later the sheriff of Kennebec County. He also served as a brigadier general during the war of 1812. His military background was reflected in his personality; Hatch describes "his stiff and erect form, and somewhat brusque and abrupt manner of speech."

These men were capable, ambitious, and occasionally unscrupulous, and they put the lie to one reason anti-separatists said Maine wasn't ready for statehood—because there weren't enough talented people in the district.

Another factor working in favor of separation was increasing political division. Massachusetts remained strongly Federalist but Maine and its growing population began tilting toward the Democratic-Republican Party. Massachusetts Federalists realized it would increase their influence if the members of the rival party in Maine ended up in a separate state. (Federalists in Maine, though, resisted separation, knowing it would consign them to minority status.) In 1816 the Massachusetts General Court passed a bill for separation, provided that Maine residents voted in its favor by a factor of five to four. They did not—not quite—and at a convention in Brunswick that September, King and the junto struggled to fudge the voting results. Using some creative math cooked up by John Holmes and Harvard mathematician William Preble, they twisted the numbers until they got the result they wanted. The General Court refused to be swayed by the creative mathematics, though, and the blatant attempt to skew the results brought only scorn and derision to the proponents for statehood.

One of the biggest obstacles to separation was a federal regulation known as the coasting law. Passed by Congress in 1798, it required coastal vessels to clear customs in every state with which their home state did not share a border. A southbound vessel from New Hampshire did not have to stop in Massachusetts, which was contiguous, but it would have to stop in every other state down the coast. As long as Maine remained part of Massachusetts, a vessel from the district would have clear sailing through New York. If Maine separated, though, its ships would have to stop in Massachusetts and every other state south of it. As a result, Maine's coastal communities strongly opposed separation. After some effective lobbying by William King and his brother Rufus, Congress revised the coasting law by turning the entire Atlantic seaboard through Georgia into a single district, ending the need for reporting to customs houses in each state. That removed a major stumbling block for statehood.

The momentum had clearly shifted, and in June 1819 the Massachusetts General Court passed a bill authorizing the voters of Maine to decide the issue. This time the district's voters gave statehood a resounding victory.

Maine's constitutional convention took place that October in Portland. William King served as president. There was talk of making Maine a "commonwealth" instead of a state but it was rejected, one reason being that "state" was shorter and easier to spell. The name Columbus was also considered instead of Maine—"the name of Columbus is associated with all that is noble," said Augusta's Daniel Cony—but Maine prevailed. The citizens of Maine voted overwhelmingly for the constitution in December 1819, and the votes were officially recorded in January. According to the act of separation, Congress now had to grant statehood by a deadline of March 4, 1820. The clock was ticking.

Statehood was within reach, but then slavery almost tripped things up at the finish line. At the time the United States had 11 free and 11 slave states, maintaining a delicate balance of power. Admitting Maine as a free state would give the free states an advantage in Congress, something the slave-holding South would not accept.

Missouri offered a way out. That territory had also requested statehood, but its status, too, hung in limbo over slavery. The result was the Missouri Compromise, a pact hammered out in Congress that prohibited slavery in the territory gained through the Louisiana Purchase north of 36 degrees 30 inches—Missouri's southern border—with the exception of Missouri itself, which would enter the Union as a slave state. Maine could join the Union as a free state and maintain the balance. The legislative package passed on March 3, 1820, the day before the separation act with Massachusetts was due to expire.

Some were unhappy to see Maine become entangled in the slavery issue. Daniel Cony protested against "coupling the destiny of Maine" with "the trackless regions, the dreary wastes, the sable tribes" of Missouri. The editors of the Portland *Gazette* said they would rather see statehood fail "than bear up so wicked a freight as the slavery of Missouri." Five members of the Maine congressional delegation voted against the compromise. Two Maine congressmen who proved instrumental in passage of the compromise, John Holmes and Mark L. Hill, were attacked for their efforts and accused of having "leagued themselves with southern slave drivers."

Others accepted the compromise. Ashur Ware and William Preble of the *Eastern Argus* stated their position in the paper when they admitted that slavery was "both a moral and political evil. But having said this, it must be admitted on the other hand that it is an evil too deeply seated to admit of an immediate cure. No man in his senses, thinks of emancipation. All agree that it would be ruinous both to master and slave." (The slaves, if asked, might have thought otherwise.)

In a "Letter to the People of Maine," John Holmes defended his position on the compromise, which he said was necessary to prevent disunion and civil war over the slavery question. Holmes sent a copy of his letter to Thomas Jefferson, and Jefferson sent a long letter back. He said "the Missouri question," like "a fire bell in the night, awakened and filled me with terror. I considered it as once as the knell of the Union. It is hushed indeed for the moment, but this is a reprieve only, not a final sentence." In fact, it would take another 41 years before the nation's smoldering divisions over slavery blazed up into civil war.

On March 15, 1820, Maine entered the union as the nation's 23rd state. William King, who had done so much to achieve this result, became the new state's first governor, but he resigned the post in June 1821 and moved to Washington to oversee the claims cases made by U.S. citizens following the Florida treaty with Spain. King tried running for governor again as a Whig in 1835 but was soundly defeated. He died insane in 1852.

The *Eastern Argus* celebrated statehood in an editorial on March 21. "Thursday last witnessed the birth of a new State, and ushered Maine into the Union," it said. "The day was noticed, as far as we have heard from the various towns, by every demonstration of joy and heartfelt congratulation, becoming the occasion. . . . May the day which has so auspiciously commenced our political existence as a State, long be remembered with complacent feelings and every annual return bring with it, by the many blessings it may produce, additional inducement for its celebration."

Maine had some 298,000 residents when it became a state in 1820, and it's safe to assume that many of them didn't care whether they were citizens of Maine or Massachusetts. Certainly, when Peter Brawn was wrestling a bear in his boat on Sebec Lake at some point in the 1820s, the question of what state he was in never entered his mind.

Brawn was originally from Massachusetts and in 1805 he moved to Dover, where he built a log cabin and lived with his family. He moved to Moorstown (now Abbot) after his wife died in 1808. The "memorable cold season of 1815-16" prompted a move to Foxcroft. (It must have been *really* cold to be a memorably cold winter in Maine.) In 1826 Brawn purchased some land on Sebec Lake, which lies north of Dover-Foxcroft in Piscataquis County, and he moved there with his second wife. He made his living making shingles, shaving them from blocks of wood. An efficient "shingle shaver" like Brawn could make about a thousand shingles a day.

In 1910 Edgar Crosby Smith contributed a paper called "Peter Brawn and His Celebrated Bear Fight on Sebec Lake" to the Piscataquis County History Society. In it, Smith told the remarkable story about Brawn's struggle. It may not be a typical incident from Maine's first decade as a state, but it is an entertaining one.

The story goes that Brawn and a man named Ayer were taking a bateau down Sebec Lake with a load of shingles when they spied a swimming bear. They started chasing the bruin. Many people might consider that decision to be unwise. The bear was not pleased when it noticed its pursuers. According to Smith's account, the bear turned toward the two men in the boat "and showed belligerent symptoms, displaying a set of formidable teeth, and performing his evolutions with an activity that convinced them that they had no insignificant enemy to contend with." Events would prove that assessment to be correct.

In apparent defiance of common sense, the two men brought the boat right alongside the bear. At this point, the bear decided to climb aboard. In what could be interpreted as yet another case of bad judgement that day, Ayer attacked the bruin with an axe, but he managed only to shear off a bit of bear cheek. This angered the bear even more, and it clamped down on Ayer's wrist with its teeth and ripped open his side with its claws. Then bear and Ayer tumbled over the side of the boat and into the lake.

When the pair hit the water, the bear relinquished his grip on Ayer, who sank beneath the waves. As the bear paddled around, waiting for Ayer to surface, Brawn took action. Ayer had taken the axe with him into the water, so Brawn attacked the bear with an oar. He struck it on the nose and on the side and, when the animal decided it had endured enough, struck it once more on the rump as the bear paddled away.

Ayer, meanwhile, had bobbed to the surface. Brawn fished him aboard the bateau, where Ayer lay dripping and bleeding on the boat's bottom. Brawn decided it would be best not to chase the bear any more. Instead, he brought Ayer ashore to get his wounds patched up, and found someone else who could help him with the shingles.

Such was life on Sebec Lake during Maine's first decade of statehood.

1830s

Jonathan Cilley Fights a Duel: Maine (Almost) Goes to War

ON FEBRUARY 24, 1838, CONGRESSMEN JONATHAN CILLEY OF MAINE and William Graves of Kentucky faced each other across a cow pasture in Bladensburg, Maryland. Both men were armed with rifles. Only one of them left the field alive. Spoiler alert: It was not Cilley.

Jonathan Cilley had been born in New Hampshire in 1802. When he entered Bowdoin College in 1821 at the relatively advanced age of 19, he traveled to school with two other students who became friends— Nathaniel Hawthorne, later the author of *The Scarlet Letter* and other works, and Franklin Pierce, a future president of the United States. (Henry Wadsworth Longfellow was another member of Cilley's Class of 1825.) Hawthorne remembered Cilley as a good student of "quick and powerful intellect" who demonstrated leadership qualities and a natural eloquence that served him well in debates. "In private intercourse, Cilley possessed a remarkable fascination," Hawthorne said. "It was impossible not to regard him with the kindliest feelings, because his companions were intuitively certain of a like kindliness on his part. He had a power of sympathy which enabled him to understand every character, and hold communion with human nature in all its varieties." But Hawthorne also detected "harsher and sterner traits" in Cilley's personality—characteristics that helped him face adversity without flinching.

After graduation, Cilley moved to Thomaston to study law with John Ruggles, a Democrat who had been elected to the Maine legislature, where he later served as speaker of the house. Ruggles was also a lawyer and editor of the *Thomaston Register*. Cilley helped out with the paper and the law practice, especially when Ruggles was off in Portland or Augusta for his legislative duties. As a Democrat, young Cilley became a strong supporter of Andrew Jackson, who had been elected president in 1828.

On April 4, 1829, Cilley married Deborah Prince of Thomaston, the sister of a friend. Their first son, Greenleaf, was born on October 27. Anyone doing the math will understand why the marriage was scheduled with some haste.

Working with Ruggles taught Cilley much about Maine's politics. He learned even more when he was elected to a one-year term to the state legislature in 1831. Ruggles had been appointed a judge, but had set his eye on a seat in the United States Senate. Democratic politics in those days was something of a snake pit, with dueling factions, ambitions, and rivalries. When Cilley ran for reelection, he learned that his friend, mentor, and next door neighbor—John Ruggles—was one of the head snakes.

Somehow Ruggles had gotten the idea that Cilley was going to stand between him and the Senate seat he wanted so badly. He did everything he could to prevent Cilley's reelection, including distributing pamphlets that attacked Cilley "in the most virulent and abusive terms." Cilley managed to win reelection, but the Ruggles faction challenged the results and refused to seat him. Cilley returned to Thomaston in defeat. Nonetheless, he was elected again in 1834, but Ruggles and others continued their attacks with "unrelenting malignity" and had Cilley expelled from the party's caucus. Despite the fierce opposition from within his own party, Cilley won the post of speaker of the Maine house in 1835.

Cilley was obviously a young man with a future, and the future lay in Washington, D.C. It required three votes before he gained the majority necessary for election to the U.S. House of Representatives, but he finally prevailed in February 1836.

Hawthorne visited his friend in Maine shortly before the new congressman headed south to Washington. The author, who had not seen Cilley since college, described him as having a "thin face, sharp features, sallow, a projecting brow, not very high, deep-set eyes; an insinuating smile and look, when he meets you, or is about to address you." The novelist expressed mixed feelings about his old friend. "He is a singular man, shrewd, crafty, insinuating, with wonderful tact," Hawthorne wrote, and he marveled at how Cilley could subtly manipulate people without them knowing it. He also admired his "natural feeling" and "frankness." "He by no means feigns the good feeling that he professes, nor is there anything affected in the frankness of his conversation; and it is this that makes him so very fascinating." Hawthorne decided he was "a daring fellow as well as a sly one," but seemed somewhat ambivalent about Cilley's character.

Cilley served in Washington for less than two years before his fatal meeting with Graves. The duel that led to his death was a tangled affair that combined personal honor, sectional differences, and political rivalries. The delicate dance to preserve honor and navigate the tricky etiquette of dueling would have seemed farcical if it hadn't ended so tragically.

Cilley first clashed with Virginian Henry Wise over the issue of the Seminole War in Florida. Wise was against it. Cilley, on the other hand, proposed pushing the war against the Native Americans "with vigor, on the old New England plan, where the Indians had been wholly exterminated." (Looked at from a 21st-century perspective, that was not the most admirable of sentiments.) In addition, Cilley attacked Wise for "this sympathy for the dark red man which seemed to be akin to that expressed in some quarters for the man of a yet darker hue." Cilley could never be mistaken for an abolitionist. (South Carolina's Francis Pickens later said that Cilley "was the first northern man who openly denounced the abolitionists and spoke as a Southern man.") Looking at the clash between Cilley of Maine and Graves of Kentucky as one between North and South becomes a little difficult.

Wise was no stranger to dueling, having wounded a man in an affair of honor in January 1835. "He is pale and thin, about thirty years of age, perhaps not so much," wrote a reporter around this time. "He dresses like an old man, though his general appearance is very youthful. He is very slovenly in his apparel, his coat hanging like a miller's bag on his shoulders. . . . His forte lies in invective; then he becomes, to those whose party sympathies follow his own excited train of feeling, thrilling; his pale and excited face, his firm and compact head thrown back, his small bony hand clenched in the air, or with the forefinger quivering there, his eyes brilliant and fixed, his voice high yet sonorous, impress a picture too vivid to be easily erased from the mind."

On February 12 Wise asked Congress to investigate charges printed in the New York *Courier and Enquirer* alleging that a fellow congressman had indicated a willingness to accept bribes. Wise did not name the congressman, but said he was a Democrat. (Strangely enough, the unnamed Democrat turned out to be Maine Senator John Ruggles.) Cilley responded, saying he did not think it right to take action based on the accusations of a newspaper editor who had also been accused of taking a bribe. That editor was James Watson Webb, a Whig who helmed the New York *Courier and Independent*. One accusation circulating about Webb was that he had abandoned President Andrew Jackson after the U.S. Bank—which Jackson opposed—loaned him $52,000.

Webb was a cantankerous and confrontational individual. Hearing of Cilley's remarks, Webb traveled to Washington and wrote a note to Cilley requesting that he clarify his comments. He asked Graves, a man he barely knew, to deliver the message. Cilley refused to accept it. Graves and Cilley remembered their conversation differently. Cilley said he told Graves he did not wish to be drawn into a quarrel with Webb and declined to comment on his character. He said he did not intend this to mean any disrespect to Graves. The Kentuckian said Cilley claimed congressional privilege concerning his remarks about Webb and was impugning Graves's honesty when he denied saying that. Graves interpreted this as an attack on *his* honor. On February 23 he demanded "satisfaction," probably expecting that an anti-dueling New Englander would not accept a challenge. Cilley, proud and determined, accepted it.

Graves selected Henry Wise—whom Cilley thought was the real force behind the escalating conflict—to serve as his second. Cilley picked John W. Jones of Wisconsin, mainly because he had few other options. The seconds began making the arrangements for the duel. On the afternoon of February 24, the two parties rode out of Washington and into the Maryland countryside, where they found a cow pasture that met their needs. Each congressman took a rifle and separated until they were 80 yards apart, and waited for the signal to fire. On the first round, Cilley shot too early and fired into the ground. Graves had a similar misfire on the second round. After each shot, Cilley announced that he bore no ill will toward Graves, probably thinking that honor had been satisfied and the duel would end.

Honor, apparently, required further sacrifice. Instead of stopping the duel, Wise suggested that if it continued past a third round, the two men should move closer to each other. "They thirst for my blood," Cilley remarked to one of his friends.

There was no need for a fourth round. Graves's third bullet struck Cilley in the stomach. "I am shot," Cilley said and fell. He was dead within minutes. Only 35 years old, he left behind a grieving widow and three children.

The reaction in the North was outrage. "Murder Most Foul!" declared the Maine *Eastern Argus*. "New England should never humiliate herself by being represented in any body which ruffians like Wise and Graves are permitted to disgrace," the paper said. "The North, depend on it, will not submit to have her representatives shot down like dogs, by the trained assassins of any section of the country."

Many saw Wise as the affair's true villain. The seconds in a duel were supposed to do everything in their power to resolve things without bloodshed, but critics charged that Wise, instead, did everything he could to force the issue. "A challenge was never given on a more shadowy pretext," wrote Hawthorne; and "a duel was never pressed to a fatal close in the face of such open kindness as was expressed by Mr. Cilley: and the conclusion is inevitable, that Mr. Graves and his principal second, Mr. Wise, have gone further than their own dreadful code will warrant them, and overstepped the imaginary distinction, which, on their own principles, separates manslaughter from murder." John Quincy Adams castigated Wise on the House floor, saying he had returned to the chamber "with his hands dripping with human gore, and a blotch of human blood upon his face." Congress launched an investigation into the affair and recommended expelling Graves and censoring the seconds. In the end, though, nothing was done. Wise remained in Congress and went on to become governor of Virginia.

Hawthorne remained mystified why his college friend had accepted Graves's challenge in the first place. "Why, as he was true to the Northern character in all things else, did he swerve from his Northern principles in this final scene?" he asked. "But his error was a generous one, since he fought for what he deemed the honor of New England; and, now that death has paid the forfeit, the most rigid may forgive him." In his biography of Cilley, Roger Ginn blames the tragic sequence of events on "a mistaken sense of honor, faulty thinking, and impulsive decision making on the part of the principals neither of whom had experience with dueling protocol." Jonathan Cilley had paid the ultimate price for his inexperience.

John Ruggles, Cilley's mentor turned archenemy, remained in the Senate. He even had the temerity to sue Cilley's widow for money he said her dead husband owed him. As a senator, though, Ruggles had issues other than the Cilleys to handle. On February 27, 1839, Ruggles addressed the Senate to announce that war had broken out on Maine's northern border. It appeared that the long-simmering issue between Great Britain and the United States over the border between Maine and Canada had led to bloodshed.

It hadn't—not quite.

The border between the United States and Canada had not been properly defined by the Treaty of Paris that ended the Revolutionary War. The treaty's ambiguous wording meant both Great Britain and the United States claimed land along the St. John River and its tributaries, including a stream called the Aroostook. The area was largely wilderness, with the only settlement of note a cluster of huts inhabited mostly by French Canadians who had fled Arcadia in Nova Scotia when the British took over. They called the place Madawaska.

One of the Americans who settled in Madawaska was John Baker, who established a sawmill there. Living in the nearby settlement of Kent on the St. John was George Morehouse, who served as a magistrate for New Brunswick. The two men soon clashed. "Magistrate Morehouse seems to have spent considerable time in harassing the settlers on the Aroostook in devious ways," noted historian John Francis Sprague. Morehouse believed that the region lay under his legal authority and occasionally instigated legal actions against the inhabitants—at one point he confiscated lumber he said Baker had illegally harvested on crown lands.

When Morehouse heard that Baker was asking people to sign a paper stating they lived on American soil and were not bound by British law, he set out to investigate. He reached Madawaska on August 7, 1827, and was infuriated to see that Baker and others had erected a "liberty pole" that bore a homemade and apparently custom-designed American flag, a white field with an eagle and a semicircle of red stars. Morehouse ordered the pole taken down. Baker refused. In the predawn hours of September 25, Morehouse had Baker hauled off to jail in New Brunswick.

"I am a citizen of the United States, and owe allegiance to that country," Baker declared at his trial. He refused to recognize the court's authority over him. The judge sentenced him to two months in jail and a fine of 25 pounds.

After his release, Baker and another American settler, James Bacon, traveled by canoe to Augusta to set their case before Governor Enoch Powell. The governor issued a proclamation protesting the "unauthorized acts" by the British authorities, and the legislature resolved that the governor should "use all proper and constitutional means in his power, to protect and defend the citizens aforesaid in the enjoyment of their rights."

Something had to be done before the situation erupted into war, so the United States and England agreed to find a neutral arbitrator to define the border. They picked King William of the Netherlands. The king studied the treaties and the maps and announced his decision in January 1831. Both sides rejected it.

The cold war began to heat up again in 1837. Congress, eager to maintain this toehold in the wilderness, sent Ebenezer Greely of Dover to Madawaska to conduct a population survey and distribute "surplus" money from the U.S. Treasury that President Andrew Jackson had designated to be returned to the states. The British governor in New Brunswick, Sir John Harvey, interpreted this as a bribe intended to buy the inhabitants' loyalty to America. He had Greely arrested and thrown into prison in New Brunswick. "A flame of indignation" swept over the state.

After Maine's Governor Robert P. Dunlap called out the militia, Harvey wisely decided to release his prisoner.

In preparation for hostilities, General John E. Wool traveled to Maine to investigate fortifications there. He visited the Moosehead Lake region and suggested building an outpost near the Moose River, then went to Houlton, which he considered "well calculated for the defense and protection of that region of country." He also suggested stationing infantry and artillery at Calais and building an arsenal in Bangor and forts at the mouths of the Penobscot and Kennebec Rivers.

Matters were about to come to a head. The tipping point was not the abstract issue of a border, but the more concrete matter of money—specifically money from logging. When officials in Augusta heard that Canadians were logging in territory claimed by Maine, they took action. The legislature ordered a force of 200 volunteers to head north and drive the interlopers out. The first troops departed Bangor on February 5, 1839, and easily captured the foreign lumbermen and brought them to Bangor.

Retribution wasn't long in coming. Rufus McIntire, the state's land agent, Captain Stover Rines, Major Hastings Strickland (the sheriff of Penobscot County) and a company of men were fast asleep in the disputed territory on the night of February 12 when 40 armed men from New Brunswick surrounded their camp. They woke the Americans and told them they were under arrest. "By whose authority?" McIntire demanded. The commander of the armed party pointed his musket at the land agent. "This is my authority," he said. The Americans were taken to Fredericton and imprisoned, but Major Strickland managed to slip away in the darkness and immediately set out for Augusta to warn the new governor, John Fairfield.

The news from up north "roused to a high pitch the indignation of the people of Maine," said historian John S. C. Abbott. The Bangor *Whig* was incensed and in an editorial said, "[W]e stand ready to shoulder our musket and take our chance in the front rank of the militia—and entertain not the slightest doubt but that the whole body of our citizens would rise as one man, to defend the territory purchased by the blood of our fathers." The legislature appropriated $800,000 to respond and ordered more than 10,000 men from the state's militia groups to prepare for action. In the words of historian Sprague, "Patriotic sons of the Pine Tree State left their homes and firesides in the most inclement season known to our rigorous climate and marched through the deep snows of a wilderness, two hundred miles, to defend our frontier from foreign invasion, when the federal government was needlessly procrastinating and turning a deaf ear to the cries of suffering and oppressed pioneers in the upper St. John valley."

The Augusta Light Infantry headed north to Bangor. Cavalry arrived from Waldo County. So did militia companies from Piscataquis County, Brewer, Bangor, Dexter, Lincoln, Castine, and Blue Hill. Hiram Burnham, who commanded a well-drilled company of militia in Cherryfield, marched his men to Calais and waited to be called into action. John Hodsdon, who would serve as Maine's adjutant general during the Civil War, was only 16 and the major of a militia division when he and his men were dispatched to Fort Fairfield to protect the border.

People even composed war songs. One of them, the "Maine Battle Song" promised,

> *Britannia shall not rule the Maine,*
> *Nor shall she rule the water;*
> *They've sung that song full long enough,*
> *Much longer than they oughter.*

War seemed inevitable, and it promised to be a very cold war indeed. "It was midwinter in Maine, and bitter cold," wrote John Abbott in his history of Maine. "The regular uniforms afforded no sufficient protection for a winter campaign, through drifted snows and freezing gales, in a region where the mercury often sank twenty-five or thirty degrees below zero. Extra garments were speedily supplied, of thick red shirts and pea-green jackets. Within a week ten thousand American troops were either in Aroostook County, or on the march there."

Congress authorized the use of 50,000 troops to settle the border dispute, should that become necessary. First, though, President Martin Van Buren decided to dispatch a single soldier to Maine to deal with the issue. The soldier was General Winfield Scott, a hero of the War of

1812 (and a future hero of the Mexican War). Standing at a strapping six feet five inches, General Scott looked every bit the military man. Before heading into war with Britain, though, Scott hoped to defuse things with diplomacy. He reached Augusta on March 5, made his headquarters at the Augusta House, and established communications between Governor Harvey in New Brunswick and Governor Fairfield.

It helped that Scott and Harvey had developed a personal friendship when they served on opposite sides during the War of 1812. On one occasion Scott's forces just failed to capture Harvey, but did snag his personal baggage. Scott personally obtained Harvey's uniform coat and a miniature of his wife and he returned them to the Englishman. The two men met as negotiators during the conflict and continued a correspondence after it. In fact, when Scott reached Augusta, he brought with him a letter from Harvey that he had yet to answer.

The personal diplomacy paid off. Both governors agreed to stand down and release their prisoners. The Aroostook War ended before it even began, and without a single casualty. On April 12, the Bangor *Whig* was able to announce that the Maine soldiers were going home. "We were rejoiced to perceive so much interest and spirit manifested at their return. They marched with a firm and elastic step, to the tune of Home! Sweet! Home!"

"Thus ended the famous 'Aroostook War,' and fortunately for the people of the State and the province it was a bloodless one," wrote historian Abbott. "It has been derided and scoffed at and regarded as a huge international joke, and often has it been the subject for jest and laughter on the stump, and ever a fertile field for the grotesque wit of newspaper writers.

"And yet it is an incident in international history, in the history of the nation, and of the State of Maine, that is of supreme importance and interest."

The border issue was finally resolved after Secretary of State Daniel Webster and British Ambassador Lord Ashburton negotiated a treaty that the Senate ratified on August 20, 1842. If the United States was going to fight another war with England, it wasn't going to be over the Maine border.

1840s

Thoreau Goes Wild

When Henry David Thoreau moved into his little cabin near Walden Pond in Massachusetts on July 4, 1845, he was pleased to be living in the woods—but it was not the *woods*. Thoreau, not quite 28 years old, didn't really face the powerful, primal forces of nature until he ventured into the Maine wilderness in 1846. "Nature was here something savage and awful, though beautiful," he wrote after his Maine expedition. "I looked with awe at the ground I trod on, to see what the Powers had made there, the form and fashion and material of their work. This was that Earth of which we have heard, made out of Chaos and Old Night." Thoreau's Maine experiences made a profound impact on him and his writing.

Thoreau was older than Maine, having been born on July 12, 1817, near Concord, Massachusetts. His family ran a boardinghouse there and his father manufactured pencils. After graduating from Harvard in 1837, Thoreau returned to Concord, where he took a job as a teacher. That lasted only a couple of weeks, until he quit over his distaste at having to whip misbehaving students and started helping his father make pencils. Later Thoreau and his older brother, John, started their own school—one that did not employ corporal punishment—but they closed it shortly before John's death from tetanus.

One of Thoreau's Concord neighbors was Ralph Waldo Emerson, a writer and philosopher. Emerson was a founder of Transcendentalism, a school of thought that stressed the individual's direct connection to nature and the world. Emerson's emphasis on one's own experiences resonated with Thoreau, and the older man became a mentor to him. For a time, Thoreau lived with the Emersons and he contributed material to the short-lived Transcendentalist journal the *Dial*.

On Emerson's recommendation, Thoreau began working as a handyman for a new arrival in Concord, Nathaniel Hawthorne, Jonathan Cilley's friend from Bowdoin. Like many others, Hawthorne found Thoreau to be "a singular character—a young man with much of wild original nature still remaining in him; and so far as he is sophisticated, it is in a way and method of his own. He is ugly as sin, long-nosed, queer-mouthed, and with uncouth and somewhat rustic, although courteous, manners, corresponding very well with such an exterior." He called Thoreau "a wild, irregular, Indian-like sort of fellow." Thoreau probably would have appreciated the Indian reference. From a young age he had been fascinated by stories about the region's Native Americans and he was an avid collector of arrowheads he found during his hikes around Concord.

In May 1845, Thoreau enlisted some Concord friends to help him raise his tiny cottage near Walden Pond, only about two miles from town. Emerson had recently purchased the land, and he gave permission for Thoreau to build there.

The life he wrote about in *Walden; or, Life in the Woods* (1854) was hardly a wilderness experience and Thoreau was no hermit. A public road passed nearby, and Thoreau often entertained visitors at his cabin. With Concord only a mile or two away, he also spent time at his parents', at the Emersons', or visiting other people in town.

But Thoreau did march to a different drummer, and in July 1846 he spent a night in jail for not paying his poll tax. For Thoreau, it was a way to protest the Mexican-American War. One of his aunts paid the tax for him, much to his displeasure, and Thoreau emerged from jail a free man after his night's stay. He used his experience as the basis for an essay that became known as "Civil Disobedience."

Thoreau had visited Maine for the first time in May 1838 when he was seeking a teaching job. He had taken a boat to Portland, a mail coach to Brunswick, and eventually made his way to Bangor, where he had a memorable encounter with a loquacious Native American in Old Town. The talkative man pointed up the Penobscot River and told Thoreau, "Two or three miles up the river one beautiful country."

Thoreau yearned to discover that beautiful country for himself, and he got the opportunity when he received an invitation from George Thatcher. Thatcher was a Bangor businessman who had married Thoreau's cousin, and he invited Thoreau to accompany him on an expedition to examine his lumber interests in the Maine woods. Thoreau jumped at the chance, seeing Thatcher's invitation as a great opportunity to climb Katahdin (or Ktaadn, as Thoreau spelled it), Maine's highest mountain— and New England's second highest.

No roads led to Katahdin, which got its name from the eastern Algonquin language, meaning "principal," "pre-eminent," or "greatest." It was isolated amid wilderness that prevented all but the most determined travelers from reaching it. Writing in 1881, 35 years after Thoreau's visit, Charles E. Hamlin said, "Mt. Ktaadin is so inaccessible that practically it is remote even to New Englanders," and estimated that a hundred Bostonians had climbed the Alps for every one that had scaled this mountain in Maine. He called Katahdin the "undisputed monarch of the great wilderness he overlooks."

The first known ascent of Katahdin took place in August 1804, when seven men from the Bangor and Orono area made the climb. Three professors, one from West Point and two from Waterville (later Colby) College, climbed it in 1836, and state geologist Charles T. Jackson—who happened to be Ralph Waldo Emerson's brother-in-law—made the ascent the next year. Boston author Edward Everett Hale made an ascent in 1845 and wrote an account for the *Boston Daily Advertiser*. It's likely that Thoreau read it, since Hale's companion on the climb was the cousin of one of Thoreau's friends.

"On the 31st of August, 1846, I left Concord in Massachusetts for Bangor and the backwoods of Maine, by way of the railroad and steamboat," Thoreau wrote, "intending to accompany a relative of mine engaged in the lumber-trade in Bangor, as far as a dam on the west branch of the Penobscot, in which property he was interested." On September 1 he and Thatcher left Bangor in a buggy. As he passed through

Stillwater and Old Town, Thoreau noted the busy sawmills, which were industriously converting the Maine woods into lumber. "The mission of men there seems to be, like so many busy demons, to drive the forest all out of the country, from every solitary beaver-swamp and mountain-side, as soon as possible," he noted.

The two men took a ferry across the Penobscot, and Thoreau's romantic notions of Native American life bumped up against harsher realities as they passed the Native American settlement on Indian Island. It appeared almost deserted, "shabby, forlorn, and cheerless." It was the remnant of a once-great nation that had left traces, in the names of lakes, streams, and even the great mountain Thoreau aimed to climb, all over the map of Maine.

Thatcher thought it would be helpful to have a Native guide, so on their second day of travel the two men headed up the Houlton road until they reached a large Native American village near Lincoln. A "stalwart, but dull and greasy-looking fellow" directed them to the home of Louis Neptune, the man who had guided Jackson up Katahdin in 1837. Neptune was "a small, wiry man, with puckered and wrinkled face" and he told the two that he was about to head north to hunt moose. Thoreau suggested they rendezvous and travel together. He asked Neptune if he thought Pomola, the god the natives said inhabited Katahdin, would let him get to the mountain's top. Neptune advised Thoreau to leave a bottle of rum on the summit—he said when he had done that in the past, the rum was always gone when he returned. Neptune may have been joking, but if he was, Thoreau missed the humor. He had a complicated relationship with the Natives he met—sometimes admiring, sometimes dismissive, often baffled.

Further on, at an inn alongside the Mattawamkeag River, the party's size doubled when Thoreau and Thatcher were joined by Charles Lowell, Thatcher's brother-in-law, and Horatio P. Blood. The men continued their trek up the northern bank of the Penobscot. "There was now no road further, the river being the only highway, and but half a dozen log-huts confined to its banks, to be met with for thirty miles. On either hand, and beyond, was a wholly uninhabited wilderness, stretching to Canada."

Finally, they reached the home of George McCauslin, a one-time lumberman who had carved out a home in the woods where the Penobscot met the Little Schoodic River. McCauslin had worked log drives on Maine rivers for more than two decades; Thoreau described him as a "man of dry wit and shrewdness." His forest home was dry and comfortable, with a huge fireplace, and a big wooden chair that became a table when you lowered its back over the arms. McCauslin and his wife treated the travelers to a feast. After dinner it began to rain and it continued throughout the next day. Thoreau was content to sit out the storm at McCauslin's and wait for Neptune.

When Neptune failed to show, Thoreau talked McCauslin into accompanying them instead. He agreed, being "not unwilling to revisit the scenes of his driving." Four miles further on, the party found Thomas Fowler working on a new cabin, and they talked him into coming along. They would need him to help with the bateau, the flat-bottomed boat they planned to use to get as close as they could to Katahdin by water. They continued up the Millinocket to the cabin of Tom Fowler's older brother, six miles from McCauslin's, and exchanged their leaky bateau for a sturdier model. Fowler's brother agreed to help transport the heavy boat cross country on a horse-drawn sled to bypass the Great Falls of the Penobscot.

There were now six in the party, including the two boatmen, with McCauslin poling in the stern and Fowler in the bow. At a logging camp where they stopped for dinner, the last human habitation along their route, Thoreau found, thrown on the ground and covered with leaves, a pamphlet by his friend and neighbor, Ralph Waldo Emerson. It would have seemed like an incredible coincidence, but it turned out Thatcher, Emerson's brother-in-law, had left the pamphlet there on an earlier visit. After dark the party left the camp and set out by moonlight in the direction of Katahdin, which lay about 20 miles away as the crow flies, but 30 by their planned route.

On their way toward the mountain, Thoreau and his party poled up streams, paddled across lakes and ponds, and hauled their bateau on grueling portages past rapids and falls. The place names testified to the Native American presence in the region—Katepskongegan Lake,

Pockwockomus Lake, and Katelskonegan Stream among them. At the Passamagamet Falls the boatmen decided to pole the boat up the rapids, perhaps to show off their expertise. With Thoreau remaining in the bateau to trim it with his weight, McCauslin and Fowler used their poles to push the boat forward against the rushing waters. The attempt almost ended in disaster when McCauslin's pole snapped, but he managed to jam the remaining fragment against a rock and steady the boat before it capsized.

Even here in the wilderness, Thoreau was surprised by all the traces humans had left behind. He spotted booms that lumbermen had rigged to hold timber, and scattered logs left behind by log drives. He was startled to see an iron ring driven into a rock at the head of Ambejijis Lake. At another location he saw an advertising handbill for a Boston clothing store pasted to a tree.

Stopping to camp on the Aboljacknagesic Stream one night, the men fished, hauling in trout hand over fist. Nearby, Thoreau found the skeleton of a moose that Indians had picked clean. The next morning, they left the boat behind and struck out overland for the mountain. McCauslin, who had never been this close before, reckoned it was about four miles away, but Thoreau later calculated the distance as closer to 14.

As they made their way through the woods they saw scores of moose tracks and places where the huge animals had eaten branches and bark from trees. Thoreau could even see their teeth marks. The forest here was so thick, McCauslin had to climb a tree to make sure were still heading for the mountain. Thoreau called it "the worst kind of traveling."

The exhausted men camped for the night in a wild and inhospitable ravine somewhere on the side of the mountain. Thoreau went ahead by himself to explore, climbing up a steep slope and clambering across krummholz, a tangled net of fir trees bent horizontally to the ground. Thoreau peered down through the bent trees and believed there were bears living in the rocks below. Finally he turned back to the camp. He would attempt the mountain in the morning.

He set out the next day and was soon climbing by himself. It was a gray, cloudy and windy day. "The mountain seemed a vast aggregation of loose rocks, as if some time it had rained rocks, and they lay as they fell on the mountain sides, nowhere fairly at rest, but leaning on each other, all rocking-stones, with cavities between, but scarcely any soil or smoother shelf," Thoreau wrote. "They were the raw materials of a planet dropped from an unseen quarry, which the vast chemistry of nature would anon work up, or work down, into the smiling and verdant plains and valleys of earth."

The summit was veiled in mist and Thoreau, alone, climbed up into the clouds. Sometimes the wind blew the mist aside for a brief promise of sunshine, but then the clouds rolled back in. "It was like sitting in a chimney and waiting for the smoke to blow away," he wrote. "It was, in fact, a cloud factory." He felt alone amid the vastness of nature. "The tops of mountains are among the unfinished parts of the globe, whither it is a slight insult to the gods to climb and pry into their secrets, and try their effect on our humanity," he said. "Only daring and insolent men, perchance, go there. Simple races, as savages, do not climb mountains,— their tops are sacred and mysterious tracts never visited by them. Pomola is always angry with those who climb to the summit of Ktaadn."

It turned out that Thoreau did not need to fear Pomola's wrath, for the wind and clouds kept him from the top. He did not reach South Peak, which it appears he was aiming at, or the mountain's highest point, now called Baxter Peak, which was even further on. Fearing his comrades would be eager to strike out for the river, he turned back to their camp. As he descended, the clouds occasionally parted to reveal nothing but vast wilderness dotted by countless lakes and streams. "Perhaps I most fully realized that this was primeval, untamed, and forever untamable *Nature*, or whatever else men call it, while coming down this part of the mountain," Thoreau wrote.

On the return journey, as they reached the Millinocket opposite Tom Fowler's home, they encountered two canoes. Louis Neptune was in one of them, on his way to hunt moose. Neptune said he had missed the rendezvous because he had been sick, but Thoreau blamed it on "a drunken frolic." He did not know whether he admired or disdained the Natives he met. "Met face to face, these Indians in their native woods looked like the sinister and slouching fellows whom you meet picking up strings and paper in the streets of a city," he said. "There is, in fact, a remarkable and unexpected resemblance between the degraded savage and the lowest classes in a great city. The one is no more a child of nature than the other. In the progress of degradation the distinction of races is soon lost."

At the end of the journey the party passed through Old Town, "where we heard the confused din and clink of a hundred saws," the sound of the mills turning the primeval forest into lumber for civilized man. Thoreau was on a Massachusetts-bound steamer the next morning, with much to ponder after his experiences in the "howling wilderness" that began only a few miles outside the city of Bangor. "I am reminded by my journey how exceedingly new this country still is," he wrote, how much of it remained unsettled and unexplored, and how little people understood their relationship to the natural world. "The very timber and boards and shingles of which our houses are made, grew but yesterday in a wilderness where the Indian still hunts, and the moose runs wild," he mused.

For the rest of his life, Thoreau remained fascinated by Maine. He returned in 1853, once again at Thatcher's invitation. He visited Moosehead Lake and traveled down the Penobscot to Chesuncook Lake. This time he hired a Native American guide, Joe Aitteon, who was the son of the Penobscot's governor. And this time Thoreau finally saw moose, although he was sickened when Thatcher shot one. "The afternoon's tragedy, and my share in it, as it affected my innocence, destroyed the pleasure of my adventure," he wrote. "Every creature is better alive than dead, men and moose and pine-trees, and he who understands it aright will rather preserve its life than destroy it."

An old friend named Ed Hoar joined Thoreau in 1857 for his final journey into the Maine woods. This time their guide was Joe Polis, a prominent member of the Penobscot tribe who had represented his people in Augusta and Washington and had once called on Daniel Webster in Massachusetts. Polis—whom Thoreau usually referred to as "the Indian" in his writing—taught Thoreau much about Native American life and culture during their travels. They paddled up Moosehead in Polis's canoe, explored the East Branch of the Penobscot, and visited the Allagash region. Thoreau saw another moose killed—Polis shot it—and rekindled his fascination with Native Americans.

Thoreau's writings about his visits to the wilderness were published as a collection titled *The Maine Woods* in 1864. By then Thoreau was dead, a victim of the tuberculosis that ran in his family. As Thoreau lay dying on May 6, 1862, a friend heard what he said were the last intelligible words he uttered. They were "Indian" and "moose," evidence that his experiences in Maine resonated with him to the very end.

1850s

Portland Riots Over Rum; Harriet Beecher Stowe Writes a Book

AMERICANS IN THE 19TH CENTURY LIKED TO DRINK. PEOPLE HAD HARD cider for breakfast, whiskey for lunch, and rum for dinner. Parents gave their children alcohol; farmers nursed sick horses with whiskey, and workers expected a dram or two to get through the day. According to Portland's Neal Dow, no one outdrank the people of his native Maine. "At the time of the admission of Maine to the Union, and for thirty years thereafter, her people probably consumed more intoxicating liquor in proportion to their numbers than the people of any other state," he wrote. He did not intend that as a compliment. Dow saw alcohol as a scourge on society and devoted his life to stamping it out. Thanks in large part to Dow's work, Maine passed the nation's first prohibition law in 1851. Known as the Maine Law, it became the model for similar attempts at prohibition in other states. It also led to a spasm of violence in 1855 that became known as the Portland Rum Riot.

Dow was a native Portlander, having been born there in 1804 in his parents' house on Congress Street. His parents were members of the Society of Friends—the Quakers—so they did not drink alcohol. Dow's great-grandfather on his mother's side bore the name of Hate-Evil Hall. So perhaps Dow was destined to fight against the evils of drink.

In addition, Dow's father was an abolitionist and helped escaped slaves who reached Portland. One 14-year-old girl who had run away from a Virginia plantation lived with the Dows for several years.

Young Neal worked in his father's tannery and in 1830 he married and moved into a house he built that still stands on Congress Street. Later he became a bank director and had other business interests until the temperance cause began to take up more and more of his time.

Dow made his first temperance speech in 1822 after he joined the Deluge Engine Company, a firefighting organization. (He eventually became the city's fire chief.) Fire companies at the time were as much about socializing as fighting fires, and hard drinking was the norm. Although just a lowly clerk, Dow made a speech and persuaded the company to ban alcohol from an upcoming anniversary event.

Not all the city's fire companies were so disposed. Dow recalled attending a gathering with another company when a toast was proposed. The other chief raised his glass, which he had filled with water in deference to Dow. "Brandy and water—water for the fire, and brandy for firemen," he said. Then Dow raised his glass, also filled with water. "Brandy and water," he said, "water extinguishes fire, and brandy extinguishes firemen."

Firemen weren't the only drinkers, of course. The state was awash in liquor. "Town-meetings, musters, firemen's parades, cattle-shows, fairs, and, in short, every gathering of the people of a public or social nature resulted almost invariably in scenes which in these days would shock the people of Maine into indignation, but which then were regarded as a matter of course," Dow said. He saw the effects of alcohol in homeowners who allowed their dwellings to fall into disrepair, farmers who let their lands go fallow, and inebriates who blocked the sidewalks in front of drinking houses.

In 1833, Dow helped form the Portland Young Men's Temperance Society. The society did not preach total abstinence, though, and merely advocated drinking in moderation. More ardent advocates split off to form their own organization, the Maine Temperance Society. The new society advocated lobbying the state legislature to outlaw the sale of alcohol—prohibition.

31

Dow himself came to believe in total abstinence and state-controlled prohibition and began crisscrossing the state to make speeches on behalf of the cause that now possessed him. As he became the public face of the movement, the liquor interests pushed back. On one occasion, rum sellers hired a sailor to beat Dow in the streets of Portland. Dow, never one to back away from a fight, turned the tables on his assailant, chased him down, and forced him to reveal who had hired him. At other times people tossed foul-smelling asafetida through his window or left trash and dead cats on his front steps. He remained undeterred.

In 1851, Dow ran as the Whig candidate for mayor of Portland. He won despite opposition from his own party leaders, with many pro-temperance Democrats crossing party lines to vote for him. Inaugurated as mayor on April 24, Dow predictably included temperance language in his speech. "There is no fact better established than this, that the traffic in intoxicating drinks tends more to the degradation and impoverishment of the people than all other causes of evil combined; its existence is incompatible with the general welfare and prosperity of the community," he said.

Dow did not let his new mayoral duties limit his battle against alcohol statewide, especially now that public opinion seemed to be tilting in his favor. Opponents called him a fanatic, but Dow achieved the victory he had sought for so long when the Maine legislature passed its prohibition law in 1851. Titled "An Act for the Suppression of Drinking Houses and Tippling Shops," it outlawed the sale of alcohol for everything but "medicinal and mechanical purposes."

After the law went into effect on June 2, Dow demonstrated his intentions to enforce it energetically by making an example of one retailer who continued selling rum. He directed the city marshal to issue a warrant and proceeded to the store in question to supervise the confiscation of the alcohol. A crowd had gathered to watch. Dow took control, told the loudly protesting store owner to be quiet, and ordered the marshal and his men to remove the liquor. Someone in the crowd cut the rope being used to hoist the barrels out of the building, but it was quickly repaired and the confiscation proceeded without further difficulty. "The effect of that first seizure was marked," Dow wrote. "It was an object lesson at once of the determination of the authorities to do their duty, and of the efficacy of the law."

Nevertheless, some people broke the law. Like the speakeasies of the 1920s, illegal drinking holes sprang up throughout Portland. Individuals devised clever ways to hide their liquor and drink on the sly. Outsiders found ways to smuggle alcohol into the state.

Dow insisted the overall effects of prohibition were almost uniformly positive. According to him, prohibition helped usher Maine into a new Golden Age, where farmers improved their land instead of venturing into town to drink, husbands and wives devoted themselves to each other and their homes instead of alcohol, and people in general found productive pursuits to replace drinking. Poorhouses and jails emptied. There remained plenty of people who opposed the law, but Dow claimed that most of them were "foreigners."

Contrary to his somewhat rosy appraisal of the new law, Dow lost reelection as Portland's mayor. He blamed outside liquor interests and widespread voter fraud. Even in defeat, though, he remained a prominent voice for temperance, going on speaking tours that took him as far west as Detroit and to appearances in Toronto, Montreal, Quebec, and even in Great Britain.

He ran unsuccessfully for mayor again in 1854. He tried once more in the spring of 1855, running now as a Republican, the new political party that supported temperance and opposed slavery. This time Dow won.

The rum riot of 1855 was sparked by the arrival of $1,600 worth of alcohol that had been legally purchased by Portland's liquor agency. The Maine Law did allow for "medicinal and mechanical" needs, and in Portland those sales were overseen by the mayor and aldermen and conducted from an agency shop in City Hall on Congress Street.

On June 2, a broadbill began circulating throughout Portland in response to the alcohol's arrival. "The mayor of the city has no more right to deal in liquors without authority than any other citizen," it stated, and called for the seizure and destruction of the agency liquor. "The old maxim reads: '*Fiat juxtitia mat caelum,*' which means, 'Let the lash which Neal Dow has prepared for other backs be applied to his own when he deserves it.'"

Citizens—one of whom, Dow said, was a liquor seller who had been driven out of business by the Maine Law—swore out a complaint that the mayor was selling liquor illegally. A judge dutifully issued a warrant and a deputy marshal went to secure the liquor at the agency store as an angry mob began gathering at City Hall. Some people in the crowd were distributing handfuls of rocks and stones.

Estimates of the crowd size varied widely—from 200 people to 1,500 or more. Backed by some armed policemen, Dow arrived and urged the crowd to disperse, but his pleas were greeted by groans, hisses, and a shower of stones. Sometime around 9:00 that night, Dow felt compelled to summon two companies of militia, the Rifle Guards and Light Guards. Around 20 members of the Light Guards, under the command of Charles H. Green, arrived first. Dow accompanied them to confront the crowd at city hall. When the mayor again demanded that the mob disperse, he was answered with another fusillade of rocks.

Dow ordered the militia to fire. Green implored him to reconsider. Dow relented and told him to wait. Rather than let more of his men get hit by rocks, Green had the Light Guards retreat to their armory, which was on the third floor of City Hall. On the way they encountered members of the Rifle Guards, commanded by Charles Roberts. The Rifle Guards had no ammunition, so Dow told Green to arm them with muskets from the Light Guards' armory. After some grumbling about giving a rival militia their weapons, the Light Guards complied. Then the Rifle Guards descended the stairs to Middle Street. "During all this time were heard from below the ferocious sounds of the mob, the clatter of stones and other missiles, the rattle of broken glass, and the crash of breaking blinds, shutters, and doors," read one account.

About 15 policemen had remained behind in the agency store as the situation began to spiral out of control. Rioters broke in a section of the main door and one especially vocal rioter urged the mob forward. The policemen fired a volley through the broken door and over the rioters' heads. Someone in the crowd shouted that the defenders had only blank cartridges; the rioters pushed forward again. One man thrust his head through the broken door and reached in to pull up the cross bar. This time the police fired "with effect." The man fell back, mortally wounded. He was John Robbins, a sailor from Deer Isle.

The Rifle Guards returned shortly after Robbins had fallen and entered the agency store from the Middle Street entrance. Stones were flying through the shattered front door. Once again Dow ordered the militia to fire. This time they did, shooting through the broken door into Congress Street and then emerging from the building with lowered bayonets. The show of force dispersed the mob. Robbins had been the only fatality, but several members of the militia had been injured by rocks.

Put on trial on the charge of illegally possessing alcohol—a charge heavily underscored with irony—Dow was acquitted. However, not only did he lose his bid for reelection, the Maine Law was also repealed later that year. Dow blamed "misrepresentation" of the June riot for the downfall of prohibition and the reverses the Republican party suffered in the elections of 1855.

The Maine Law was watered down, so to speak, when a less stringent version passed in 1858, but prohibition advocates celebrated a major victory in 1884 with the passage of the 26th Amendment to the Maine Constitution, which outlawed the "sale and manufacture of intoxicating liquors, excluding cider." The amendment remained in effect until it was repealed by the 54th Amendment in 1934. By then prohibition had been attempted on a national scale, an experiment that also ended in 1934.

Dow never again served as Portland's mayor although he was elected to the state legislature and continued to support prohibition. When the Civil War broke out, he became colonel of the 13th Maine Volunteer Infantry. Promoted to brigadier general, he served in Florida and was wounded and captured during the fighting for Port Hudson, Mississippi, in 1863. He spent time in the miserable conditions of Richmond's Libby Prison. According to *Maine in the War for the Union*, Dow "impressed himself favorably upon all with whom he came in contact, even those in the South who had been taught to despise him for his zealous advocacy of temperance principles." In 1880 he ran for president as the candidate for the Prohibition Party. He did not win. Neil Dow died in 1897 at the age of 94 and is buried in Portland.

While the subject of prohibition was roiling the state of Maine, an even more divisive issue was threatening to tear apart the entire nation. The issue was slavery, and a woman writing from her home in Brunswick heaped fuel on the fire.

The woman was Harriet Beecher Stowe. Her book, *Uncle Tom's Cabin*, became a flash point that widened the divide between North and South over the contentious issue of human bondage.

Stowe was not a Maine native. Born in Litchfield, Connecticut, in 1811, she belonged to a prominent religious family. Her father was Lyman Beecher, one of the nation's best-known Congregationalist ministers. One of her brothers was Henry Ward Beecher, who would achieve worldwide fame as the minister of Plymouth Church in Brooklyn. Her sister Catherine founded the Hartford Female Seminary in Connecticut and in 1837 wrote *Essay on Slavery and Abolitionism with Reference to the Duty of the American Females.* Her brother Edward led the Illinois Anti-Slavery Society.

Harriet was already a published author when she married widower Calvin Stowe in January 1836. He was a noted mathematician who had graduated as valedictorian from Bowdoin College in 1824. Calvin was teaching in Ohio when he received a job offer from his alma mater in Brunswick. He remained behind in Ohio to finish up the school year while his wife, three of their five children, and Harriet's Aunt Esther Beecher made the trip to Maine without him. Harriet was six months pregnant at the time and was still in mourning for an 18-month-old son who had died of cholera.

Professor William Smith from Bowdoin had arranged to meet the Stowes' boat when it reached Bath, but in a somewhat slapstick case of miscommunication they managed to miss each other—Harriet and her five children somehow slipped off the steamer while the professor poked around onboard looking for them—so both parties traveled to Brunswick separately, Smith convinced the Stowes were not coming after all. Harriet and her brood surprised everyone when they showed up.

The Stowes lived in Brunswick for only two years (and Calvin for less than that, for he soon accepted another offer from the Andover Theological

Seminary in Massachusetts and was often absent), but she said it was the happiest time of her life. It wasn't always easy, though, for the family was living in straitened circumstances. "Cincinnati had not made them rich, and their apparent poverty when they came into Maine excited surprise and compassion," wrote Nehemiah Cleaveland in his 1919 history of Bowdoin. The house they rented on Back Street (now Federal Street) was "a decayed and uncomfortable mansion." (Years before, Bowdoin student Henry Wadsworth Longfellow had rented a room there). When Calvin arrived, he found his new dwelling to be "most miserably out of repair, and certainly unfit to offer for rent to any body," thanks to its broken windows, useless door latches, and tumbledown fences and gates. In the Maine winter, water in buckets turned to ice overnight, biscuit dough froze as it sat by the kitchen fire, and the children complained about having to go upstairs to freezing bedrooms. "I was bred to such hardness from the cradle & so did not mind it but they feel it," Harriet wrote.

Rent for the big, drafty house was more than the Stowes had budgeted, so Harriet resumed her writing to help make ends meet. She was writing when she went into labor on July 8, 1850, and gave birth to another son.

Harriet's best-known work came to her, the story goes, while she was attending a service at Brunswick's First Parish Church and had a vision of a slave who had been murdered by his cruel owner. She rushed home and began to work on his story.

The Beechers were noted abolitionists, and Harriet's dislike of slavery had only increased in 1850 with the passage of the Fugitive Slave Law, which made it a crime for any U.S. citizen to refuse assistance to slave catchers apprehending runaway slaves. When a fugitive appeared on the Stowes' doorway in Brunswick, Harriet willingly violated the law to put him up for the night before he resumed his trek north to Canada and freedom. "Now our beds were all full, & before this law was passed I might have tried to send him somewhere else—As it was all hands in the house united in making him up a bed," she told her sister.

Harriet began writing her story of slavery at her rented home, and she wrote some more in her husband's office in Bowdoin's Appleton Hall. On Saturdays she liked to read from the work in progress for gatherings in her parlor. One student who visited the Stowes' on those Saturday evenings was a young man from Brewer named Joshua Lawrence Chamberlain. "On these occasions a chosen circle of friends, mostly young, were favored with the freedom of her house, the rallying point being, however, the reading before publication, of the successive chapters of her Uncle Tom's Cabin, and the frank discussion of them," he recalled years later.

The first installments of *Uncle Tom's Cabin* appeared in the June 2, 1851, edition of an antislavery weekly called the *National Era*. Readers were captivated by the story of Christ-like Uncle Tom, who is sold to the brutal slaveowner Simon Legree in Louisiana, and the slave Eliza, who escapes across ice floes in the Ohio River to safety in the North. The two-volume hardback edition appeared in March 1852, a month after the Stowes had left Brunswick for Andover. The book was an immediate sensation, selling 300,000 copies in the United States in one year, and two million copies worldwide. While it may not be a work of great literature (George Orwell called it "[p]erhaps the supreme example of the 'good bad' book"), it had explosive repercussions. Abolitionists hailed the way it exposed the horrors of slavery, while Southerners condemned it as a work of fantasy. Abolitionist William Lloyd Garrison said the novel would prove to be "eminently serviceable in the tremendous conflict now waged for the immediate and entire suppression of slavery on the American soil."

Books alone wouldn't end slavery in the United States, and it took a long and bloody Civil War before America experienced what Abraham Lincoln called "a new birth of freedom." But the book that Harriet Beecher Stowe wrote in Brunswick, Maine, certainly stoked passions that led to the conflict. According to one story—perhaps apocryphal—when Lincoln met the author for the first time, he greeted her by saying, "So you're the little woman who wrote the book that started this great war!"

1860s

Maine Defends the Union

SOUTH CAROLINA DECLARED ITS SECESSION FROM THE UNION IN December 1860 following the election of Republican Abraham Lincoln as president. Other states followed, and the nation teetered on the brink of civil war. It tumbled over after Rebels fired on Fort Sumter in Charleston harbor on April 12, 1861. Maine was quick to answer the call to restore the Union. By war's end, 73,000 of its citizens had served in the Union army, the largest number *per capita* from any northern state. Some 118,000 of them became casualties.

Not all Mainers remained loyal to the Union, though. Two became Confederate generals. Danville Leadbetter, born in Leeds in 1811, served as a military engineer for the Confederacy and rose to the rank of brigadier general. A member of West Point's class of 1836, Leadbetter oversaw the construction of Rebel fortifications at Mobile, Alabama, and in Chattanooga and Knoxville, Tennessee. He died in Canada in 1866.

Zebulon York was born in the Franklin County town of Avon in 1819 and studied at the Wesleyan Seminary in Kents Hill. He later earned a law degree in Louisiana and was a wealthy slave owner there when war came. He formed a regiment, the 14th Louisiana, and fought well with it. Promoted to brigadier general in 1864 and given command of a brigade, York was wounded in the Shenandoah Valley and had his left arm amputated. After the war, his assets gone, he ran a hotel in Natchez, Mississippi, where he died in 1900.

There were Maine soldiers in the Confederate ranks, too. While fighting outside Richmond during Maj. Gen. George McClellan's Peninsular Campaign in 1862, Captain John W. Channing of the 7th Maine was conversing with Rebel pickets from a Georgia regiment in front of his position when he realized one of them was an old friend he had known back in Winslow. After the battle of Middleburg in the Shenandoah Valley in June 1863, Captain Walter Morrill of the 20th Maine was surprised when he recognized a man among the Rebel prisoners that he had lumbered with on the Penobscot River.

Still, the vast majority of Maine's citizens remained loyal to the United States and contributed to the Union cause. That included the state's women, not just the men who marched off to war. More than 21,000 women from the North worked in military hospitals, and among them were Maine women such as Isabella Fogg, Harriet Eaton, Rebecca Usher, and Amy Morris Bradley. Sarah Smith Sampson of Bath was another. An 1865 history of Maine's war effort said Sampson's work was "invaluable" and that she "has been truly a 'ministering angel' to our sick and wounded soldiers, attending as she has, in every possible way to their wants. Her unremitting attentions have won for her everlasting gratitude and honor."

Sarah and Charles Sampson were living in Bath when the war began, and Charles joined the 3rd Maine Volunteer Infantry regiment. Sarah traveled with him to Washington, where, she said, "I pledged myself to the relief of the sick and suffering soldiers of our army while the war should continue." (Because she was not working as an official army nurse, she was not under the jurisdiction of Dorothea Dix, the Maine native who was commissioned in 1861 to head the Office of Army Nurses.)

Sampson visited the sick in the regimental hospital every day and traveled into Virginia when her husband's regiment marched off to fight in the First Battle of Bull Run that July. "From this time to the embarkation of the army in March of 1862, never a day passed that I was not with the sick in the hospital," she said. She remained with her husband when the regiment moved south to take part in McClellan's campaign against Richmond that spring. When Oliver Otis Howard, the 3rd Maine's first commander, and his brother Charles were both wounded at the battle of Fair Oaks, Sampson helped get them both back to the federal base at Fortress Monroe, where she found them medical attention and made sure they got onto a steamer for Baltimore. She then returned to the field to help with the wounded. "Such suffering and confusion I never before witnessed," she said. Sampson had a close scrape when she had to flee a Confederate attack. She lost her lists of wounded Maine soldiers and all her possessions in the ensuing "skedaddle" and took refuge on a U.S. navy gunship on the James River.

Shortly afterward, Charles Sampson fell ill and resigned his commission, and Sarah returned with him to Bath. "It is with great reluctance that I leave at a time when my services are so much, ever so much needed; and when my opportunities and facilities for affording relief to the suffering are daily extending," she wrote to Maine's adjutant general, John Hodsdon, "and it is made still greater by the earnest persuasions and importunities of many that I should remain from a sense of duty—But I feel my first duty is to my husband, who would not on any account permit me to remain even were I disposed to."

She must have overcome her husband's objections, because Sampson returned to the nation's capital that October to work for the Maine Soldiers Relief Association of Washington. She received a salary of $40 a month (later raised to $60) and the use of a wagon and a driver so she could visit area hospitals. When scores of wounded soldiers flooded into Washington after the Battle of Fredericksburg that December, Sampson was there. "Some of them recognized me, and begged me with tears to take them where they might die (if die they must), within reach of their friends," she wrote.

Another wave of wounded soldiers arrived the next May after the Battle of Chancellorsville. Sampson made a tour of all the army corps hospitals to gather names of the Maine soldiers and, when possible, have them sent home. She recalled how one man, Jackson Ballard of the 3rd Maine, implored her to stay with him as he lay dying. She did, and once he died she found a coffin for him and had his body sent home to Palermo.

After the Union and Confederate armies clashed in Gettysburg that July, Sampson traveled to Pennsylvania with as many supplies as she could gather, including fresh eggs and brandy to make eggnog. She remained in Gettysburg until August 15. "We did what we could, but 'twas little to what we would," she said.

When the bloody Overland Campaign began in May 1864, Sampson went to work in Fredericksburg, where she "beheld such wretchedness and suffering as we had never before seen." Wounded soldiers filled houses, stores, and churches. Many lacked blankets, food, and water. "It encouraged them to feel that some friends from their own State had come to their relief; some of them cried for joy, and we cried with them," Sampson recalled. She accompanied some of the wounded on their grueling trip by steamer back to a hospital at White House Landing on the York River in Virginia. When that hospital was broken up, Sampson moved further south to City Point at the confluence of the Appomattox and James Rivers, where General-in-Chief Ulysses S. Grant had established his headquarters as his armies made unsuccessful attempts to capture the railroad terminus at Petersburg. Sampson shared a tent with two other nurses from Maine, Ruth Mayhew and Harriet Eaton.

Sampson continued her work with Maine soldiers—treating their wounds, writing letters for them, keeping their family members informed of their circumstances, and providing moral support—until she returned to Maine in September 1864. Perhaps the strain was too much, for she became seriously ill at home and didn't return to Washington until February, when she resumed her work for the Maine Soldiers' Relief Association. As Grant began the final push of the Appomattox campaign that spring, Sampson set up shop in the Virginia town of Burkesville. She was there when Robert E. Lee surrendered the Army of Northern Virginia and when word arrived that Abraham Lincoln had been assassinated.

Sampson ended her work in Washington that October. The number of soldiers under her care had dwindled to a final five, and she left with them on a train for Augusta, reaching Maine's capital on October 9, 1865. Looking back at her years of service, she said she had "been rewarded a thousand times for all I have sacrificed or endured for the soldiers. Sacred tears of gratitude, blessings from pale lips, and seats beside the death-beds of our country's noblest sons, have been mine; and though some still live who remember the 'cup of cold water,' the many have 'sealed their devotion to the country with their lives.'"

When she died in 1907, Sarah Sampson was buried in Arlington National Cemetery.

~ ~

The war unfolded on battlefields far from Maine, but the conflict made its impact felt at home in other ways—in the empty places at the dinner table or in the newly dug graves in the cemetery. In June 1863 the war reached Portland in a much more direct manner.

The first Mainers to sense the impending threat were Albert T. Bibber and Elbridge Titcomb, fishermen out of Falmouth who owned a sloop called the *Village*. On June 26, the men were in their dory when the schooner *Archer* hailed them. The schooner lowered a boat and the five men aboard rowed over to the fishermen. They said they were Confederate privateers and they brought Bibber and Titcomb back to the *Archer*.

The Falmouth men later testified they didn't believe the sailors' story, thinking instead that they were "a merry crew of drunken fishermen on a frolic." The man in charge on the *Archer*, though, appeared to be neither drunk nor a fisherman. He carefully quizzed the two men about Portland, especially about what ships were in port, and asked for their assistance in navigating into the harbor.

The leader was Lt. Charles Read of the Confederate Navy. A Mississippian and a graduate of the Naval Academy in Annapolis, Read was described as "little more than a boy, bright faced, alert, twenty-three years of age, rather slight, with brown whiskers and a thin, sharp face." He and his crew were on a voyage of destruction up the East Coast. It had started when Read was an officer aboard the CSS *Florida* under John Maffitt. When the *Florida* captured the brig *Clarence* on June 6, Read took command of that vessel and used it to burn or capture some 19 other ships. When he and his crew took the bark *Tacony* outside Mt. Desert Island on June 12, Read had everything transported to the better ship and set the *Clarence* on fire. On June 25 he captured the *Archer*, transferred his operations to that vessel, and set his sights on Portland. When the two captured fishermen told him that the revenue cutter *Caleb Cushing* and a passenger steamer were both in port, Read found his targets.

The rebels kept their 12-pounder cannon and other arms hidden as they brought the *Archer* past the guns of Fort Preble and into Portland harbor. No one challenged them. Once anchored, they used binoculars to make a careful survey of the town. The raiders planned to row over to the *Caleb Cushing* and board her, capture the crew, and sail out to the *Archer* to transfer arms and equipment. Read hoped to burn two U.S. gunboats under construction at one of the wharves and capture the steamer *Chesapeake* to prevent her from being used for pursuit. But Read's engineer, Eugene H. Brown, doubted he could get the steamer underway without assistance from another engineer, so Read decided to focus on the cutter. If Bibber and Titcomb had really been fooled about the crew's true nature, they must have realized the truth when the Confederates had them confined belowdecks and told them to keep quiet. From overhead they heard the mysterious sailors make their preparations for the night.

The *Caleb Cushing* was a brigantine of 200 tons that was armed with two cannon, a 32-pounder and a 15-pounder. Essentially a patrol boat, she had no engines and was powered only by the wind. Read had targeted her at an especially opportune time. The *Caleb Cushing's* captain had recently died, leaving Lt. Dudley Davenport—a Georgian suspected of Southern sympathies—in command. Furthermore, much of the crew had gone ashore to spend the night in Portland.

The Rebels rowed to the cutter, their oars muffled, around 1:30 that morning, and found it surprisingly easy to take control. Davenport was in his berth when he heard noises on deck. He emerged to investigate and found himself confronted by lowered pistols. The men aiming them said they would kill anyone who resisted. Davenport surrendered. The Rebels put him and the 20 crew members remaining on board in irons and locked them up belowdecks. There were some tense moments when the Rebels had trouble slipping the anchor cable, but after some frustration they were able to make headway out of the harbor with the aid of a slight wind. The skeleton crew left aboard *Archer* prepared to follow.

Sometime around 7:30, observers in the tower on Munjoy Hill noticed the *Caleb Cushing's* departure. The initial belief was that Davenport must have taken the ship. "The city was thrown into a state of excitement bordering on consternation," the *Eastern Argus* reported. As soon as he received word, the port's collector, Jedidiah Jewett, sent out a summons to members of the 17th U.S. Infantry at Fort Preble and members of the 7th Maine under Col. Edwin C. Mason who were on recruiting duty at nearby Camp Lincoln. Jewett sent the steamer *Forest City*, a 700-ton side wheeler of the Portland & Boston line under command of a Captain Liscomb, and a smaller steamer called the *Casco* to Fort Preble to get arms, and he dispatched the steam tug *Tiger* to fetch Mason and his men—including the regimental band—and get them aboard the *Chesapeake*. William Leighton, the naval agent in Portland overseeing the gunboat construction, assumed command of the *Chesapeake*. A crowd of excited civilians crowded aboard the steamships, eager to take part in the chase. One of them was Charles Mead Gould, a combat veteran who had fought with the 10th Maine. When he had heard about the excitement in the harbor he had grabbed his pistol and headed for the wharf.

As protection from enemy fire, the men aboard the *Chesapeake* stuffed bales of cotton along her sides and around the engines. This was done as the steamship company's local agent protested loudly about the confiscation of his vessel. Mayor Jacob McLellan brushed aside his objections and said he and the city would be responsible for any loss. He told Leighton, "Catch the damned scoundrels and hang every one of them."

The *Caleb Cushing* had a head start, but the wind dropped and her captors had to use her small boats in an attempt to tow her out of the harbor. The raiders could see the steamboats in pursuit and began to search the captured vessel for ammunition. They found powder but no shot, and none of the captured crew would tell them where it was stowed. The Rebels stuffed whatever scrap metal they could find into the *Caleb Cushing*'s guns and fired at the oncoming *Chesapeake*.

"That means business," Leighton said to Colonel Mason. "Steer for her," he told the helmsman, "and we'll run her down or go to the bottom."

The cutter fired two more shots at its pursuers, neither of which found its target. The *Chesapeake* returned fire with a 6-pounder gun it had taken aboard. According to an account in the *Portland Daily Press,* one of the men aboard the *Chesapeake* was a sailor who had served under Admiral Farragut. "After the *Chesapeake* fired at the cutter, making a good shot for a small piece, the old tar rushed up, embraced the gun and affectionately patted her as though she was a pet child, with a hearty expression of approval for her good shot."

Leighton hailed the *Forest City* to determine a course of action. Captain Liscomb hesitated to take the initiative. "All right," Leighton said, "we shall steer straight for her and run into her any way we can, and you can take what's left."

Ahead, they could see that the cutter was lowering a small boat full of men. It began heading toward the *Chesapeake*, apparently with the intention of boarding her. "Stand ready, men," Col. Mason ordered the soldiers of the 7th Maine. More shots from the *Caleb Cushing* came whistling past. The *Chesapeake* fired at the small boat but missed. Someone aboard the boat waved a white handkerchief. Leighton ordered everyone to hold their fire as the boat came alongside. Aboard her were Davenport and the crew from the *Caleb Cushing*. Gould wrote that some of the armed citizens, thinking Davenport had been part of the plot, wanted to take immediate retribution. "'Shoot 'em, kill 'em, hang 'em,' they cried and commenced aiming their guns, fixing their bayonets and unfixing them and such a rumpus I never saw," Gould said. More responsible citizens restrained them.

Davenport was not pleased that the *Chesapeake* had fired at them. "It is hard, after a man has been taken prisoner, ironed, and his life threatened by pirates, to be shot by his own friends," he complained once he came aboard. Leighton, still suspicious of the Georgian, had the crew members sent below.

Meanwhile, the *Caleb Cushing* had lowered more boats, which began heading in the opposite direction. Wisps of smoke began to rise above the cutter. It appeared her captors had set the vessel on fire and were attempting to escape. The *Forest City* headed off to capture the men in the boats.

Both vessels now stood by and watched as the *Caleb Cushing* burned, aware that the powder aboard her would eventually explode. Some men talked Leighton into letting them take a small boat and attempt to extinguish the fire, but they realized the hopelessness of the task before they got too close. Three men, though, remained determined to save a small boat tied to the cutter's stern and they managed to cut it loose just before the ship exploded. "The smoke rolls up in vast columns," read an account in the *Argus*, "fragments of shells, masts and spars and blackened timbers are seen hundreds of feet in the air, falling all around, the cutter begins to sink, her stem disappears, the guns fall off the deck into the fathomless deep, she careens, she gives one lurch—and the *Caleb Cushing* sinks beneath the waves." (The three men renamed the recovered boat the *Trio* and put it on display at the North Star Boat Club.)

The *Forest City*, in the meantime, captured the *Archer* and its skeleton crew as they attempted to slip out of the harbor and the victorious flotilla made its way back to port. "As we passed the forts in the harbor guns were fired, bells rung and other lively demonstrations were made," said the account in the *Argus*. "The wharves and all available points were alive with people, who cheered again and again, and they were responded to from the decks of the *Chesapeake* by cheers and the firing of guns."

It took some time for Portland to catch its collective breath. "You can form but a faint idea of the excitement now existing among the citizens of Portland and vicinity," said Major George L. Andrews of the 17th U.S. Infantry. "Rumor follows rumor in rapid succession, and just before daylight this morning someone from the vicinity of the post went to the city with a fresh rumor which set the whole city in a ferment. The bells were rung and men, women, and children soon filled the streets, and were rushing hither and thither in aimless fright."

The city eventually recovered its equilibrium and, despite the loss of the *Caleb Cushing*, chalked up the outcome as a victory for Portland. "Too much credit cannot be given to Mr. Collector Jewett for the promptness with which he acted on this occasion, and to our citizens for the alacrity with which they hastened to offer their services," wrote the *Daily Press*. "The results reflect credit upon the city. It has upset the calculations of these piratical villains, and instead of finding themselves on the high seas with a well appointed vessel, committing degradations on our commerce, they are ironed and confined, waiting their trial as pirates." The *Daily Press* would be disappointed on that last point, however. The Rebels were not treated as pirates but as prisoners of war and were eventually exchanged for Union prisoners.

—◦—

At the time of the Civil War (and to the present day), the population of Maine was overwhelmingly white. According to the census of 1860, only 1,140 African Americans lived in the state. Nonetheless, not all the soldiers from Maine were white, even though the state did not raise any African American regiments once Abraham Lincoln's Emancipation Proclamation cleared the way for black soldiers to serve. Yet non-whites from Maine did fight for the Union. Some of them joined black regiments formed in other states, such as the 14th Rhode Island Heavy Artillery or the 5th Massachusetts Cavalry. Surprisingly, though, some black men joined the 1st Maine Heavy Artillery, which was not a "colored" regiment. "Lemuel W. Carter, George A. Freeman, and Franklin Fremont, of Company M, and Aaron Williams, of Company G, were of African descent," noted a 1903 history of the regiment. "Thomas Loren, Louis M. Thompson, Thomas Dana, Thomas Lewis, Supple Orson, and John Tomar, of Company B, John Saul, of Company E, and William H. Over, of Company M, were Maine Indians, all except the latter belonging to the Penobscot tribe.

Little is known about these men, although pension records at the National Archives in Washington provide a few scraps of information. George A. Freeman was a seaman from Bath when he mustered into the 1st Maine Heavy Artillery on January 5, 1864. The regiment initially received the relatively cushy assignment of manning the defenses of Washington, D.C., until the bloody Battle of the Wilderness required a fresh infusion of soldiers for Ulysses S. Grant's Overland Campaign in the spring of 1864. The 1st Maine Heavy Artillery received orders to move out into Virginia, where it received its baptism of blood during the fighting around Spotsylvania Court House on May 19. Freeman was wounded when he received a bullet through his right hand. The wound left his hand useless for labor and following his discharge from the army he applied for a soldier's pension. After the war, Freeman divorced his first wife and married Sarah Watson. Her first husband, Thomas Watson of China, Maine, had been killed while fighting with the 43rd United States Colored Troops. Freeman died in Brunswick on January 8, 1887.

Lemuel W. Carter enlisted as a private in company M of the 1st Maine Heavy Artillery on January 1, 1864. In June he began suffering from a cough that led to hemorrhaging of his lungs, which may have been tuberculosis. He was honorably discharged on August 17, 1865. When Carter applied for a pension in 1889 he was 47 and living in Brunswick, where he worked as a hostler and a teamster.

Emerson Peters was one of the soldiers who joined a black regiment. He was born on April 4, 1839, in Warren, Maine, and was working as a "horseler" when he enlisted in Co. B of the 5th Massachusetts Cavalry in September 1864. Like many soldiers, he became afflicted with what he called "chronic diarrhea" and "malarial poisoning" while fighting the Army of Northern Virginia. "Had another attack of Malaria and Chronic diarrhea about the time the Regiment started in pursuit of General Lee's Army," he noted in his pension claim. "At the time of the surrender I was sick and unfit for duty and so continued to suffer until discharged." He had married his wife, Jane, in Augusta on May 4, 1862, and they had one daughter, Susie, born in 1874 in Richmond. His pension claim was initially rejected because he didn't furnish the proper documentation, but he eventually got it straightened out (and one of the men testifying to his veracity was George A. Freeman). By 1918 Peters was receiving $32 a month. He died on June 13, 1920, at the National Soldiers' Home in Togus.

When the war began in 1861, many people, North and South, thought it would be short and relatively bloodless. They were wrong. The First Battle of Bull Run, in July 1861, shattered that illusion. In Bangor, Marcellus Emery, editor of the *Bangor Democrat*, gloated in an editorial about the Southern victory. Enraged citizens broke into his office and destroyed his printing press and equipment. Emery narrowly escaped from the mob.

As the war dragged on, anti-war sentiment grew, especially among Democrats. When Lincoln announced his intention to issue an Emancipation Proclamation in September 1862, it further alienated those who had not wanted the war to become a campaign to end slavery. Resistance stiffened.

There was more resistance in 1863 when Lincoln announced plans for a draft to fill the Union's needs for soldiers. The response was especially virulent in New York City, where anti-draft rioters went on a three-day rampage in July. The rioters targeted African Americans, lynching an unknown number and burning the Colored Orphan Asylum. Troops from the Army of the Potomac, fresh from the Battle of Gettysburg, had to be rushed to New York to help put down the disturbances.

Even Maine saw resistance to the draft. From the town of Buckfield, outside Lewiston, an anonymous letter writer unloaded on the state's adjutant general. "I don't know that you are aware of the state of feeling in this vicinity in regard to drafting, but I know that the people have borne this tyranny as long as they will: the strings are ready to snap," he wrote, warning that "you will see the blood run in the streets and the torch of the incendiary will be applied to the buildings right away."

Similar sentiments were doubtlessly expressed in the tiny western mountain town of Kingfield, which attempted an organized resistance to the draft. This part of Maine leaned Democratic, and that was due in part to Eben F. Pillsbury, a Kingfield native who became a prominent Democratic politician. Pillsbury became known for his "abusive denunciation" of Lincoln before Fort Sumter temporarily changed his tune and Democrats united with Republicans to support the Union cause.

In Kingfield, the draft called for 12 men. The man in charge of it was a Republican named Nathan Saunders. When he announced the names of the draftees, people noticed a disproportionate number of Democrats among them, even for Democratic-leaning Kingfield. A mob gathered to express its displeasure with the proceedings, but when they reached Saunders's house, they found he had left town. The mob painted his house with black stripes to mark it as the home of a "black Republican" and left things at that.

By this time Pillsbury, strongly opposed to both emancipation and the draft, had reverted to his denunciations of Lincoln and the administration's war policy. He attended an anti-draft meeting in Kingfield, and when asked if there was any way to resist, he held up a glass of water and said, "The United States Government is as weak as this water. You can draw your own conclusions." People at the meeting took this as encouragement, and when a man named Lambert reached Kingfield to officially summon the drafted men, a mob greeted him, demanded his paperwork, and chased him out of town.

When word of Kingfield's rebellion reached Augusta, Governor Abner Coburn called out the Lewiston Light Infantry, under the command of Jesse Stevens, to handle the situation. To bolster his volunteers, Stevens also received about 30 soldiers from Augusta. One was Lewiston native Leroy H. Tobie, who came from an abolitionist family that had helped escaped slaves reach Canada. When the war began Tobie was not yet 18, but he obtained his parents' permission to enlist in the 10th Maine. He served with the regiment until he was mustered out in May 1863.

Tobie had little respect for militia groups like the Lewiston Light Infantry, especially when some of its members found excuses to avoid going to Kingfield. "Now it happened that many members of that organization were suddenly very much devoted to business and could not possibly go with the company, so they did the next best thing—they secured substitutes," he said. For combat veterans like Tobie, though, the expedition promised "plenty of fun" and a great opportunity to laugh at the green militiamen. "They had smelled powder, had faced the brave men of the southern army in hard-fought battles, and did not think of being frightened until they saw something to be frightened at."

The small force took a train to Farmington, where they heard rumors of the "blood-thirsty and desperate character of the rioters and the people at Kingfield." The stories made one militiaman so nervous he loaded a cartridge into his rifle backwards, much to the amusement of the veterans. On the 22-mile march toward Kingfield the veterans took the lead, where they ate all the berries they found along the road before the militiamen could find them, and sent back frightening stories to the captain about bushwhackers. "But they only laughed in their sleeves at him, not being at all frightened at the thought of bush-whackers in the good old State of Maine." When the veterans fired at crows flying overhead, the militiamen behind them panicked and formed into lines of battle.

It turned out that the militia had little to fear. When they approached the town of New Portland and took shelter from a thunderstorm in a barn outside town, some citizens arrived to give them doughnuts.

Kingfield lay 6 miles away. Two captains rode ahead on horseback with the draft notices. They reached Kingfield at 10:00 in the morning and delivered the draft notifications without incident. The town even sent out a fife and drum band to greet the rest of the approaching force. When the militia heard the martial music they thought they were going to be attacked, but instead they received a friendly escort into town, where they set up camp in a hayfield for the night. The next day Kingfield treated the militia to a picnic lunch. One of the soldiers—Private Nelson Dingley, Jr.—used the occasion to deliver a short speech. "We expected a volley of bullets and cannon balls, but instead we have been met by a volley of baked beans, doughnuts and custard pie," he said. "We can hardly believe that there is any disloyalty in this town, judging from our reception, or that there were ever any riotous proceedings."

Their mission over, the soldiers marched back to Farmington in the rain and were back in Lewiston that night. The Kingfield Rebellion was over.

Private Dingley went on to become the governor of Maine. Wrote his son and biographer, "The cap and uniform Mr. Dingley wore, and the musket he carried on this memorable occasion, were interesting relics in the family homestead for years after; and the owner of them was very fond of relating the amusing incidents of the Kingfield campaign in which 'he fought, bled and died for his country.'"

1870s

Maine Teeters on the Precipice

POLITICS TODAY MAY BE FRACTURED AND CONTENTIOUS, BUT THAT'S nothing compared to Maine in the late 1870s, when disputed state elections threatened to flare into civil war. Things got so bad that the outgoing governor brought a cache of weapons to the statehouse and hired mercenaries to protect the building from political rivals. As historian John J. Pullen described the situation in *Joshua Chamberlain: A Hero's Life & Legacy*, "In late December 1879 and early January 1880, the state of Maine . . . almost became a banana republic, with gangs of armed men trying to seize control of the government and the streets of the capital about to be stained by rivulets of blood."

How did Maine come to this deplorable situation? The answer lay in party politics. The Republican Party had dominated the state since shortly after its founding in the 1850s and had an uninterrupted hold on the governorship since 1856, much to the Democrats' frustration. Things began shifting in the later 1870s thanks to the rise of a third party, the Greenbacks, which backed soft money over the hard money represented by gold and silver. Paper money, it was felt, was better economically for Maine's agrarian economy.

For their gubernatorial candidate in 1878, the Greenbackers selected Joseph L. Smith, a lumberman from Old Town. The Republicans renominated Governor Selden Connor, who had commanded the 7th Maine Volunteer Infantry during the Civil War and had been badly wounded during the Battle of the Wilderness. The Democrats chose Alonzo

Garcelon, a former Republican from Lewiston. A Bowdoin College graduate and a doctor, Garcelon had served as Lewiston's mayor and as Maine's surgeon general during the Civil War.

Republican Connor received the most votes in the election, but he did not win the majority required by law. That meant the Senate would choose between two candidates selected by the House. The House picked Smith and Garcelon. Republicans saw the Democrat as the lesser of two evils, and Garcelon became governor.

The governor's term was for a single year, and in 1879 the Greenbackers nominated Smith again at a raucous convention in Portland. The Republicans met in Bangor and nominated a relatively unknown named Daniel F. Davis. The Democrats, also meeting in Bangor, nominated Garcelon for another term.

The election took place on September 8 and for the second time in a row, no candidate won a majority. Davis came in first, Smith second, and Garcelon a fairly distant third. Once again the choice fell to the Senate, but now the makeup of the legislature was being called into question. It appeared that Republicans had won a majority of 29 seats in the House and 7 in the Senate. According to Maine law, community selectmen, supervisors, or aldermen used forms provided by the state printer to record their election returns, and then sent the forms to Augusta for the governor and his executive council to certify. As this process got underway, rumors began circulating that Garcelon and his executive council planned to "count out" victorious Republican candidates on technicalities and award their seats to "Fusionists," an alliance between the Democrats and the Greenbackers. Once the Fusionists gained a majority in the Senate, they would make Smith governor.

It was an audacious scheme, and for a time it looked like it would work. When the election results were announced on December 17, the Republican majorities had been wiped away to give the Fusionists control of both houses. The executive council had found creative ways to disqualify Republicans. They threw out votes in Republican-dominated Skowhegan because the ballot had been printed in two columns instead of one, as required. Some results were discarded because the certifying official had written in a candidate's initials, not his full name, or left out a "Jr." In the return from Gouldsboro, someone had changed the middle initial of Republican candidate Oliver P. Bragdon to a B, so it was disqualified. (Later examination showed that the return had obviously been tampered with. "If there be a lower depth than this to which men can sink, it is not on God's green earth," said the Ellsworth *American*.) The executive council counted out the returns from Webster and Lisbon because they said one person had signed for all three selectmen, contrary to law. The selectmen in question protested that they had all signed the return as required.

A wave of anger and revulsion swept across Maine. Republicans (and fair-minded members of the other parties) began attending "indignation meetings" all over the state. At a meeting in Augusta, a minister preached a sermon where he said, "Mob violence would settle nothing whatever, but open, systematic war would if it must be had." There were "bold and stirring speeches" in Bangor, where Norumbega Hall was "packed to almost suffocation" and Mayor William H. Brown denounced the counting-out as "the blackest crime ever perpetrated in the United States." In their speeches, speakers compared the situation to Fort Sumter, the Revolutionary War, the French Revolution, and the Bible's Book of Revelation. Violence seemed imminent. "I thank God that I am not too old to carry a musket," said one Bangor speaker. In Winthrop, 800 people crowded into Packard Hall, where the governor and the council "were handled without gloves."

Such talk appears to have rattled Governor Garcelon. On Christmas morning, strangers arrived in Bangor and were reported to be busy in the state arsenal. Mayor Brown and several other men set out to investigate. They reached the arsenal just after two wagons loaded with arms and ammunition had departed for the train station. The delegation set off in pursuit. They found the wagons at the Kenduskeag Bridge, where a mob of concerned citizens had blocked them from crossing. The man in charge of the wagons, a clerk named French from the adjutant general's office in Augusta, said he was acting under verbal orders from Garcelon to bring weapons to the capital. Brown suggested that French return everything to the arsenal before the situation got out of hand. As the wagons turned around, the crowd gave a hearty three cheers and dispersed.

In Augusta, Mayor George E. Nash advised the governor against calling out the militia. Nash said he could deal with any trouble with 200 special policemen. Despite Nash's assurances, Garcelon remained determined to get weapons from Bangor. He had better luck with his second attempt at acquiring them, and on December 30, 120 rifles and 20,000 rounds of ammunition reached Augusta on a train from Bangor and were taken on a two-horse sled to the capitol. "There were large crowds in the streets through which the teams passed, and the bells of some of the churches were tolled, but no attempt was made to interfere with the transfer," The *Kennebec Journal* reported. It appeared that Maine was on the brink of a new civil war.

To protect the statehouse from insurrection, Garcelon and his council recruited a paramilitary force. Some of the recruits had spent time in the state and county prisons. The statehouse took on the appearance of an armed camp. "The doors are locked, the windows guarded, and the approaches watched," noted an account in the Boston *Herald*. "On trying to enter, a rifle pointed at the stranger warns him to go slow. His business stated, he proceeds through the half dozen men about the door, but at every turn, on every flight of stairs, in every room, he finds armed men."

Republicans wanted Garcelon to ask the Maine Supreme Court to render an opinion about the electoral issue, but the governor resisted. When he finally did submit questions to the court, the justices sided with the Republicans. Garcelon, whose term of office was due to end on January 7, ignored the ruling. Chaos and anarchy threatened. Fearful of what might happen next, Garcelon turned to the one man he thought could steer Maine through the crisis—the hero of Little Round Top.

Joshua Lawrence Chamberlain had been a professor at Bowdoin College when the Civil War began. In 1862 he volunteered to fight, resigned his professorship, and became lieutenant colonel of the 20th Maine Volunteer Infantry. He was in command of the regiment at Gettysburg, where the 20th Maine made a valiant defense of a rocky hill called Little Round Top. Chamberlain was badly wounded outside Petersburg in 1864 but returned to the field by the spring of 1865 and was the officer who oversaw the official surrender of Robert E. Lee's army at Appomattox. After the war he served two terms as Maine's governor before returning to Bowdoin as the college's president. In 1874 Chamberlain had faced a serious crisis at Bowdoin when the students staged a mutiny over his program of mandatory military drill. Chamberlain dismissed the rebellious students and sent a letter to their parents, saying their children would be allowed back if they signed a letter promising to follow the college's rules. Almost all the students did, and the college board compromised by making drill optional. (It was eliminated completely in 1882.)

That was small potatoes compared to the turmoil roiling Maine now. Chamberlain had mostly stayed out of the fray, although he was not pleased by what was happening. "The intense greed,—not to say need,—of getting possession of the government led to practices not contemplated by the constitution, nor accordant with truth and right," he said later. Chamberlain had encouraged Garcelon to consult the Supreme Court, but he had not attended any indignation meetings. When James G. Blaine, chairman of the Republican Party, asked Chamberlain to attend a meeting in Brunswick, the ex-governor demurred, saying that "what we now need to do is not to add to the popular excitement which is likely to result in disorder and violence, but to aid in keeping the peace by inducing our friends to speak and act as sober and law abiding citizens." Resorting to bloodshed, he said, would be "deplorable." "I cannot bear to think of our fair and orderly state plunged into the horrors of a civil war."

Even though Chamberlain was a Republican, Garcelon asked him to come to Augusta and take charge of the militia. On January 5 he issued an order: "Major-General Joshua L. Chamberlain is authorized and directed to protect the public property and institutions of the State until my successor is duly qualified."

When Chamberlain reached Augusta he found the state capitol barricaded and patrolled by Garcelon's mercenaries. "We have no right to keep these armed ruffians here, and I will not remain if they are not sent away in half an hour," he reportedly told the governor. Chamberlain also had the arms from Bangor returned and warned local militia that they should follow only his orders. He notified three nearby militia companies and an artillery battery to be ready to come to Augusta immediately if needed. As he surveyed the situation, Chamberlain remained determined to remain above partisan politics, a tightrope act that opened him to attacks from both sides. Republicans railed against him as "The Republican Renegade," "The Fusionist Sympathizer," and "the Most Dangerous Man in Maine." Fusionists called him "The Lawless Usurper," "The Tool of Blaine," and "The Serpent of Brunswick."

Republican attacks and the upswell of indignation were having an impact. A Democrat from Farmington, the ironically named Louis Voter, sent a letter resigning from the seat he had received when the Fusionists had counted out his Republican opponent. Other Fusionist candidates followed Voter's example. Despite the cracks in their front, the Fusionists moved forward with plans to form a legislature. When the party met in Augusta on January 7, a great mass of interested citizens gathered at the Statehouse to follow the proceedings, causing a commotion and clogging the hallways and stairs. Most of the Republican members stayed away. Despite protests by the few Republicans present, Garcelon swore in the members of the House and Senate. The Senate voted for James D. Lamson as its president and the House chose John C. Talbot as its speaker.

The Republicans convened to elect their own legislature on January 12, even though Brandon Lancaster, the Fusionist building superintendent, tried to stop them by locking the doors and taking away the lamp oil. The Republicans chose Joseph A. Locke as Senate president, and George E. Weeks as speaker of the house and voted to submit questions about the election to the Supreme Court.

When Lamson met with Chamberlain and asked to be recognized as governor, Chamberlain refused. He asked him to refer the question to the Supreme Court. "There are only two ways to settle the question at issue and quiet the public minds," Chamberlain said, "by following strictly the constitution and laws or by revolution and blood." When Republican Joseph Locke asked Chamberlain to recognize *his* claim to the governorship, the general refused to do that too. He later said that both sides had dangled the possibility of a U.S. Senate seat if Chamberlain backed their claims.

Chamberlain heard rumors that he was going to be arrested for treason, or that he would be kidnapped by the Fusionists and spirited away.

Republicans were not happy with him, either. Thomas Hyde, a Civil War veteran and a friend of Chamberlain's, arrived in Augusta with a warning that Republicans were willing to use force and "pitch the Fusionists out of the window." "Tom, you are as dear to me as my own son," Chamberlain replied. "But I will permit you to do nothing of the kind. I am going to preserve the peace. I want you and Mr. Blaine and the others to keep away from this building."

"I wish Mr. Blaine & others would have more confidence in my military ability," Chamberlain complained to his wife. Too many people, he said, were worried about "their precious pink skins." Chamberlain had reason to worry about his own. Mayor Nash assigned policemen to escort the general in Augusta, and Chamberlain had his son bring him two of his pistols from Brunswick.

For Chamberlain, January 14, 1800, was "another Round Top," the day that Maine's fate swayed in the balance. Things appeared to reach a climax when a mob showed up outside the state capitol with blood on its mind. "There were threats all morning of overpowering the police & throwing me out the window, & the ugly looking crowd seemed like men who could be brought to do it (or to try it)," Chamberlain later told his wife. Chamberlain appeared on the main steps outside to confront the gathering. "Men, you wish to kill me, I hear," he said. Nonetheless, he announced that he intended to follow the dictates of law. He threw open his coat. "If anyone wants to kill me for it, here I am. Let him kill!"

Instead, the members of the mob crept away in shame.

On January 16 Chamberlain wrote to Blaine. "A storm is raging around me here in the State House; & I have no doubt of the designs of wicked men inside this building as well as outside," he said. Chamberlain continued to resist Republican demands that he call out the militia. "Whoever first says '*take arms!*' has a fearful responsibility on him, & I don't mean it shall me be who does that."

He did not have to. Although the Fusionist legislature elected Joseph L. Smith as governor on January 16 and inaugurated him, time was running out on the great counting-out conspiracy. Smith tried to remove Chamberlain from his post, but Chamberlain refused to budge, even when threatened with arrest. The Supreme Court issued a unanimous decision the next day and ruled that Garcelon and his council could not determine the qualifications of the members of the legislature. The Republicans, triumphant, voted for Daniel F. Davis as governor. As Davis arrived to take the oath of office, "the audience rose up as one man, and the sound that followed was like the roar of the sea, steadily increasing in volume, until the old Capitol building fairly rocked." To add insult to injury, Fusionists had locked the door to the governor's office and taken the keys, so Davis had to have someone pick the lock so he could get in.

The *Kennebec Journal* celebrated with its headline the next day:

HALLELUJAH!
The Victory won!

Chamberlain considered his duty done and returned to Brunswick.

The Fusionists hadn't quite given up, though. On January 19 they attempted to gain entry to the capitol but were denied admittance. They gathered elsewhere and considered taking the capitol by force. Davis summoned militia units from Auburn and Richmond to Augusta, and had a Gatling gun set up on the capitol grounds.

The Fusionists met for the last time on January 28 and adjourned their legislature until August. It never met again. Instead, legitimately elected Fusionist candidates joined the legally recognized legislature. The crisis was over.

In February the state appointed a committee of seven representatives and three senators to investigate the events surrounding the disputed election and its aftermath. In his testimony, Garcelon denied any knowledge of returns being altered. He also admitted to a remarkable ignorance about the political makeup of Maine's towns or the political parties to which various candidates belonged. "So far as that matter is concerned. I presume there is not a man in the State who knows so little about the political complexion of towns or members of the Legislature as I do," he told his examiners. "It is a matter I never inquired into." No one was prosecuted for the apparent vote tampering, perhaps to avoid reigniting the passions that had almost plunged the state into civil war.

Ironically, Chamberlain's handling of the crisis probably ended his hopes for a future in politics. On January 12, at the height of the crisis, he had sent a letter to Chief Justice John Appleton, recommending that Fusionist Lamson "is entitled to be recognized." What Chamberlain meant, he explained later, was he believed Lamson should be allowed to present questions to the Supreme Court, not that he should be recognized as governor. When word of the letter got out, though, Republicans became convinced that Chamberlain had intended to betray the party. Chamberlain was supposedly interested in becoming a U.S. senator, but uproar over the letter, which Chamberlain biographer John Pullen said "was perhaps too hastily written," doomed his chances.

Despite the blow given to his political hopes, Chamberlain remained pleased with the way he had handled the events of 1879-1880 and steered Maine away from the precipice. Looking back on those tumultuous days years later, he said it was "by far the most important public service he ever rendered."

1880s

James G. Blaine Runs for President

BLAINE MEMORIAL PARK OCCUPIES AUGUSTA'S HIGHEST HILL, NEXT TO the airport and overlooking Forest Grove Cemetery. It's named after James G. Blaine, the man who is interred here. The accomplishments engraved on the slab over his grave provide a sense of his life. He was a member of the Maine House of Representatives, and then its speaker; a member of the U.S. Congress and then Speaker of the House; a U.S. Senator, Secretary of State, and president of the first Pan-American conference. The list fills the entire slab.

There's a second Blaine buried here in the park. The life summary on her slab is a bit more succinct. "His Wife," it reads.

If it weren't for Harriet Stanwood Blaine, though, there's little chance that Pennsylvanian James G. Blaine would have ended up in Maine. Only after relocating to his wife's hometown of Augusta did Blaine begin his climb to prominence. His ascent took him agonizingly close to the White House in 1884, in a presidential campaign season chock full of scandal and innuendo. "Such a campaign as that of 1884 had never been known in this country," wrote Blaine biographer Charles Edward Russell. "When it was done, men prayed that its like might never come again."

Before he became presidential timber, Blaine had already made an indelible mark on Maine politics. "James G. Blaine was the most widely known, the best loved and the most hated man in Maine History," wrote

Louis Clinton Hatch in his multi-volume history of the state. He was accomplished and controversial—loved by his followers, and possessed of such charisma that he became known as "the magnetic man." Like the best politicians, he had a nearly infallible memory for names and faces and a talent for making people feel they were the focus of his attention. On the other hand, Blaine was so dogged by rumors of personal corruption that his adversaries called him "the Continental Liar from the State of Maine." One biographer described Blaine's career as "the greatest wonder ever known in American politics, a phenomenon, a portent, a thing to move the thoughtful patriot to pondering and maybe to fear. For this man had two paths that he walked; one in the daylight that was straight, one in the dark that was twisted as a ram's horn."

In his history, Hatch seems eager to place some distance between Blaine and the state he came to call home. "Unlike all other citizens of Maine who have attained great prominence in the political life of the State and nation Mr. Blaine was not a New Englander by either blood, birth or breeding," he noted. He was, in fact, born on December 31, 1830, in the western Pennsylvania town of West Brownsville. He did not appear to be a promising child, and he didn't learn to read until he was seven. In 1848 Blaine began teaching at a school in Kentucky, and that's where he met Harriet Stanwood.

Born in Augusta on October 12, 1828, Harriet was the daughter of Jacob Stanwood, a wool merchant who had moved to Maine from Ipswich, Massachusetts, in 1820 with his second wife, Sally. Harriet was the Stanwood's seventh child. After attending the Cony Academy in Augusta, Harriet studied at a girls' school in Ipswich before finding a teaching position in Millersburg, Kentucky, where she met her future husband.

The match appears to have been love at first sight, or nearly so, but there is some mystery about the marriage. The Blaines apparently got married twice—the first time a secret marriage in Kentucky in 1850, and the second one performed in March 1851 in Pennsylvania, supposedly because Blaine worried the first marriage might not have been legal. Their first child, Stanwood, was born a mere three months after the second ceremony, and the timing may have been a factor.

Whatever the circumstances, the marriage appeared a happy one. Blaine learned to depend on his wife for advice and she vehemently defended him when necessary. "Mrs. Blaine was a woman of brilliant mind and of keen wit, a fitting mate of her husband in mental quality," wrote Edward Stanwood in an early biography. (Stanwood was Harriet's cousin, so he may have been biased.) "More than this, she was able to enter to the fullest extent into the subjects which interested him. Her literary tastes were in strict agreement with his. Together they read and enjoyed the works of the great writers of fiction, poetry and history. She not only sympathized with her husband in politics and shared and incited his ambitions, but she brought so good a judgment to the consideration of public questions that Mr. Blaine habitually talked over political questions with her, and frequently sought her advice."

Blaine studied law in Philadelphia before taking a teaching position at the Pennsylvania Institute for the Blind. When young Stanwood died at the age of three, the grief-stricken parents relocated to Harriet's Augusta, where James had received an offer to edit the *Kennebec Journal* and later the Portland *Advertiser*. But it was clear his future lay outside publishing, and he quickly became a rising star on the Maine political scene, his Pennsylvania roots notwithstanding. Said former governor Edward Kent, "There was a sort of western dash about him that took with us downeasters; an expression of frankness, candor and confidence that gave him from the start a very strong and permanent hold on our people." In 1856 Blaine served as a delegate at the Republican national convention; two years later he was elected to the state legislature, and he became speaker of the Maine house and then the head of the state Republican Party. He moved to the national stage in 1862 when he became the U.S. Congressman from the district around Augusta, and he was appointed to a Senate seat in 1876.

Blaine did not serve in the Civil War. Instead, he sent a substitute to fight in his place and remained in Maine to pull political levers. One Maine man who did fight in the war, Oliver Otis Howard, noted his impressions of Blaine in the early days of the conflict. "Nobody in the Maine House of Representatives, where he had been for two years and of which he was now the Speaker, could match him in debate," Howard wrote. "He was, as an opponent, sharp, fearless, aggressive, and uncompromising; he always had given in wordy conflicts, as village editor and as debater in public assemblies, blow for blow with ever-increasing momentum. Yet from his consummate management he had already become popular."

Even though he had not fought, after the war Blaine became known for "waving the bloody shirt" to stir up the war's passions in the aid of Republican causes. After Blaine made one powerful "bloody shirt" speech on the House floor, a colleague compared him to "a plumed knight" who "threw his shining lance full and fair against the brazen forehead of every traitor to his country and every maligner of his fair reputation." The "plumed knight" nickname stuck, although enemies learned to wield it sarcastically when discussing Blaine's reputation for corruption.

Blaine dominated Maine politics for the rest of his life. "He dictated platforms; the candidates were, with some exceptions, those whom he favored," Hatch said. But biographer Stanwood hesitated to call him a "boss"; instead, he says Blaine was a leader more interested in helping the party than himself.

In truth, Blaine was interested in helping himself, and his willingness to sell his office for personal gain threatened to derail his career in 1872. When Arkansas was set to receive land from the U.S. government if it started a railroad line by a certain deadline, Blaine shepherded bills through Congress to extend the deadline, while gaining a financial interest in the Little Rock & Fort Smith line for himself. Blaine vehemently denied any wrongdoing and appeared to be exonerated, until a man named James Mulligan came forward and said he had letters between Blaine and a broker for the deal, one James Fisher, implicating Blaine in improprieties. Somehow Blaine obtained the letters, either by simply taking them after Mulligan let him look them over, or by threatening to kill himself unless Mulligan handed over the correspondence. But Blaine refused to make the letters public. They were his private correspondence, he insisted. Instead, he made an emotional speech on the House floor, proclaiming his innocence and reading selected passages to back himself up. Later revelations would show that Blaine was not being honest—his speech, Hatch wrote, "was entirely misleading and contained absolute falsehoods"—but it was good enough for his supporters, although the scandal did help deny him the Republican presidential nomination in 1876. That went to Rutherford B. Hayes, who won the election that fall.

Harriet remained unwavering in her support of her husband. Writing to a friend in June 1876, she said that "those who know him most, love him best. I dare to say that he is the best man I have ever known. Do not misunderstand me, I do not say that he is the best man that ever lived, but that of all the men whom I have thoroughly known, he is the best."

Blaine almost won the Republication nomination in 1880, but on the 34th ballot the delegates voted for James Garfield instead. Garfield won the election and selected Blaine as his secretary of state, but then the president was mortally wounded by an assassin's bullet—Blaine was standing at his side when he was shot—and was replaced by his vice president, Chester A. Arthur. Blaine tendered his resignation and returned to Augusta. There he bided his time and sowed the newspapers with articles attacking his enemies and praising his allies. At the Republican convention in 1884 he prepared to receive the nomination he had sought for so long.

Historian Mark Summers called the election of 1884 and its package of sex, corruption and scandal "one of the gaudiest in history." At the Republican convention, some delegates refused to back Blaine because of his shady reputation. They became known as "Mugwumps," supposedly after an Algonquin word for "big chief." In *Puck* magazine, cartoonist Bernhard Gillam depicted Blaine as a "tattooed man," stripped to his underwear and covered with the names of the institutions he had corrupted himself before. Someone printed up knockoffs and distributed them at the convention. Even as a "tattooed man," Blaine did not have much competition at the convention, not even from Arthur, an incumbent but accidental president. Summers reports that "when the roll call reached Maine, and the presentation of its favorite son's name, there was a roar so loud that it drowned out the thirty-piece brass band. The walls shook. The gaslights guttered." For his running mate, Blaine chose Civil War general John Logan.

Blaine's Democratic opponent was Grover Cleveland, the governor of New York. He had a reputation for honesty and seemed a good alternative to the wily Blaine. A cartoon by Bernhard Gillam, the same artist who tattooed Blaine, called him "Cleveland the celibate" and showed him turning away from various temptations.

It turned out that the bachelor Cleveland was not exactly celibate. On July 21, 1884, the Buffalo *Evening Tribune* published an article titled "A Terrible Tale." According to the paper, Cleveland had once had an affair with a widow named Maria Halpin, and she had borne his son, whom she named Oscar Folsom Cleveland.

Republicans sought to make the child more than just an aberration in Cleveland's personal life. They painted a picture of a man awash in debauchery, who was often drunk and consorting with prostitutes, the kind of man who tried to cover up his illegitimate child by having the mother thrown into an insane asylum. During one drunken spree, the stories said, Cleveland's law partner had been killed in a riding accident. During another, Cleveland and another man fought over a prostitute "till they were both nearly naked and covered with blood." Compared to this portrait of Cleveland, Blaine looked like a plumed knight indeed.

Cleveland responded quickly to the Halpin story. "Tell the truth," he reportedly said. Yes, he had enjoyed a relationship with the widow, but when she became pregnant and bore a child, he provided support, even though he was not certain the child was his. The other stories were soon exposed as part of a Republican smear campaign. According to one investigator, Cleveland's behavior after the child's birth "was singularly honorable, showing no attempt to evade responsibility, and doing all he could to meet the duties involved, of which marriage was certainly one." Still the story had damaged Cleveland's reputation.

The Democrats responded to Republican smears in kind, spreading a story that Blaine's marriage to Harriet had taken place under duress. "There is hardly an intelligent man in this country who has not heard that James G. Blaine betrayed the girl whom he married, and then only married her at the muzzle of a shotgun," reported the Indianapolis *Sentinel*. Blaine sued the paper, but quietly dropped the suit after the election.

Sometime in August, an unknown person stole into Augusta's Forest Grove Cemetery, where young Stanwood Blaine was buried, and tried to chisel the date of birth from the tombstone. Whether this was done to damage or help Blaine remains a mystery. "There is great indignation among all classes of people over the sacrilegious act," reported the *Kennebec Journal.*

As if that weren't enough, the Indianapolis *Sentinel* tried to drum up another scandal against Blaine, this time by accusing him of being a bit too forward in showing affection to other men on the campaign trail. "Now, if ladies were voters, and it were ladies he practiced his osculatory art upon, we should not object—i.e. if the ladies did not. But this thing of his kissing men—of pressing his bearded lips upon bearded lips—is too aggressive."

The scandal of the Mulligan letters resurfaced in 1884 as well. Back in April 1876, as the Little Rock & Fort Smith charges threatened to derail Blaine's hopes for the nomination, he wrote to James Fisher and asked him to write a letter absolving Blaine of any wrongdoing. Blaine helpfully included a draft of what he hoped Fisher would write. As a postscript, he added, "Burn this letter."

Fisher did not burn it. When the letter emerged during the 1884 campaign, it provided Blaine's enemies with a perfect slogan, and "Burn this letter!" became a popular chant at Democratic rallies. Republicans responded with their own anti-Cleveland chant: "Ma! Ma! Where's my Pa?"

Senator John Sherman suggested that Blaine campaign personally, so Blaine hit the road. Ex-president Ulysses S. Grant appeared at a speech in New York, ex-president Rutherford B. Hayes in Ohio. His central campaign issue was the tariff, which the Republican Party supported. His personal appearances helped sway one of the swing states, Ohio, to his side, but whenever Blaine made an appearance, the Democrats had a stenographer on hand in case he said anything damaging.

It appeared that New York would be pivotal to the election, so Blaine gamely made a tour through the Empire State, with a final big event in New York City on October 28. Part of the festivities was a gathering of ministers who could be counted on to harp on Cleveland's personal vices. One minister present was Samuel D. Burchard, from a Presbyterian church in New York City. When it was his turn to speak, he told Blaine, "We are Republicans and don't propose to leave our party and identify ourselves with the party whose antecedents have been rum, Romanism, and rebellion." Blaine may not have paid attention to the remark, but a newspaper reporter did, and word spread about Burchard's appeal to anti-Catholic prejudice. The issue created a political firestorm on the eve of the election, and "the three Rs" angered Catholics who might otherwise have been willing to vote Republican.

In the end, Blaine lost New York by 1,149 votes, out of almost 1,200,000 cast. Burchard—"an ass in the shape of a preacher," in Blaine's embittered description—may have helped tip the balance, though some Republicans were quick to raise accusations of voter fraud.

Blaine may have been secretly relieved to have lost. Harriet was not. "You need not feel envious of any one who was here during those trying days," she wrote a friend after the election. "It is all a horror to me."

Despite his defeat and his legacy of scandal, James G. Blaine remained a favorite among Republicans for the nomination in 1888. He refused to be considered, citing "considerations entirely personal to myself." Those reasons, it appeared, stemmed from his wife. "In the campaign of 1884, the scandalmongering and mud-slinging had filled her with an uncontrolled and almost hysterical terror," wrote biographer Charles Edward Russell, and Harriet believed "she could not endure another such ordeal." Instead, the Republicans chose Benjamin Harrison. After he won, Harrison asked Blaine to be his secretary of state.

The Blaines's son Walker and daughter Alice both died of pneumonia in January 1890. Their son Emmons died in June. After a long period of illness, James G. Blaine died on January 27, 1893. Harriet followed him into the grave on July 15, 1903. They were initially buried in Washington, but in 1919 the state legislature passed a resolution calling for the bodies to be exhumed and reburied in Augusta.

The reinternment took place on Sunday, June 13. Blaine's former newspaper, the *Kennebec Journal*, described it as "a perfect June day amid the splendors of bounteous and beautiful nature." The remains arrived in Augusta via a special train car and members of the James Fitzgerald Post, No. 2, of the American Legion escorted the coffins to their new resting places. The honorary pall bearers included Governor Carl E. Milliken and other political luminaries. Dr. James H. Ecob of Augusta's South Parish Congregational Church, which the Blaines had attended, preformed the committal service, which the paper said, was "perfect in every detail," words that do not describe the checkered career of James G. Blaine.

1890s

Louis Sockalexis Socks It to Them

PEOPLE WHO SAW LOUIS SOCKALEXIS ON THE BASEBALL DIAMOND SAID he was one of the best players ever—even better than greats like Ty Cobb, Honus Wagner, or Rogers Hornsby. "He had a gorgeous left-hand swing, hit the ball almost as far as Babe Ruth," recalled one man. "He was faster than Ty Cobb and as good a baserunner. He had the outfielding skill of Tris Speaker. He threw like Bob Meusel, which means that no one could throw a ball farther or more accurately."

Sockalexis, a Penobscot Indian from Maine, blazed like a supernova during the first half of the 1897 baseball season and then burned out as quickly. Today, much of his story appears shrouded in legend. Some of the feats attributed to him—such as throwing a baseball across Indian Island—are implausible or even impossible. He may or may not have been the first Native American to play major league baseball, or the inspiration for the Cleveland Indians' name. One thing that does emerge from the mists of legend is that, for a brief time, Louis Sockalexis was a unique talent and a true star. "He was a baseball meteor, who burned brightly but flamed out too quickly," wrote biographer David L. Fleitz. He called Sockalexis "the Native American version of Jackie Robinson," the player who broke baseball's color barrier in 1947.

Louis Sockalexis was born to a prominent family in the Penobscot tribe on October 24, 1871, on Indian Island in the Penobscot River north of Bangor. He attended Houlton Academy, a prep school in northern Maine, and played baseball there. It appears he also took classes at the Catholic school in Old Town.

In 1894 the Poland Spring House, a resort hotel, organized its own baseball team and hired Sockalexis, who had been demonstrating his prowess at the sport. He displayed impressive skills at the plate and in the field. He had such a strong throwing arm that improbable stories began to circulate about how far he could throw. On one occasion while playing for Poland Spring he did hurl a ball 408 feet. "Sockalexis is the best thrower in New England," the hotel noted.

While playing for the hotel and the local Knox County League that summer, Sockalexis met Michael "Doc" Powers, who played baseball for Holy Cross College in Worcester, Massachusetts. Powers thought Sockalexis would be an asset for his team and Holy Cross accepted him, even though he was about to turn 23. He began attending the college's preparatory school, probably on a scholarship.

Powers had judged wisely. Sockalexis became a star at Holy Cross, where he pitched and played outfield. In his two seasons at the school he batted .444 and .436 and often demonstrated his cannon of an arm from center field. "Despite his brief tenure at the college, Sockalexis helped transform Holy Cross into an eastern baseball power, for which he later earned posthumous induction into the college's Athletic Hall of Fame as one of its six charter members," noted historian Daniel P. Barr. Historians have speculated that Sockalexis's college career inspired Maine author Gilbert Patten to create the character Frank Merriwell, a baseball player for Yale who appeared in a popular series of novels.

Sockalexis also became known for his speed on the base paths, stealing six bases in one game with Holy Cross. (Because the rules at the time allowed a team to use an opposing player to run the bases if necessary, Sockalexis stole four of his bases for the other team.) According to another story, he corralled a ball that had rolled out of the outfield and threw it 414 feet to stop the runner at third.

At Holy Cross, Sockalexis also ran track and played on the football team. Baseball back then was a bruising, tough game but it was nothing compared to football. In the days before the forward pass was legalized, football was a game of brute force as teams powered their way over the goal line. Sockalexis played in a legendary game against Boston College on November 14, 1896. Holy Cross led 6-4 at the end of the game, but Boston College claimed the clock had not run out. After Holy Cross left the field, the Boston College team returned and scored on a final unopposed play. Holy Cross protested, and both teams claimed victory.

When Doc Powers transferred to Notre Dame in the fall of 1896, Sockalexis followed and played center field on the university's baseball team during the spring of 1897. One of his teammates later said that Sockalexis "was just as great a ball player as they say he was," citing his hitting and throwing ability and his speed. The major leagues were already showing interest. It appears that James "Chippy" McGarr, a coach at Holy Cross and a third baseman for the Cleveland Spiders, had informed the team about Sockalexis. Cleveland's manager, Oliver Wendell "Patsy" Tebeau, directed Worcester resident, occasional Holy Cross coach, and future hall-of-famer Jesse Burkett to sign the promising young Penobscot. By then Sockalexis had departed for Notre Dame, so Tebeau went to South Bend himself to secure the signature. Sockalexis signed the contract but said he wanted to finish the school year before joining the team. Instead, in an ominous foreshadowing, Sockalexis and another student went on a drunken spree in March 1897, busted up a local brothel, and landed in jail. Notre Dame expelled both students, and Sockalexis boarded a train for Cleveland. "They're Indians Now," read a headline in the *Sporting News* about the team after Sockalexis joined.

Even in the rowdy, no-holds-barred game of baseball in the 1890s, Tebeau's team had a reputation for aggressive, profanity-filled play, second only to the notoriously dirty Baltimore Orioles. Cleveland players argued and sometimes fought with umpires and often found themselves on the receiving end of rocks and bottles thrown by opposing fans. Still, the team had potential, with a roster that included pitcher Cy Young, center fielder Burkett, and third baseman Bobby Wallace, all of whom would eventually get inducted into the Baseball Hall of Fame.

Sockalexis stood out as the only Native American in the major leagues. But was he the first? Some historians give that distinction to James Madison Toy, who played in Cleveland in 1887 and Brooklyn in

1890. Sockalexis biographer Ed Rice disputes that notion. Toy supposedly had a Sioux father, but he did not look Native American or identify himself as one. "Louis Sockalexis, on the other hand, was clearly recognized as an Indian by all of his contemporaries, and was accordingly both heckled and acclaimed throughout his debut season with Cleveland in 1897," Rice wrote in *Baseball's First Indian, Louis Sockalexis: Penobscot Legend, Cleveland Indian.* "It is he who deserves recognition for being the first Native American to play major league baseball."

Whether he was first or not, Sockalexis created a sensation when he arrived in Cleveland. Tall, good looking, and clearly of Native American ancestry, he was unique, for better or worse. As one writer put it, Sockalexis had "the racial features of the redskin, but in his civilian clothes he passes as a handsome fellow." One sportswriter noted, "There is no feature of the signing of Sockalexis more gratifying than the fact that his presence on the team will result in relegating to obscurity the title of 'Spiders' by which the team has been handicapped for several seasons, to give place to the more significant name 'Indians.'"

Initially, Tebeau's faith in Sockalexis proved justified, behind the plate and in the field. His Native American heritage also provided fodder for a press corps eager to brandish Native American stereotypes. "Indians Hang One Little Scalp on Their Belts" read a typical headline after a Cleveland victory. Opposing teams and their fans tried to taunt the young Penobscot with war whoops and "Indian" dances. When the team played hated rival Baltimore, the Orioles' captain, third baseman John McGraw, showed up on the diamond wearing a huge Indian headdress. Sockalexis did not seem to mind. "No matter where we play I go through the same ordeal, and at the present time I am so used to it that at times I forget to smile at my tormentors, believing it to be a part of the game."

For the beginning of the season his coverage was mostly positive. After a game on April 26, the Cleveland *Plain Dealer* noted, "The bright particular start of the game was Warrior Louis Sockalexis. He was naturally the center of attraction after the visitors reached the grounds. He was greeted with war whoops and Indian yells, but as the game progressed and Socks began to hit and field, he was given an ovation. The Indian is a star, at least that is the impression that the 4,420 fans drew from his work today." After a game against Chicago on May 1, the *Plain Dealer* said, "The man who said that there is no good Indians except dead Indians, or words to that effect, surely never saw one Louis Sockalexis, late of the Penobscot tribe, but now of the tribe of Tebeau."

After the Indians played in Boston in June, a local reporter noted, "I never saw a deer run, but if a deer can run as fast as Sockalexis, then I can understand what a tough time my hunting friends have annually in the Maine woods." He confessed that Sockalexis was a "sensation," and concluded with a string of stereotypes. "He is a good Indian, a mighty big chief among the great medicine men, and our bonnets are off to him."

Cleveland's Indian was frequently saluted in poetry on the sports pages, sometimes in parody of "The Song of Hiawatha" by Henry Wadsworth Longfellow (another Maine native). Read one attempt:

This is the bounding Sockalexis,
Fielder of the mighty Clevelands,
Like the catapult in action,
For the plate he throws the baseball
Till the rooter, blithely rooting,
Shouts until he shakes the bleachers,
Sockalexis, Sockalexis,
Sock it to them, Sockalexis.

It had been a dizzying climb. The fall was faster. Even as Sockalexis was creating a sensation on the diamond, he was becoming a cause for concern off it. The problem was alcohol. When, exactly, Sockalexis began to drink remains in question. One legend is that he never tried alcohol until his new Cleveland teammates strong-armed him into celebrating with bourbon after one of his early triumphs, but it's clear Sockalexis had started drinking before he reached the majors. Alcohol was not a problem in the regimented, Jesuit-dominated atmosphere of Holy Cross, but Sockalexis was drinking at Notre Dame, as his expulsion demonstrates. The problem accelerated in Cleveland, where the new star developed a love for the bright lights of the big city, and his fans loved to buy him drinks. The sportswriters of the day, quick to embrace Native American stereotypes when writing about Sockalexis, blamed the problem on the supposed weakness Indians had for "firewater." "Sockalexis had succumbed to the curse which had been the bane of his nationality ever since civilization in America put whiskey in reach of the aborigines," concluded a writer for the *Sporting News*. Whatever the origin of the problem, Sockalexis's inability to control his drinking quickly took a toll.

On July 22 the *Plain Dealer* reported that Sockalexis was becoming a disciplinary problem for the team. Earlier that month, he had injured his foot, supposedly when he either jumped or fell from a hotel window during a spree. He played sporadically after that. On July 31 he received a suspension. When he returned to the team on August 14, he was a shadow of his former self. He ended up in the hospital with what was called a blood infection, which might have been caused by his injured foot. Or he may have needed some time to dry out. He played only one more game that year. Years later, Tebeau said he had even attempted to bribe Sockalexis into staying sober, saying he would pay him $6,000 for the first year and $10,000 for the year after that, "if he would stay sober and play ball. He promised, all right. But he couldn't let the strong stuff alone."

Sockalexis returned to the team in 1898, but he was not the same player he had been just a year before. He showed up late to spring training in Hot Springs, Arkansas, probably due to drinking. He played lackadaisically, but blamed his problems on making the transition from a cold winter in Maine to a warm spring in Arkansas. He knew he had no one to blame but himself for the terrible end to the previous season, and he vowed to improve. "My mind is made up and it is no joke," he told sportswriters. "I have a good future as a ball player and only have to take care of myself to keep in the game." Although he could occasionally display some of the old magic behind the plate, he hardly played during the regular season and made his final appearance on July 14.

In the spring of 1899, Cleveland owner Robison bought the St. Louis Browns. He had long been frustrated by baseball in Cleveland, especially over the city's laws prohibiting games on Sunday, so he sent all the best Cleveland players south to St. Louis. He did not send Sockalexis. He remained in Cleveland with a team of castoffs that compiled a historically bad record of 20-134, 84 games out of first place. Sockalexis played his last game in the major leagues on May 13 in Pittsburgh. "He was about as fast on his feet as a cow, didn't get within a mile of the drives to his garden and seemed to be dreaming of better days," a sportswriter noted. It appears he had been drinking, for he fell down twice in the outfield and couldn't manage a hit. Back in Cleveland he was arrested for public intoxication and spent a couple of nights in jail. Cleveland ended his contract.

Sockalexis had not hit rock bottom. Not quite. He played some semi-professional baseball in the minor leagues for the Hartford team of the Eastern League, appearing in 26 games in 1899 before his drinking became such an issue that he was released. He spent some time with the Bristol Bellmakers of the Connecticut State League, an even lower rung on the baseball ladder. He lasted around three weeks there before landing with the Waterbury team of the same league. He played well and finished the season with the team, but he did not return the next year. Instead, he spent time in jail in Holyoke, Massachusetts, and Pittsburgh on vagrancy charges. By 1902 it appears he had cleaned up his act slightly, because he was able to play for the Lowell team of the New England League.

The next year Sockalexis was back in Bangor, playing for a team in the Maine League. He remained in Maine for the rest of his life, operating the ferry that ran between Indian Island and the mainland and working as a logger. He also maintained his connection to baseball by playing occasionally, coaching the juveniles on Indian Island, and umpiring in the wild-and-wooly Northern Maine League.

Louis Sockalexis was working as a logger in the woods outside Bangor when he died of a heart attack on Christmas Eve, 1913, at the age of 41. In its obituary, the *Bangor Daily News* said, "The name of Sockalexis is yet magic with the old-time fans who remember him in his palmy days and some of them cannot be convinced that the Indian had all the physique and skill to have risen to baseball fame—as high and mighty as 'Ty' Cobb or any of the great outfielders of those and former days." He was buried on Indian Island.

Just over a year after Louis Sockalexis died, his old team in Cleveland needed a new name. They had been playing as the Naps, after their most popular player, Napoleon Lajoie. But Lajoie had moved on to Philadelphia. The team turned to the baseball writers in Cleveland to pick a new name. They chose the Indians, "it having been one of the names applied to the old National League club of Cleveland many years ago." The writers did not cite Sockalexis as a reason for their choice, but the name originally dated to 1897 and the excitement created by the exotic rookie from Maine and his apparently bright future in baseball.

The Cleveland *Plain Dealer* made the connection with Louis Sockalexis, though. On January 18, 1915, the paper said the new name looked back "to a time when Cleveland had one of the most popular teams in the United States. It also serves to revive the memory of a single great player who has been gathered to his fathers in the happy hunting grounds of the Abenakis."

More than a century after his death, people remain fascinated by the stunning rise and tragic fall of Louis Sockalexis. Within a year, in 2002 and 2003, three biographies of the original Cleveland Indian appeared, by Ed Rice, Brian McDonald, and David L. Fleitz. Bill Felber included a chapter about him in his 2007 book about the 1897 baseball season. Part of the fascination is Sockalexis's role as a pioneer—the man who may have broken the major leagues' color barrier. Part of it is a compelling sense of promise unfulfilled and the wonder of what might have been. Another factor may be the appeal of a classic "fish out of water" story, the tale of a Penobscot Indian from Maine struggling to find his way in the big cities of the white man. "So let us begin by considering the dimensions of the Sockalexis phenomenon," wrote Felber in his book: "He could hit a baseball harder than almost any man alive. He was an Indian playing a white man's game. His presence in the major leagues fed still-fresh stereotypes regarding the strength of the 'noble savage.' His downfall validated the classic cautionary tale of all great stories, be they comedies or tragedies. In the case of Sockalexis, it turned out to be tragedy."

1900s

The Stanleys Get Steamed

THE VEHICLE IN THE PHOTOGRAPH LOOKS LESS LIKE A CAR AND MORE like a canoe turned upside down and placed on wire-spoked buggy wheels. The photo was taken in 1906 on the hard-packed beach near Daytona, Florida. The man sitting inside the low-slung vehicle is Fred Marriott, the fastest man in the world. Standing behind the car is one of the men who created it, Francis Edgar Stanley. He and his twin brother Freelan Oscar had been born and bred in Kingfield, Maine, and had made their name synonymous with steam-powered vehicles. In 1906, Marriott drove Stanley's vehicle to a speed record of 127.66 miles per hour. More than a century would pass before another steam-powered vehicle went faster.

F.E. (called Frank) and F.O. (Freel) were born in Kingfield on June 1, 1849. "They were industrious, resourceful, and exceptionally fine students, their talent for acquiring knowledge far out-running the limits of the common schools of their vicinity," read a biographical sketch in Hatch's history of Maine. The twins demonstrated their ingenuity and eye for business at a young age. They started a maple sugar business, raising the money for some of the equipment by shooting a mink and selling its fur. They also earned money by whittling tops they sold to other children in Kingfield.

The twins attended the Western Maine Normal School, although F.E. dropped out after he was falsely accused of cheating. He began a career as a teacher and was toying with taking up law, until his artistic ability, especially portrait drawing, pulled him in another direction. He invented an airbrush to use for his portraits and also became a successful photographer. While living in Lewiston, he developed a new form of dry-plate photography, a much more efficient means of taking photographs than the wet-plate method. As word of his technique spread, F.E. founded the Stanley Dry-Plate Company in 1881.

F.O. had also embarked on a teaching career after spending a single year at Bowdoin. (He was one of only three students who did not return to school following the "mutiny" over the mandatory military training that college president Joshua Chamberlain had started.) In 1884 F.O. joined his brother in the business. "I doubt any enterprise was ever started in a more primitive manner than ours," he wrote. "We had, practically, no capital, no factory and no customers." But F.O.'s dry-plate process caught on, and soon the brothers were so successful they decided to relocate to Massachusetts to be near the transportation hubs there. In 1904 they sold the company to Eastman Kodak.

Hatch described F.E. in a biographical sketch, but he could have been writing about F.O. as well. "He was proud of his New England lineage, and of his birth on a farm in Maine," Hatch wrote. "He was devoted to his family and his home. His personal life was absolutely clean and pure. He thought on high lines and lived as he thought. He had, in short, the energy and uprightness, intellectual ability, common sense and sound judgment that distinguish the best New England blood. In addition to these qualities he was a man with an infinite capacity for enjoyment of the righteous things of life, and had a most cheerful nature, a kindling wit, and powers of mind and body of the highest order." Both twins were good musicians and natural storytellers, loved the outdoors, and had good senses of humor. Fred Marriott later recounted how the brothers reacted almost identically to the punchline of a funny story. Both would bend over and slap a leg. The only difference was that F.E. would say, "Godfrey mighty," while F.O would exclaim, "Gee cracky."

In Massachusetts, the brothers became interested in using steam to propel a personal vehicle. They were not the first people to consider the idea, which had been in circulation for centuries. Sir Isaac Newton even sketched out a steam-propelled carriage in 1680. Locomotives and boats used steam propulsion, but they required huge boilers and big engines. Over the years, inventors had developed a proliferation of steam carriages, coaches, wagons, buggies, and bicycles. Starting in 1887, Ransom E. Olds, later of Oldsmobile fame, had built a series of steam-operated vehicles. Unlike the Stanleys, though, none of these early inventors put their cars into production.

Steam-powered cars did have some advantages over the nascent internal combustion engines. In a gasoline car, the controlled explosion of fuel within the cylinders moved pistons up and down, and these drove a crankshaft that turned the wheels. In a steam car, burning fuel—which could be gasoline, kerosene, or even paraffin—heated water in a boiler to create steam pressure. The release of steam from the boiler provided the motivating power for the car. A throttle controlled the release of steam, without the violent explosions of the internal combustion engine. Unlike gasoline cars, steamers did not require gears and clutches and they were quiet, efficient, and quick to accelerate. Their one major drawback was that it could take time before the pressure in the boiler was sufficient to move the car, although efficient "flash boilers" could generate steam relatively quickly.

"The performance of a steam car at times is startling," wrote steam enthusiast Thomas Derr in a 1932 history. "Its instantaneous leap in response to the throttle is unmatchable by any gasoline car. This is all the more striking because accomplished without any apparent effort on the part of the engine. If the steam pressure is high enough to slip the wheels, the steam car then has the greatest acceleration that is possible in an automobile."

The Stanleys knew little about the technology when they made their first sketches of steam designs in 1896. They just thought it would be fun. They decided they would like their first car to weigh only about 500 pounds, but the engine they commissioned from the Mason Regulator Company in Massachusetts ended up weighing more than 400 pounds alone. They had the Roberts Iron Works make them a boiler; it weighed another 200 pounds. "Yet we were not discouraged," F.O. remembered. They later turned to a company in their home state, J.W. Penny and Sons of Mechanic Falls, which built them a motor that weighed only 35 pounds. And they designed their own boiler, which could withstand 600 pounds of steam pressure, which weighed in at a mere 90 pounds.

But it was the heavy Mason motor that powered their first steamer, which they finished in September 1897. A famous photograph taken in Watertown shows the brothers, two identical bearded men wearing bowler hats and with a lap robe draped across their legs, sitting in their car, which looks like a sleigh mounted on four bicycle wheels.

"I shall never forget our first ride," F.O. related. As the twins drove down a street in Watertown, the car startled a horse hitched to a wagon. The animal snapped its harness and galloped out of town. That afternoon its owner got in touch with the twins and told them they owed him $25 for the horse. Instead, in a typical example of their Yankee thrift, they had his broken harness repaired for $2.00.

The next day the brothers ventured all the way to Cambridge, spooking another horse along the way. "We naturally concluded from those two trips that the life of an automobile driver was not a happy one," F.O. said. The advent of the horseless carriage made things difficult for horses, as well.

By the spring of 1898 the twins had built three more cars with the lighter engine and boiler. "These boilers were a marvel of lightness and strength," said F.O. They were made of copper and steel and three layers of steel wire wrapped around the outside helped contain the pressure. The Stanleys sold one of the cars for $600, but at this point considered the whole thing a hobby, not a business.

That began to change after the twins participated in New England's first automobile show, which took place in Boston in October 1898 and included an outdoor meet at the Charles River Park in Cambridge. The Stanley car outperformed all the others at the meet and set a speed record of 2 minutes and 11 seconds for a mile. It also showed up the other entries in a hill climbing exhibition. By the end of the day, the Stanleys had received 200 orders for their car. Suddenly they were in the automobile business. They bought a bicycle factory next door to the dry-plate business and began to make cars.

On August 31, 1899, F.O. and his wife drove in a Stanley car to the top of Mt. Washington, the first time a self-propelled vehicle made the ascent. There is no record that they pasted a "This Car Climbed Mt. Washington" bumper sticker on the back of the vehicle.

In 1899 John Brisben Walker, owner of *Cosmopolitan* magazine, offered to buy the Stanleys' new company. He offered $250,000. The twins were a bit taken aback by the magnitude of the offer, having invested only $20,000 or so in the business to date, but they eventually accepted and sold their patents to Walker's new company, Locomobile. At this point things became a little confusing. Locomobile split into two companies, and one twin served as advisor to each. When the brothers decided to start producing steamers again, Locomobile sued them for infringing on their own patents. The Stanleys revised and improved their designs but, when Locomobile decided to abandon steamers in favor of gasoline cars, they got their patents back.

In the early 1900s, Florida promotors, including the managers of the beachside Ormond Hotel, began spreading word about the suitability of the state's Atlantic beaches for automobile racing. The hard-packed sand offered a smooth, dust-free surface that was better than most roads at that time. The first Ormond-Daytona races took advantage of the beaches on March 26-28, 1903, the start of a tradition that led to the formation of the National Association for Stock Car Auto Racing, better known today as NASCAR.

No world records were set on the first day of that first event, although one competitor did establish a new American record for the measured mile, driving an Oldsmobile at an average speed of just over 54 mph. On the first day, one of the beach's promotors, Massachusetts businessman J.F. Hathaway, drove a Stanley Steamer for a mile in just under a minute and a half, at an average speed of almost 41 mph. Stanley vehicles would go much faster than that within just a few years.

At the 1904 races, Louis S. Ross, an inventor and firefighting afi- cionado from Newton, Massachusetts, drove his 6-hp Stanley to a speed record for steam cars in the mile course, at an average speed of a little more than 55 mph. Ross also won a five-mile race, although he had only one opponent. The 1905 races were marred by the event's first fatality, an accident involving the Stanley twins' nephew, Newton Stanley. Newton was driving a motorcycle down the beach when he suddenly swerved into the path of a car driven by racer Frank Croker. Stanley broke his leg and went flying into the surf in the ensuing crash. The car went tumbling into the water, too, mortally injuring Croker and instantly killing his mechanic, Alexander Raoul.

Louis Ross returned to Florida in 1905 in a vehicle that he had designed himself. It was powered by two Stanley steam engines and earned the nickname "Wogglebug" thanks to the way it wobbled as Ross attempted to synchronize the two throttles. The streamlined vehicle looked a bit like a life-size Pinewood Derby racer and sprayed steam into the air from an exhaust pipe mounted just behind the cockpit, but it set a world record of 38 seconds for the mile—an average speed of almost 95 mph. Ross retained his record for a good five minutes, until an English racer bested it. (That record stood for 15 minutes until it, too, was topped.) Ross and his Wogglebug also beat three other entries in a one-mile race to win the Thomas Dewar Trophy. "It was the Cinderella story of the year," wrote Dick Punnett in his book *Beach Racers: Daytona Before NASCAR*.

F.E. designed his own car for the 1906 events, where it would compete against drivers with names like Henry Ford and Louis Chevrolet. F.E. designed his new steamer for one purpose only: speed. He had the lightweight body constructed of cedar strips and canvas and painted red. The driver sat on the floor and steered with a steel bar instead of a wheel. The 30-hp engine was powered by a boiler that could reach 1,000 pounds per square inch of steam pressure. To keep the boiler from disintegrating if it should explode, it was wound with 30 miles of piano wire.

F.E. assigned Fred Marriott, the foreman of the company's repair department, to drive the racecar, which journalists initially dubbed the Teakettle. On the third day of racing Marriott became the fastest man alive, setting a new record for the mile when he reached 127.66 mph. He also briefly set the world record for two miles, 59⅗ seconds, the first time anyone had done it in less than a minute, but a French car soon made even better time.

Marriott returned for the 1907 races, with a modified version of the car from the year before. On the race's third day he fell short in his first two attempts to best his 1906 record. The third try was not the charm. As Marriott accelerated across the beach, his front wheels hit some ripples in the sand, bouncing the front of the car into the air. "It then swerved side-wise, and when the front wheels again came in contact with the ground, it was headed toward the sea, the wheels of course went down and the car rolled over and over, breaking to fragments," said motorcyclist Glenn Curtiss, not yet a pioneering aviator, who witnessed the accident. "The boiler kept on going, and rolled several hundred feet farther than the balance of the car, the escaping steam giving the appearance of a meteor rushing through the surf."

Amazingly, Marriott survived the crash, even though he was thrown out of the car and suffered cuts, bruises, and broken ribs. F.E., who had been watching the run with stopwatch in hand, estimated that Marriott might have been able to reach 150 mph. F.O., who was not there, later recounted an embellished account of the accident, claiming that Marriott's car left the ground completely and that the injured driver was found with one eye dangling from its socket. While not as bad as that, the crash was distressing enough. F.E.'s wife, Augusta, dubbed the day "Black Friday." "The car was dashed to atoms and Fred inside!" she wrote in her diary. "He looked so dreadfully—pale and the bloody face—I can never forget it."

The accident ended F.E. Stanley's interest in racing. "The most valu-able lesson learned by this accident was the great danger such terrific speed incurs," he said. "So we decided never again to risk the life of a courageous man for such a small return." The record Marriott had set in 1906 remained the top speed ever attained by a steam car until a British car beat it by reaching 140 miles an hour in 2009.

The Stanleys were done with racing, but not with the business of steam-powered cars. F.E. continued running the Stanley Motor Carriage Company in his own low-key, idiosyncratic fashion, even as the internal combustion engine dominated the field. "We do know, however, that during all these years we have quietly stood on the side-lines, as it were, and have viewed with calm and peaceful mind the frantic endeavors of those engaged in our line of business as they collided with each other in their efforts to adapt the internal-explosive engine, which is essentially a constant speed motor, to automobile service, which is about the most inappropriate use to which it could possibly be put."

Inappropriate or not, the internal combustion engine became the mammal to the Stanley's dinosaur. Steam cars developed a fervent following from people who extolled their silence and simplicity, but that was not enough. Even F.O. eventually conceded the field to the gas-powered cars. "I regard the invention of the internal combustion engine one of the most valuable inventions made by man," he wrote near the end of his life. "And all the time, and all the money spent in trying to make a steam car as good, or better, than a gas car is time and money wasted."

F.E. retired from business in 1917. He did not enjoy his retirement for long. On July 21, 1918, he was driving one of his steam cars down a narrow country lane near Ipswich, Massachusetts, when he suddenly found the road blocked by a pair of farm wagons. F.E. swerved to keep from crashing into them and smashed into a wood pile. The car overturned, fracturing his skull. F.E. Stanley died in the ambulance on the way to the hospital. He was 70 years old.

The Stanley Motor Carriage Company continued to produce steamers until it went bankrupt in 1923. Reorganized, the company staggered along until it built its last car in 1925. F.O. had left the business long before that. In 1903 he was diagnosed with tuberculosis and the next year he visited Colorado for health reasons. There he founded the Stanley Hotel, a sprawling resort nestled against the mountain in Estes Park north of Denver. He designed the hotel, which opened in 1909. Guests were chauffeured around in a Stanley Mountain Wagon, a specially designed, 12-passenger, steam-powered car. F.O. also turned his attention to making violins. He died on October 2, 1940.

The Stanley Hotel has another Maine connection. In 1974 Bangor's Stephen King and his wife stayed there for a night. It was at the end of the tourist season and the staff had started to close down the big old hotel for the winter. As he wandered through the nearly deserted hallways of the massive building, King got an idea for a book he was working on. In his imagination, the Stanley Hotel became the haunted Overlook, and the idea turned into his third novel, *The Shining*.

Maybe it's just a coincidence, but in King's novel the Overlook Hotel is destroyed when its steam boiler explodes.

1910s

Hiram Maxim Invents Modern War

ON JANUARY 28, 1915, THE *WILLIAM P. FRYE*, A STEEL-HULLED, FOUR-masted ship that had been built in Bath, Maine, was making its way across the South Atlantic with a cargo of wheat. The vessel had left Seattle, Washington, on November 4, 1914, with a destination of Queenstown, Ireland. She never reached port. Instead she encountered the German cruiser *Prinz Eitel Friedrich*. Although the United States was neutral in the war that was consuming Europe, the *Prinz Eitel Friedrich* ordered the American vessel to halt and sent over a boarding party. After examining the *Frye*'s papers, the German captain had the American crew transferred to his cruiser. Then the *Prinz Eitel Friedrich* fired its guns and sent the *William P. Frye* to the bottom of the Atlantic. The Maine ship had the unfortunate distinction of being the first American vessel sunk by Germany during the growing conflict we now call World War I.

The United States did not enter the war until April 1917. By the time the armistice was signed in November 1918, some 32,000 soldiers from Maine had fought in the conflict, with about 1,000 of them paying the ultimate price. How many of them realized that the war had been shaped, in large part, by a man from their own state?

—❦—

Sir Hiram Stevens Maxim died on November 24, 1916, just a few weeks after German machine guns based on his invention killed some 60,000 British soldiers during the Battle of the Somme. Thanks largely to the machine gun, the war in Europe had turned into a bloody stalemate, with contending armies facing each other across a network of trenches that zig-zagged across the continent. "The Maxim gun and its offspring had altered how armies were organized and how war was waged, and killed men in quantities beyond counting," wrote C.J. Chivers in *The Gun*, his history of the AK-47 and the automatic weapons that preceded it.

Although he was a British citizen when he died, Hiram Maxim was a son of Maine. He had been born near the town of Sangerville, south of Moosehead Lake, on February 5, 1840, the eldest son of Isaac Weston Maxim and Harriet Boston Stevens. It appears that Maxim was an unusual child. In his memoirs, he recalled that "the proudest moment" of his life was when he managed—working methodically over the course of two weeks—to chop down a neighbor's huge balsam tree with only a butcher's knife. The neighbor was not amused, but it was typical behavior for young Hiram, who was "overflowing with latent exuberance and energy which oftimes found vent in pranks and boyish schemes which annoyed and sometimes confounded the wiser ones around him," as Maine historian John Francis Sprague noted.

Such behavior earned young Maxim a reputation as "the worst boy for miles around," the kind of child who pulled the wings off flies (which he did, he said, in the spirit of scientific inquiry.) People might have said he became the worst man for miles around, for Maxim grew up to be something of a jerk. He was a serial womanizer, a bigamist, and an unabashed racist. He was vain and quarrelsome and had a liking for cruel practical jokes. He referred to his hired servants by the generic name of "Stupid." On one occasion he tricked his cook (Stupid Number Five, his son recalled) into believing he had branded her with a red-hot poker, when it was really ice cold. She screamed, fainted, and—once she regained consciousness—quit.

Maxim was decidedly eccentric, a character trait one of his biographers blamed on his native state. "He was, after all, from Maine," wrote

Arthur Hawkey in *The Amazing Hiram Maxim: An Intimate Biography*, "and for a Maine Yankee eccentricity was almost a way of life and remains one of the characteristics of the hardy, independent and shrewd people of that small and most easterly State of the USA."

His personal life was eccentric, too. In 1867 he married Louisa Jane Budden of Boston, although she initially found his appearance and manners embarrassing. In 1878, Maxim met Helen Leighton on a streetcar. He was 38 and she was 15. Despite the age difference and his own marital status, Maxim wooed and won Helen, arranged some sort of marriage ceremony, set her up in a house, and got her pregnant. He later met and fell in love with Sarah Haynes of Boston and brought her with him to Europe as his secretary. After Maxim's first wife divorced him in 1888, he married Sarah. Later he successfully defended himself against Helen's charges of bigamy, even though she had the backing of Maxim's estranged brother Hudson. (Hudson was an inventor, too, and had developed smokeless gunpowder.)

Despite his character flaws and idiosyncrasies, Maxim was a gifted inventor and, although largely self-taught, he made pioneering contributions to everything from electric light to aviation.

It appears Hiram inherited some of his abilities from his father, whom Hiram credited with first giving him the idea for the machine gun. Isaac Maxim said he had received it in a vision, and that the gun "would be so powerful and deadly in its work that its practical effect would be to eventually abolish war and hasten the millennium." In 1854 father and son made some drawings of their idea and submitted them to a gun maker in Bangor, but nothing happened with it until Hiram resumed his research years later in London.

The path that took him to England was a long and winding one. When Hiram was 14, he started working for a carriage maker in East Corinth. He later found a job making rakes and then worked for another carriage maker. Maxim had a natural aptitude for mechanics and was skilled at drawing and painting. He literally invented a better mousetrap, and he built a tricycle with wooden spokes that "for a time was a nine days' wonder," as he recalled in his memoirs.

When the Civil War broke out in 1861, Maxim was working as a wood turner in Dexter. He joined a local militia company but quickly decided that war was not for him. Two of his brothers served but he never did. Still, he bridled at reports that he had deserted and fled to Canada, although that might have been the case. The man who would later revolutionize war never experienced it himself.

"It has often been said that Maine is the best State in the Union to emigrate from, and I had long wished to get out of it," he wrote. He ended up in northern New York and then in Canada, working as a painter and taking delight in his ability to lick anyone who challenged him in a fight. His memoirs brim with accounts of how he always bested the toughest men around in fisticuffs.

Then he was off to Fitchburg, Massachusetts, to work for his uncle in a brass foundry, followed by stints in Boston and New York, where he began working at an iron works. Here Maxim developed an improved apparatus for gas lighting that he began selling through a company called the Maxim Gas Machine Company. He also invented a more efficient lamp for locomotives. Maxim began experimenting with incandescent light and claimed that Thomas Edison had to rely on some of his work with carbon filaments to make his own light a success. Although Edison patented his invention first, Maxim got a job as the engineer for the US Electric Lighting Company and continued his research and development.

When his company sent him to London to oversee its operations there, Maxim resumed work on the automatic gun he and his father had discussed. (He would become a British citizen in 1900, and Queen Victoria knighted him the next year.) Maxim purchased a milling factory in Bankside, hired a couple of mechanics, and set to work. People he talked with, including one manufacturer of rifle barrels, attempted to warn him off the project. "You don't stand a ghost of a chance in competition with regular gunmakers—stick to electricity," he supposedly told Maxim. "I am a totally different mechanic from any you have ever seen before—a different breed," Maxim supposedly replied. Despite the apparent ineptitude of practically everyone he encountered—as recounted in his memoirs, at least—he managed to develop a gun that used the energy of its own recoil to slide the barrel back, open the chamber, eject the spent cartridge, and insert a new bullet. In June 1883 he patented his invention, which he described as "Improvement in and relating to Mechanism for Facilitating the Action of Magazine Rifles and other Fire-Arms." A month later he was issued a second patent for a "Machine or battery gun. . . . In which the feeding, firing, extracting and ejecting devices are operated by the force developed by the recoil of the breech block." With his new gun, Maxim could fire 10 bullets a second.

He wasn't the first person to make rapid-firing weapons. Richard J. Gatling had created a rapid-fire machine gun with multiple barrels, which revolved when its operator turned a crank. Gatling tried to get the federal government interested during the Civil War, with little luck. Repeating rifles saw some service in the Franco-Prussian war, starting in 1870, and the English and the Russians started using Gatling guns. Other inventors and manufacturers, including Hotchkiss, Nordenfeldt, and Gardner, developed their own weapons. Those guns were big and cumbersome and had a tendency to jam if the operator turned the crank too quickly. Maxim's gun was clearly superior.

Maxim gave a public demonstration of his weapon in London in 1885 and piqued the interest of Britain, Germany, Italy, and France. When British forces used Maxim's guns to deliver a "frightful rain of bullets" that decimated a West Africa tribal uprising in 1887, the history of warfare had reached a pivotal point. As one Englishman wrote, "In most of our wars it has been the dash, the skill, and the bravery of our officers and men that have won the day, but in this case the battle was won by a quiet scientific gentleman living down in Kent." That gentleman, of course, was Maxim.

He continued to demonstrate his gun throughout Europe. After one trial in Switzerland, an officer told him, "No gun has ever been made in the world that could kill so many men and horses in so short a time." In Austria, the Archduke William told Maxim the gun was "the most dreadful instrument that I have ever seen or imagined."

When Edward Albert, the Prince of Wales, visited Kaiser Wilhelm II of Germany, he arranged a demonstration of the Maxim gun and its competitors. "Once the Kaiser had seen the efficiency and ease of use of the automatic machine gun, Maxim had offered his weapon for sale to the powers that would become the central military actors in World War I," wrote C.J. Chivers. Germany began ordering the new weapon. Russia did, too, and put them to use against the Japanese in the Russo-Japanese War. According to Maxim, "more than half of the Japanese killed in the late war were killed with the little Maxim gun." Maxim merged with his rival Nordenfeldt in 1888, and then with the Vickers company in 1896. (Upon Maxim's retirement in 1911, the company changed its name from Vickers, Sons & Maxim, Ltd. to simply Vickers, Ltd.)

When war broke out in Europe in 1914, Maxim's gun ensured that it would be a war like none that had been fought before. The machine gun turned offensive attacks against fixed positions into mass suicide. Writing about Maxim in his history of World War II, Sir Basil Liddell Hart said, "His name is more deeply engraved on the real history of the World War than that of any other man. Emperors, statesmen and generals had the power to make war, but not to end it. Having created it, they found themselves helpless puppets in the grip of Hiram Maxim who by his machine gun, had paralyzed the power of attack. All efforts to break the defensive grip of the machine gun were in vain; they could only raise tombstones and triumphal arches." The inventor from Sangerville had transformed the face of war.

Maxim did not limit his work to his automatic rifle. "I also designed an air-gun which was much more efficient than any other air-gun that had ever been made," he writes, in a characteristically immodest passage from his memoirs. He experimented with a better method of roasting coffee and, although not a coffee drinker himself, he wrote that he made "a few cups of the best coffee ever made on this planet." When he turned his eye toward aviation, he constructed a steam-operated machine in 1894. After the bulky apparatus broke free from the track on which Maxim tested it, he claimed, "This was the first time in the history of the world that a flying-machine actually lifted itself and a man into the air." (An appraisal in *Air Force Magazine* begged to differ, labeling Maxim's claims as "outlandish boasts," and saying that "he wasted more money to produce fewer results than almost any other experimenter.")

But he will always be best known for the gun that bore his name. "It is astonishing to note how quickly this invention put me on the very pinnacle of fame," Maxim wrote in his memoirs. After he developed a medical inhaler for bronchitis, Maxim received much criticism for turning his talents to a seemingly mundane invention. "I suppose I shall have to stand the disgrace which is said to be sufficiently great to wipe out all the credit that I might have had for inventing killing machines," he noted sarcastically.

In his memoirs, Maxim describes an editorial cartoon that depicted him shooting his gun while the angel of death stood behind him, holding a crown over his head. He did not say what he thought about the depiction.

～～

Once the United States entered the war, Maine men began getting killed by the gun Maxim invented. One of them was Moses Neptune, the son of the governor of the Passamaquoddy tribe. Neptune was one of six Passamaquoddy who enlisted in April 1917. The other five were Samuel Dana, Charles Lola, Henry Sockbeson, David Sopiel, and George Stevens, Sr. Like Louis Sockalexis before them, Neptune, Dana, and Sopiel loved baseball and played on the team in their community of Pleasant Point on the Passamaquoddy reservation near Eastport. The six young men joined the Maine National Guard's 2nd Regiment of Infantry, which became part of the 26th Division, known as the Yankee Division, and were assigned to Company I of the 103rd Infantry regiment.

The 103rd shipped out for Europe in September 1917. During a German attack on the Toul sector on June 16, Charles Lola was killed by machine gun fire and Samuel Dana received a wound that cost him a leg. Henry Sockbeson was wounded in combat on July 16 but elected to remain with the regiment. Machine gun fire wounded David Sopiel on July 22, leaving Neptune and Stevens the only two Passamaquoddy who remained untouched, even as they endured grueling combat, including the battle of Verdun in the fall of 1918. Their luck turned on November 10—the day before the armistice took effect. During an attack against the machine guns of an entrenched German position near the town of Flabas, Stevens was shot in the legs. Neptune was killed.

When these six Passamaquoddy men enlisted, they were not even U.S. citizens, a status denied to Native Americans until 1924. "They enlisted to protect their homeland," wrote Maine National Guard historian Jonathan D. Bratten, "just as their forefathers had done in other U.S. wars going back to the American Revolution, when they sided with the colonials."

⌒⌒

Walker Blaine Beale was the grandson of James G. Blaine and had been a student at Harvard when the United States entered the war. He decided to leave school to join the 310th infantry. Before he left for war, Beale let the state use the family mansion in Augusta to coordinate its war activities. Today the building, known as the Blaine house, serves as home to the state's governor.

Beale's uncle was conductor Walter Damrosch, who wrote about his nephew in his autobiography. He recalled the last time he saw Walker, on Christmas Day in 1916, when the young man was training at Fort Dix and his family met him at a nearby hotel. "We all did our best to make it gay in that hotel dining-room, the rain falling dismally," he remembered. "We were so proud of our young khaki-uniformed lieutenant!" Beale was dead within a year of that bleak Christmas, dying on September 18, 1918, at the age of 22. "Reconnoitring [sic] to assure the safety of his men, he leaped a fence to join three fellow officers," his uncle wrote. "A shell tore them to pieces. This was in the early afternoon. Walker was taken to a field hospital and died at eleven that night."

⌒⌒

Sumner Sewall, from the Bath shipbuilding family that constructed the ill-fated *William P. Frye*, was more fortunate. He was born in Bath in 1897 and, like Beale, was a Harvard student. He left college to serve in the American Ambulance Field Service, and later joined the American Air Service while in Paris. After some training, he joined the 95th Pursuit Squadron as a 1st lieutenant in December 1917.

Sewall flew his first combat mission in March, piloting an unarmed French-built Nieuport on a patrol. Before long Sewall had a plane equipped with machine guns (Hiram Maxim's presence making itself felt even in the air), and by war's end he had shot down seven enemy airplanes, making him an official "Ace." He received awards for his service from France (the Legion of Honor and Croix de Guerre), and Belgium (the Order of Leopold and Order de la Couronne). His own country awarded him the Distinguished Service Cross "for repeated acts of extraordinary heroism" over France on June 3 and October 13, 1918. On the first date, Sewall attacked six enemy planes with two other pilots. The other pilots' guns jammed, but Sewall remained in the fray alone for 15 minutes and shot down one of the hostile planes. On the second date, Sewall saw a German Fokker and eight other planes attacking an American observation aircraft. He flew to the American's defense, shot down the Fokker, and managed to escort the observation plane back to its own lines. He received an oak leaf for an action in December, when he attacked five enemy Fokkers and destroyed one, "following it within 30 metres of the ground in spite of severe fire from a machine gun, rifles, and anti-aircraft guns, bullets from which passed through his clothing."

Sumner Sewall survived the war and returned to Maine. In 1941 he became Maine's governor, and he served until 1945, through a second world war that was even more dreadful than the first.

1920s

Lindbergh Comes to Town

IN OUR 21ST CENTURY WORLD OF SATELLITES, CELL PHONES, AND ROU-tine transatlantic flights, it may be hard to understand the impact 25-year-old Charles Lindbergh made when he flew his single-engine *Spirit of St. Louis* nonstop from New York to Paris in May 1927. By the time he touched down at Le Bourget airport, 33½ hours after he took off from Long Island's Roosevelt Field, Lindbergh was an international celebrity—the most famous man in the world.

The instant adulation didn't come because Lindbergh was the first person to fly across the Atlantic—that had been accomplished eight years earlier, when a U.S. Navy seaplane had made the trip, which took 19 days and required multiple stops. The Lone Eagle wasn't the first to fly non-stop across the Atlantic, either. English officers John Alcock and Arthur Whitten-Brown had flown without stopping from Newfoundland to Ireland in 1919. Lindbergh was, however, the first to fly nonstop between New York and Paris, winning a race to capture a $25,000 prize put up by hotelier Raymond Orteig. Several other, better-known, aviators had also been vying for the prize, and some of them had died trying. The previous September, famed French World War I ace René Fonck had crashed while trying to take off from Roosevelt Field; two of his crew died. Two other Frenchmen, Charles Nungesser and François Coli, had attempted to fly from Paris to New York just days before Lindbergh's attempt but disappeared along the way. (Some theorized that the aviators crashed in the Maine woods outside Machias.)

Even more than *what* Lindbergh had done, the *how* he had done it captured the world's imagination. Lindbergh was a young, unknown airmail pilot flying a plane built by an obscure San Diego company. He did have financial backers, but the "Lone Eagle" made the flight solo—a quintessential plucky American going it alone against great odds. His story galvanized the world. When the *Spirit of St. Louis* appeared in the skies above Paris on the night of May 21, more than 150,000 people were waiting at Le Bourget, delirious with excitement. They mobbed the field when he landed, tore pieces of fabric from his airplane, and overwhelmed the pilot, who was hustled into a car by some helpful Frenchmen and sheltered in a hangar until he could be safely transported to the American embassy.

Upon Lindbergh's return to the United States, more than 4 million people gave him a rapturous welcome in a New York City ticker-tape parade that left 2,000 tons of confetti littering the city's streets. Everyone was mad for Lindy. People wrote songs and poems about him and they danced the Lindy Hop. Movie producers vied to sign him up; manufacturers of everything from fountain pens to breakfast cereal wanted the Lindbergh name on their products. "One of the salesmen of the Thompson Manufacturing Company in Belfast, Maine, realized they could move their breeches faster if they started calling it the 'Lindy' pant," wrote biographer Scott Berg. That salesman was hardly the first or the last person to capitalize on Lindbergh's fame.

Observers marveled at the figure at the center of this maelstrom. He seemed like such a nice young man—quiet, polite, modest. He was everything an all-American hero was supposed to be, and America embraced him passionately, fervently, and feverishly.

Shortly after his return home, Lindbergh decided he would use his new stature to awaken America to the potential of air travel. He accepted a proposal from the Daniel Guggenheim Fund for the Promotion of Aeronautics to fly his famous airplane to every state in the Union and preach the gospel of commercial aviation. He planned to depart on July 20 from Long Island and head north to New England, with his first stop in Hartford, Connecticut. His schedule had him reaching Portland, Maine, on Saturday, July 23.

Portland had a brand-new airport—so new it hadn't officially opened yet—just outside the city in Scarborough (or Scarboro, as the *Portland Press Herald* spelled it). Lindbergh expected to land there at 2:45 on Saturday. "Every precaution humanely possible will be taken at the Portland Airport at Scarboro to make Lindbergh's arrival not only safe and convenient for the pilot, but an event which can be witnessed in comfort by the maximum number of visitors," the *Press Herald* told its readers. The Portland Chamber of Commerce issued a warning that the aviator would turn back to Boston if Portland residents rushed the field, as Parisians had done at Le Bourget. Once on the ground, Lindbergh would be whisked into a waiting car and driven into the city, escorted by motorcyclists of the Maine State Police.

The parade route was planned to avoid as many trolley tracks as possible to prevent the Lone Eagle from being jostled. A guard of honor, consisting of an infantry company, a Marine detachment, sailors from the USS *Seattle*, three batteries of artillery from the Maine National Guard, and 1,000 "citizen soldiers" from Fort McKinley Citizens' Military Training Camp planned to display their drill routines for Lindbergh. If they had enough time, they also planned a display of "mass calisthenics."

After the parade, Lindbergh was scheduled to address the gathered hordes in a field at Deering Oaks at 3:45. The reception committee prepared for a crowd of 30,000 people. Lester C. Ayer of the New England Telephone and Telegraph Company set up a P.A. system to ensure that everyone in the crowd would be able to hear. The committee also made arrangements to park an "extraordinary number of automobiles free of charge." After his address, Lindbergh would return to the Eastland Hotel in Portland in preparation for a dinner there that evening. All 700 tickets were sold out by Thursday.

Philip J. Deering, the head of the reception committee, asked that everyone in Portland who owned American flags display them during Lindbergh's visit. The fire department planned to blow its whistles to announce Lindbergh's arrival. "When Colonel Lindbergh arrives, he will discover at first hand that New England restraint itself has limits which yield to feats of importance equal to his flight across the lonely Atlantic," the paper said.

Lindbergh and the *Spirit of St. Louis* began the tour as scheduled. He was accompanied by a second plane, provided by the department of commerce and piloted by Phil Love, an old friend of Lindbergh's from his days as an airmail pilot. Serving as Lindbergh's aide was Donald Kehoe, who worked for the commerce department. The only other member of the team was mechanic Ted Sorenson. At Hartford, 50,000 people turned out to see the Lone Eagle. "A slender fair-haired young fellow who appeared to be just out of his 'teens, rolled and slipped and dived his way into the hearts of 50,000 usually staid, Connecticut citizens at Brainard Field today," reported the Associated Press.

Lindbergh stopped in Providence, Rhode Island, on Thursday and reached Boston on Friday, leading to the death of one man from "over-excitement" in the delerious horde at the airport. During Lindbergh's appearance on Boston Common, members of the National Guard "rescued 17 women who had been knocked down and trampled by the surging crowd." Lindbergh, the paper said, spent his day at "the center of a howling mob of devotees who made any sacrifice of their personal safety for one glimpse of their hero." Maine's Governor Ralph Brewster was in Boston to greet Lindbergh but had to miss his Portland appearance so he could attend a governor's conference in Michigan.

At one of the first stops, Lindbergh demonstrated his single-mindedness—as well as his growing dislike of the press—when a reporter tried to get him to talk about his private life. "Is it true, Colonel, that girls don't interest you at all?" she asked.

"If you can show me what that has to do with aviation, I'll be glad to answer you," Lindbergh said.

"Then aviation is your only interest?"

"That is the purpose of this tour, to promote aviation."

"Are you always so evasive?" the reporter asked.

"I shall be glad to tell you everything I know—on aviation," Lindbergh answered.

As Lindbergh made his way north, Portland braced for impact. In a boxed item on Saturday's front page simply headlined "Please!" the *Press Herald* implored people to keep off the airfield until Lindbergh had landed, and repeated the aviator's request that no other pilots attempt to rendezvous with him in the air.

The sun rose on Saturday behind a thick bank of clouds and fog. In Scarborough, contractors had been working feverishly to get the new airfield ready. In Portland, thousands eagerly anticipated sighting the famous aviator. "Maine turns its eyes to the Western sky today to catch the first glint of silvered wings, for the hearts of the people are impatient to welcome and honor Charles Augustus Lindbergh, the modest representative of American youth who thrilled the world with his spirit and made his countrymen proud of their birthright," said the *Press Herald*. "One thought is uppermost in every mind. Men, women and children have determined to show the young aviator the admiration they feel for his courage, skill and daring. They seem to chafe under the restraint of their New England nature, lest he fail to understand the warmth in their hearts for his unperishable gallantry in the face of odds."

Local businesses trumpeted their admiration for Lindy. Loring, Short & Harmon at Monument Square took out an ad to promote the impending arrival of *We*, Lindbergh's book about his flight, priced at $2.50 and due "to be published shortly, probably late this month." Chapman's, at 245 Middle Street, took out an ad to welcome Lindbergh and to tout its "large assortment of white felt hats and other shades." Porteous, Mitchell & Braun used a full page to announce it would close on Saturday afternoon out of respect. "Though we live in a 'commercial' age, admiration and appreciation for deeds brilliantly conceived and carried through, is strongly entrenched in the minds and hearts of the people of Maine," the store announced. Eastman Bros. & Bancroft announced that it would close early, too, but refrained from lofty rhetoric.

In Boston, Lindbergh and his team took stock of the bad weather. Reports cited dense fog all the way into Maine, but Lindbergh was determined to make the flight on schedule. "It isn't as bad as it looks," Kehoe remembered him saying. "The flying won't be hard; I've seen worse days on the mail. The only trouble will be at Portland, if the airport is covered with fog."

Kehoe asked Lindbergh not to take any chances. "I'll be all right," the young aviator said. "With these instruments I can get through the fog, and if I can't find Portland Airport I'll drop in somewhere else." Lindbergh climbed into the *Spirit of St. Louis's* tiny cockpit and took off into the mist. Love preferred to fly alone in the support plane in such dangerous conditions, so Kehoe and Sorenson drove. It was a tense and worrying trip. As the two men neared Portland, they noticed a procession of cars and decided to follow them. The cars led them to Love, who had been forced by the fog to land in a field. Love said he had heard the *Spirit of St. Louis* flying somewhere in the clouds above him.

Portland, it turned out, was completely socked in. After circling fruitlessly around the city for more than two hours, Lindbergh decided a landing was impossible so he flew toward New Hampshire in the hopes that the weather was better there. He landed in Concord and postponed his Portland appearance for a day.

The weather was no better on Sunday when Lindbergh took off from Concord. As he had the day before, he circled around Portland for more than two hours in a fruitless search for the fogged-in airport. He finally spied Old Orchard Beach through a break in the clouds and decided to land there. He made a perfect landing and taxied up to a little airfield run by Captain Harry Martin Jones.

Like Lindbergh, Jones was an aviation pioneer. He had created a sensation in 1912 when he made the first (and last) landing on Boston Common. He flew the mail between Boston and New York for a time before setting up shop on Old Orchard Beach in 1919, offering flying lessons and giving airplane flights to tourists from his beach airstrip. He charged $25 for a round-trip flight from the beach to Portland. Old Orchard Beach even made Jones its first (and last) "aerial policeman," complete with uniform.

The arrival of the most famous man in the world at Jones's hangar must have come as quite a surprise. Mechanic Austin Thomas was the first man to greet Lindbergh, followed by Roy E. Haines, who was in town overseeing a toy factory he owned. Thomas and Haines helped Lindbergh push his airplane inside Jones's hangar before the gathering crowd could mob him. Haines offered him a ride to Scarborough but couldn't get his car to start. A nearby homeowner offered his vehicle and Lindbergh and company set off. Kehoe and a delegation from the welcoming committee met them on the way.

Other than the tricks played by the weather, Lindbergh's visit went off almost without a hitch, except when a car backed out of a driveway and hit state policeman Eugene Stevens, part of Lindbergh's motorcycle escort from the airport. Stevens suffered only some bruising and was gratified to receive a note and a box of candy from Lindbergh as he recuperated at Maine General Hospital.

Thousands of people lined the route into town, despite the threat of rain. "At every corner, crowds had congregated and the whole countryside seemed to have been swept with a wave of madness," the *Press Herald* reported. "Men and women screamed out their greetings, and above their voices rose the shriller cries of excited children." The guest of honor sat in the back seat of the car, bowing to the crowd. At one point people broke through the lines of police and swarmed into the street. After order was restored, Lindbergh finished the parade and was brought to the Eastland Hotel for a short rest before the afternoon's events. While he was there, the "little blonde" who operated the hotel's elevator couldn't resist temptation, and she surprised Lindbergh with a bear hug.

The 25,000 people who crowded into Deering Oaks that afternoon were a little less than the 30,000 predicted. In his talk to the crowd, Lindbergh referred to his issues with the weather but pointed out how technological developments in radio would soon let pilots land in the densest fog. Lester Ayer must have done his job well, for the *Press Herald* boasted that "Perfect Order Prevails While Amplifiers Enable Every Word To Be Heard." (The paper also pointed out that, according to police, pickpockets managed to extract $289 from unsuspecting celebrants.)

Lindbergh repeated his belief in aviation's future that night at the Eastland, touting developments in radio beacons, deicing equipment, and compasses. "In a few more years, planes will be flying in every kind of weather condition and schedule," he predicted. "Airports must be built, as you have done here in Portland. Build for the present, and plan for the future, too."

Seven hundred people enjoyed the festivities at the Eastland, while hundreds more waited outside, hoping for a glimpse of the guest of honor. One man who made his way up to the head table was Lindbergh's uncle, John C. Lodge of Detroit. Lodge was spending the summer in Poland Springs, but he traveled to Portland to see his famous nephew. Earlier that day he had tried to visit Lindbergh at the Eastland but Kehoe, not believing Lodge's claim to kinship, denied him admittance.

During the dinner, someone opened a door in the back of the room so spectators waiting outside could catch a glimpse of the Lone Eagle. "Fathers and mothers held simpering infants up in their arms, so that some day they can tell their own children they saw Lindbergh," said the paper. "'Lindy' is America's greatest drawing attraction. Showmen must weep when they hear about his reception." It was, according to the *Press Herald*, "Portland's biggest day in many a year." It was even bigger for Mary Elizabeth Skerrit, the wife of a Portland policeman. At 5:05 that morning she gave birth to a son. The proud parents named him Charles Lindbergh Skerrit.

Lindbergh's delayed arrival in Portland came as a great disappointment to Elise Fellows White. Something of an aviation fanatic, White was determined to see the Lone Eagle. She managed to reach Portland on Sunday, but arrived too late to see Lindbergh at Deering Oaks and policemen stopped her from entering the Eastland Hotel. Once back home she burst into tears. The next morning she took a train to Old Orchard Beach, made her way to Jones's hangar, and spotted the *Spirit of St. Louis* through its open doors. "I found myself transported from the other place straight to heaven," White wrote in her diary. She ducked under the rope that Jones had strung up as a barrier, and managed to touch one of the plane's wings.

Lindbergh arrived in a car shortly afterward. "His face was delightfully ordinary, just a clean-cut average western boy's face," White wrote. "He might have been working in a hayfield or running a tractor." After tinkering with his plane and talking with men in the hangar, Lindbergh emerged and tossed some seaweed into the air to check the wind. Police kept the crowd back as men pushed the *Spirit of St. Louis* onto the beach. Lindbergh climbed into the cockpit and started the engine. Some volunteers had to push to extricate the wheels from the wet sand, and then Lindbergh started his plane on its takeoff run down the beach. "It moved smoothly over the sand and in no distance at all—hardly more than a hundred yards—it was in the air," White wrote. "He tipped and banked and turned swooping low over the beach then rose like a silver winged bird against the blue sky."

Lindbergh flew over Portland one more time, giving residents a final chance to see his airplane. Then he turned toward Scarborough and finally landed at the new airport. He bid farewell to his reception committee and praised the airfield before taking off for his next official stop in Concord, New Hampshire. Along the way he made a short detour over Poland Springs to provide an aerial greeting to his mother's aunt, who had not been able to travel with John C. Lodge to Portland. " 'We' came, 'we' saw, 'we' conquered," said the *Press Herald*, using the personal pronoun Lindbergh used to refer to himself and his airplane, "and both Col. Charles Lindbergh and the *Spirit of St. Louis* left broken hearts behind him when he left Maine, for his charm and modesty won him followers who will never be able to forget him."

By the time Lindbergh finished his tour in late October, he had visited all 48 states and stopped in 82 cities. He was late only once—when fog kept him from landing in Portland, Maine.

For a few years after Lindbergh lifted the *Spirit of St. Louis* from its wet sand, Old Orchard Beach continued to play a role in aviation. Thanks to its long stretch of beach and its location at the edge of North America, it became a jumping-off point for transatlantic attempts after Lindbergh's accidental visit.

In mid-June 1929, there were two airplanes on the beach, poised to leap across the Atlantic. The *Green Flash* was a Bellanca J crewed by Americans. The second airplane was a French entry, a Bernard 191 called *L'Oiseau Canari* (The Yellow Bird). Both crews aimed to make nonstop flights to Europe, the Americans to Rome and the Frenchmen to Paris. The *Green Flash* crashed on takeoff, but on June 13 the French crew managed to wrestle their heavy airplane into the air and head east across the ocean.

The three Frenchmen had painstakingly calculated the weight of the plane and its passengers to determine how much fuel they needed to reach Paris. They had not calculated on the weight of Arthur Schreiber, the first person to stowaway aboard a transatlantic flight.

Schreiber, a 22-year-old Portland resident, had gone the day before with some friends to see the airplanes on the beach. When a friend suggested that he join one of the crews, Schreiber decided that wasn't a bad idea. "It was a crazy era," he remembered years later. "There was flagpole sitting, human fly feats and people eating goldfish. I believe I was a product of that era." Schreiber went home, took a leather jacket and goggles from a brother who had been in the Army Air Corps, and told his mother he was going horseback riding. Instead he returned to Old Orchard Beach and spent the night there. The next morning, he asked *L'Oiseau Canari*'s radio operator and financial backer, Armand Lotti, if he could join the crew. Lotti, naturally, said no. Later, as Schreiber was helping push the airplane onto the sand, he took advantage of the confusion to climb through an aft hatch and hide in the tail section. The crew thought the plane seemed a bit tail-heavy when they lifted off the beach, but they didn't know why until Schreiber emerged from his hiding place about 20 minutes later. "In the beginning we were unable to decide whether to strangle our stowaway or drop him out into the ocean or leave him in his cubby hole, but we realized that since we had got past the great difficulty of getting up in the air with him it would be best to take him right along," said one of the crew members. "We also thought Providence had guided us in the take-off from Old Orchard and that it was our duty to guard this daring youth who was ready to share our perils."

Schreiber's extra weight put Paris out of reach, but after almost 29 hours of flight, including some severe thunderstorms that almost knocked the plane out of the sky, the aviators landed in Spain. From there they pushed on to Paris, where Schreiber received a hero's welcome at Le Bourget. When Schreiber left Paris, Lotti accompanied him to the train that would take him to the vessel *Leviathan* for his transatlantic voyage home. A reporter noted that Schreiber seemed "contrite and somewhat anxious." He quoted Schreiber as saying, "I did a fool stunt and I am heartily sorry for it. The only consolation is I have found such a good friend in Lotti here, one of the men who suffered from my foolishness." Lotti had even bought Schreiber the stylish French suit he was wearing, as well as his boat ticket home. He and the other crew members also made sure that Schreiber signed a pledge that he would give them half of any money he made from his adventure.

Schreiber's father met him on June 26 when the *Leviathan* arrived in New York. Young Schreiber bristled when a reporter asked if he had compared himself to Lindbergh. "There is no precedent for what I did," he responded, "and there is no way to tell now what I shall do with my experience." He and his father departed for Portland from Roosevelt Field aboard a Stimson monoplane for a flight to Harry Jones's hangar on Old Orchard Beach. There a reporter from the *Portland Press Herald* loaned them his car so they could get home. "Schreiber drove, remarking with wonder that he had been away only two weeks, but had visited Spain and France," the reporter noted. His father "was greatly thrilled by the airplane trip from New York."

Arthur Schreiber later got his pilot's license and he served with the Marines in World War II. He and Lotti kept in touch, and Schreiber visited him in France on a couple of occasions. In June 1974 the two men were reunited in Maine on the 45th anniversary of the flight for a luncheon in Biddeford and a reception in Portland. Schreiber was living in California when he died on February 10, 1997, on his 90th birthday, his days as an aviation pioneer long past.

1930s

Al Brady Meets His End

IN THE FALL OF 1933, LORENA A. HICKOK VISITED MAINE TO SEE HOW the state was weathering the Great Depression. She went at the request of Harry Hopkins, an intimate of President Franklin Roosevelt and the head of the Federal Emergency Relief Administration, one of the agencies the Roosevelt administration had launched to provide assistance to Americans suffering from the economic hard times. As Hickok traveled around the state, she found that even though the Depression had hit Maine hard, Mainers resisted the idea of receiving government help. The majority of Mainers, she reported to Hopkins, were "typical 'down East Yankees.' Proud, reserved, independent. Shrewd, but honest. Endowed with all the good solid virtues on which this nation was founded." Mainers, she found, "would almost starve rather than ask for help." In some Aroostook County towns, the teachers had not been paid since January but were willing to keep teaching if they could be paid with food. Potato prices had plunged, and farmers were finding it cost them more to pick the crop than they could get by selling them. "They dumped so many into the rivers and creeks that the authorities had to make them stop for they were blocking up the streams, I was told." She found similar tales of woe throughout the state. The demand for Maine pulpwood was down; Rockland's shipbuilding was virtually nonexistent; sardine canneries were suffering; limestone quarries were idle. In Eastport, which Hickok found to be one of the "brighter spots" in Maine, local government had fixed up some shacks to house the unemployed. "They could hardly be called luxurious, but they looked fairly warm," she said.

Still, Hickok found that most Mainers were willing to tough it out. "The attitude of most of the unemployed is, I should say, almost tragically patient," she noted. "Considering the treatment I could easily imagine they were getting, they were pitiful. Now and then I'd remember some wistfulness. Seldom any bitterness." She did note some "fury" in Bangor and Portland over bureaucratic red tape and delays, which led to "semi-riots over fuel."

Bangor did experience a spasm of violence in the Depression year of 1937, but it wasn't over fuel.

On the morning on October 13, 1937, readers of the *Bangor Daily News* were greeted by a blaring banner headline. "BRADY AND PAL SLAIN HERE," it read. "America's Public Enemy Number One Killed in Battle with G-Men on Central Street—Carefully Planned Plot Traps Three of Desperate Gang—One Taken Alive in Dakin Sporting Goods Shop."

Alfred Brady, the 26-year-old criminal that FBI chief J. Edgar Hoover had named "Public Enemy Number One," had been cut down in the middle of Bangor's downtown. Lying nearby on Central Street was another member of Brady's criminal trio, Clarence Lee Shaffer, Jr. "Both were almost literally shot to pieces in the rain of lead from government guns," the *Daily News* told its readers. The third member of the gang, James Dalhover, was taken alive.

It was the biggest story to hit Bangor in years.

Before their luck ran out in Maine, the hoodlums of Alfred Brady's gang had created their own crime wave across the eastern United States. The FBI estimated that from late 1935 to April 1936 Brady and his cohorts committed around 150 robberies and holdups and at least three murders. According to one story, they bragged that their criminal exploits "would make Dillinger look like a piker."

"Whether or not they accomplished their avowed purpose is a moot question," said an FBI account of their activities, "but the fact that they met the same fate as the members of the Dillinger gang cannot be disputed."

A profile of the gang running in *Official Detective* magazine included dialogue that could have been cribbed from a James Cagney movie. The article described the "pint-sized" Brady as a "weak-chinned former Sunday school teacher" who had become "unquestionably this country's Public Rat Number One, to use the apt aphorism invented by J. Edgar Hoover.

"In a little less than two years Brady and his followers have slain three men, two of them policemen, and have taken more than $200,000 in loot," said *Official Detective*. "Suffering from delusions of invincibility, they go out of their way to fight with the law and derive a fiendish delight from murder."

Alfred Brady was just about to turn 27 when he died in Bangor. He was born on October 25, 1910, in Indiana. His father died when he was young and his mother, who remarried, died when Brady was 16. As a young man he had a series of nondescript jobs, including stints in a clothing store, a hot tamale stand, a mattress factory, and as a welder on an automobile assembly line. (*Official Detective* notwithstanding, there's no record of him teaching Sunday school.) His first arrest appears to have been for a grocery store robbery gone wrong in 1929. He was later arrested for vagrancy, and then for possessing stolen goods.

Sometime after his release, Brady met Rhuel James Dalhover. Born on August 24, 1906, in Indiana, Dalhover had done time in reform school for robbing a grocery store. He drifted about the country until he settled in Cincinnati, married, and had two children. In 1926 Dalhover was caught with a load of bootleg whiskey in Kentucky but broke out of jail, only to be arrested again with a stolen car and returned to prison. He resumed bootlegging once he got out.

Brady and Dalhover's criminal partnership started small. The pair gained a mere $18 on their first job, when they robbed a movie theater in Crothersville, Indiana. The second job, a grocery store in Sellersville, nabbed a more lucrative $190.

Clarence Lee Shaffer, Jr., joined the gang in October 1935. He was the youngest of the three, having been born in Indianapolis in 1916.

Like the others, he had drifted from job to job and also stole cars. While running a hamburger stand in Indianapolis, Shaffer got his girlfriend pregnant, but refused to marry her or help raise the child.

These three petty criminals, with occasional assistance from Charles Geiseking, embarked on a series of crimes across the Midwest, committing holdups, robbing grocery and jewelry stores, and stealing cars. They may have killed a policeman named Frank Levy in Anderson, Indiana, but the facts of the murder remain murky. Brady did shoot and kill a clerk named Edward Lindsay while robbing an Ohio grocery store in March 1936. Police wounded Geiseking in a shootout after a jewelry store robbery in Lima, Ohio, that April. The doctor who treated Geiseking tipped off the police, and a policeman, Sgt. Richard Rivers of Indianapolis, died in the resulting shootout. Brady, Dalhover and Shaffer fled to Chicago, leaving Geiseking behind.

It appeared that the gang's run was over when the three hoodlums were all arrested in May 1936 for the murder of Rivers and incarcerated at a county jail in Indiana. Yet they managed another daring escape when they attacked the sheriff, took his gun, and disappeared in a stolen car.

By this time the FBI had become involved. After the jewelry store robbery in Lima, Ohio, the gang had disposed of the empty boxes along a road in Geneva, Indiana. By crossing a state line they had entered the bureau's jurisdiction. The resulting manhunt led to the final shootout in Bangor.

After the prison break, the gang members made tracks for Baltimore, where they decided to lay low. Brady found time to indulge his love for roller skating. Shaffer married a local woman and Dalhover married her sister, even though he was already wed. When they needed money, the three men made sure to commit their robberies far from their new home base. They explained their absences by saying they owned a furniture factory in Bangor.

Local police picked up the trail after a bank job in Indiana on May 25, 1937, and set off in pursuit. The criminals pulled off the road and prepared an ambush. When a police car appeared, Brady, armed with a machine gun, and Dalhover and Shaffer, equipped with rifles, opened fire, killing state policeman Paul Minneman and wounding deputy sheriff

Elmer Craig. Before fleeing, Brady took Minneman's gun from the dying officer.

After yet another shootout, this time in Baltimore, the gang left Maryland and drifted around the Midwest until finally holing up in Bridgeport, Connecticut. They decided to head to Maine apparently because they heard they could easily purchase guns there.

On September 21, 1937, the Brady gang made their first visit to Dakin Sporting Goods store in Bangor, where they purchased ammunition. They returned on October 5. This time Dalhover went in and bought three Colt .45s and more bullets. As he was leaving, Dalhover asked store manager Everett S. "Shep" Hurd, "Where can we get a machine gun in this town?" Hurd replied that his store didn't handle them. "Well, see if you can get us one," Dalhover said. "Get all the clips you can find, too. We'll be back next Monday or Tuesday."

As soon as Dalhover left, Hurd telephoned Bangor police chief Thomas Crowley. The chief sent one of his inspectors, Frank Golden, to talk with Hurd. Crowley and Hurd figured that the man must have been Dalhover. Hurd also contacted Maine State Police Sergeant F.R. Hall, who passed the report to Chief Wilbur H. Towle of the state police at his headquarters in Augusta. Towle called the FBI's Boston office. On Saturday, four FBI agents—"G-men," in the day's slang—flew into Bangor. More arrived by car on Sunday, along with members of the Indiana State Police, including Detective Meredith Stewart. The head of the stakeout was Myron Gurnea, whom the *Bangor Daily News* described as "a tall, rangy young man with an incisive manner and a disarming smile."

Completely unaware of the reception being arranged for them in Bangor, Brady, Dalhover, and Shaffer started north for their return to Dakin's. On the night of October 11 they reached Carmel, where they rented a cabin at the Auto Rest Stop. They registered as Charles Harriss and company from Warren, Ohio. The next morning Dalhover purchased some items at the gift shop—a book of souvenir photos and some gewgaws he thought would make nice paperweights. Then the three gangsters climbed into the car and continued on to Bangor.

The FBI and the police were ready. Two men were stationed inside the store, one behind the counter and another hidden behind a partition in the back. They had rigged up a simple signal to flash the alert when the criminals entered. A string led from the counter to a piece of cardboard in the store window. The cardboard would fall when somebody tugged on the string, warning the agents outside. Some of them watched from parked cars. Others mingled with Bangor's residents on the sidewalks. Still others, armed with machine guns, waited in one of the buildings across the street.

The agent behind the counter at Dakin's with Shep Hurd was Walter R. Walsh. He had joined the bureau in 1934 at the age of 27 after graduating from Rutgers Law School. An expert marksman, Walsh had been involved in the arrest of Kate "Ma" Barker's son Doc in 1935, and was the man who discovered the body of George "Baby Face" Nelson after a shootout with the FBI the year before that.

The heavily armed gangsters cruised into downtown Bangor around 8:30 in the morning on October 12. They were driving a black Buick sedan with Ohio plates. The car was essentially an arsenal on wheels— inside they had two dozen handguns, six rifles, three machine guns, two shotguns, and plenty of ammunition.

The three well-dressed strangers reportedly had breakfast at a downtown restaurant before heading over to Dakin's. They parked just down the street. Dalhover and Shaffer got out. Brady remained in the car's back seat. Dalhover went into Dakin's, while Shaffer stayed outside to keep an eye on things.

Dalhover walked up to Hurd at the counter. He remembered the store manager from the previous visit. "Now if you've got the stuff I ordered," he began, but before he could finish the sentence Walsh stuck his gun in his ribs.

"Put 'em up," he said. Dalhover complied. "Where are your pals?" Walsh demanded. Dalhover didn't answer. Walsh slammed the butt of his gun in Dalhover's face, drawing blood. "Now will you talk?" Walsh asked.

"They're out front," Dalhover said.

Shaffer was pretending to examine the display window outside. When he realized what was happening, he pulled his gun and fired through the glass door. One bullet hit Walsh in the shoulder. Dakin employee James

Seeley, who was outside sweeping, dropped to the ground and flattened himself against the sidewalk.

Walsh remained on his feet and kept his gun pressed against Dalhover. The second agent, armed with a machine gun, ran out from the rear of the store and began firing at Shaffer through the door.

Outside, an agent dashed up to the gangsters' car, where Brady still sat in the back seat. The G-man smashed a window with the butt of his gun. "Come out!" he shouted.

"I'll come," Brady replied. Instead, he grabbed his gun and threw the door open. Then all hell broke loose. "Central Street became a madhouse—and, a moment later, a shambles," the *Daily News* reported. The agent at the car fired his machine gun, gunning down Brady as the gang leader made a dash for an alley. Brady fell onto his back in the street, dead, still clutching the gun he had taken from Paul Minneman. Shaffer backed away from the store, firing blindly. The agents in the second-story window across the street opened fire.

Fred Elias, a reporter from the *Bangor Daily Commercial*, happened to be passing by when the shooting started. "I swung around the corner and sighted a big G-man in blue with a tommy gun pumping lead and two men were in the middle of the street, prone and apparently badly hurt," he said. Elias recalled seeing agents grab a third man as he attempted to duck down an alley, but he must have been mistaken, for Walsh already had Dalhover in custody.

G.E. Huntley was one of the paper's printers, and he was also on the scene when he heard gunfire erupt. "I thought a box of shells was exploding in Dakin's," he recalled. "When I got to the corner I saw everybody was running, everybody flying around, and the cops sprinting about."

It's something of a miracle that no bystanders were shot. Two bullets went through the windows of Barnet Landon's tailor shop on the second story opposite Dakin's. Another went through a window of the Singer Sewing Machine Company. John W. Whitlock, who worked at Singer, was in Harry Johnson's barbershop when the barrage started. "Look out, Harry, some of those bullets may come this way," Whitlock said as he pulled Johnson away from the window. Another round hit the sign for

Louis Kirstein & Son. Marion Newcomb was walking to her job at a downtown store when a bullet passed through her dress, nearly hitting her in the thigh. Grace Hardy had been sitting in her car in front of Dakin's writing a letter when the shooting started. She dropped to the floor of the car and waited for the gunfire to stop.

"G-men, by this time, were converging from all sides," read an account in the *Daily News*. "Lead continued to rain from the machine-gun nest." Shaffer went down. "The lieutenant of America's most notorious criminal gang fell across the tracks; his blood mingled with that of Brady. It spread in an ever-widening, crimson lake. For a few minutes the street seemed full of it." Shaffer lived for at least eight more minutes, long enough for Dr. Harry D. McNeil, Bangor's health officer, to reach him, before the gangster expired in the middle of Central Street.

Just like that, it was over. Inspectors Frank Golden and John F. Hayes marched Dalhover to City Hall, their guns stuck in his ribs. Walsh was taken to Eastern Maine General Hospital to be treated for his wounds.

So many sightseers flooded into downtown Bangor to see the scene of the shootout, police had to direct the traffic. Fireman arrived and turned their hoses onto the street to wash the blood away.

Bangor was abuzz, but G-man Myron Gurnea remained tight-lipped about the case, to the frustration of local reporters. Rumors swirled about town. Barber Howard L. Chisolm said he was positive he had given the gangsters shaves and haircuts and that he had provided a recommendation for a nearby boarding house. Some claimed the men had visited the Bangor Public Works Department on Monday to see if they could get accurate maps of the area and had also inquired at the office of the Penobscot County Commissioner.

Other residents repeated a story that the gang had been planning a job in Bangor, and that a map of the Merrill Trust Company building had been found in the car. Dalhover reportedly denied any such plans, explaining that Maine's roads were "too rotten" for an effective getaway. As for why the gang traveled all the way to Maine, the *Daily News* quoted Dalhover as saying, "Maine is the only state where they don't want your whole life history when you go in to buy a gat." "Strikingly Easy to Buy Guns in the State of Maine," read one headline in the paper. No permits were necessary, not even for machine guns, and a customer could buy unlimited numbers of weapons.

Official Detective magazine wasted no time plugging its coverage of the Brady gang by running an ad in the October 13 edition of the *Bangor Daily News*. They also let the paper run an excerpt from the article, headlined "Inside Story of Brady Gang's Reign of Terror." In the same paper, Bangor's Bijou Theater, which was screening *Dead End*, a gangster picture featuring Humphrey Bogart, was equally quick to exploit the shootout. "If you weren't on Central St. yesterday you must see 'Dead End,' the ad said, promising the film would explain "How are these killers made . . . Where do they come from?"

Reporters in Indiana tracked down Dalhover's mother. "It's too bad he wasn't killed suddenly like the rest of them," she said. Then she reportedly fainted. Dalhover's Baltimore wife told reporters, "They had it coming to them." Paul Minneman's widow said she was glad the gang had been stopped, "but most of all I'm glad no more police officers were killed capturing them." Dorothy Rivers, widow of Sgt. Richard Rivers, said she felt her husband's murder had been "avenged." Christine Puckett, the woman in Indianapolis who had borne Shaffer's son, said his death was "probably the best for him, for his folks, for me and for the little boy." Shaffer's stepfather spoke for the dead man's mother when he said, "We expected the end would come just as it did. In a way it was a shock to us and in another way it was not a surprise."

Accompanied by Gurnea, another FBI agent, and Indiana detective Meredith Stewart, Dalhover left Bangor before dawn on Thursday on a flight to Indianapolis. He was sentenced to death for Paul Minneman's murder, and electrocuted in Indiana on November 18, 1938. In his last interview he told reporters, "All in all, I have no regrets. I had my fun while it lasted, although it didn't last long."

The coffin with Shaffer's body took a train ride back to his father in Indianapolis.

Alfred Brady, the former Public Enemy Number One, was buried in an unmarked grave in Bangor's Mt. Hope Cemetery. "In striking contrast to the gaudy and highly publicized funerals of certain big city gang chieftains, here were no mourners, no flowers, no crowds, no ceremonies," the *Daily News* reported. "Representatives of the cemetery and a Bangor undertaking firm, two photographers and two newspaper men, were all who saw the pine box, in which was encased the simple casket, lowered into the grave." The city was reimbursed for the costs with money found on the gangsters. "There was no touch of mistaken romance; it was all utterly dreary, ugly and disillusioning under the leaden skies. In this one concrete example, at least, complete oblivion was the reward of crime."

Or was it? There's a marker at Brady's grave today, placed there in 2007. "We are here, not to praise this murderous thug, but to help the public recognize some of its central history of events that happened in Bangor 70 years ago and to bring some closure to this sad story," said city councilman Gerry Palmer at the time. Palmer also played the role of Shep Hurd in a reenactment of the events of October 12, 1937.

Former FBI agent Walter R. Walsh returned to Bangor to take part in the 2007 event. Despite being wounded in the shootout, Walsh had enjoyed a long and eventful life afterward. He served with the Marines during World War II, where he trained snipers and participated in the invasion of Okinawa. In 1948 he was a member of the U.S. shooting team at the Olympics.

In an NPR interview he did in 2008, Walsh recalled the Brady shootout and was asked if he had any secrets for a long life. "To start with, you have to be lucky," he said. Walter Walsh must have been very lucky indeed, for he was the oldest living FBI agent when he died in 2014 at the age of 106.

1940s

John Ford Films Midway; German Spies Come Ashore

ON THE AFTERNOON OF DECEMBER 7, 1941, DIRECTOR JOHN FORD AND his wife were attending a luncheon at the home of an admiral in Alexandria, Virginia. The host excused himself to take a call from the War Department. When he returned, he told his guests that the Japanese had attacked Pearl Harbor. "We are at war," he said.

Ford had been born John Martin Feeney in Cape Elizabeth on February 1, 1894, the son of Irish immigrants who had settled in Portland, where the elder Feeney operated a bar on Munjoy Hill. Young John played on the Portland High School football team and graduated in 1914. His high school nickname, probably because of his football prowess, was "Bull." One of his biographers said he was "that staunchest of New Englanders, a Maine man" whose upbringing in the state taught him "the value of common people, the beauty of the natural world, and the symmetry when the two are joined." He never forgot his Maine roots.

When Feeney's older brother Francis headed west and found work as an actor and director in California, young John followed—and assumed his brother's stage name of Ford as well. Eventually John Ford began directing his own films. By the time war threatened, he was one of Hollywood's most respected directors, with films that included *The Iron Horse, The Grapes of Wrath, Young Mr. Lincoln, How Green Was My Valley*, and even a Shirley Temple film, *Wee Willie Winkie*. In his 1939 western

117

Stagecoach, Ford turned a relatively obscure actor named John Wayne into a star. It was also the first movie Ford shot in Utah's Monument Valley, a setting he turned iconic in his post-war westerns.

Yet for all his talent, John Ford was a flawed human being with a strong streak of pure New England cussedness. "Actors were terrified of him because he liked to terrify them," said John Carradine, who acted for Ford in several films. "He was a sadist." Ford became known for the way he needled his actors during filming and for his tendency to go on drunken benders between projects. According to one acquaintance, "It was as though God had touched John Ford at the beginning of his life and said, 'How would you like to be a very unique man—like no one else. However, you may scare some people.'"

Ford had always nursed a love for the sea, perhaps inspired by his youth on Casco Bay. In the 1930s he enlisted in the Navy Reserve with a commission as a lieutenant commander, and as tensions with Japan increased, he sometimes used his yacht *Araner* to surveil any Japanese vessels he encountered. He started the Naval Volunteer Photographic Unit in 1939 and began recruiting friends in the film industry to help. The Navy called Ford to active duty in September 1941 and he went to Washington, where his photographic unit was assigned to work under William Donovan, the head of the Office of Strategic Services (OSS), the precursor to the Central Intelligence Agency.

Ford was filming aboard the carrier U.S.S. *Hornet* on April 18, 1942, when General James Doolittle and his raiders took off in twin-engine B-25 Mitchells to bomb Tokyo. Although the Doolittle Raid did little physical damage to Japan, it dealt a psychological blow. Shocked by the first American attack on its mainland, the Japanese military decided to move aggressively across the Pacific to prevent any more raids. One target was a tiny island with an airstrip a thousand miles away from Hawaii called Midway.

The U.S. Navy had cracked Japanese naval codes and knew that Midway was in the crosshairs, so Admiral Chester Nimitz dispatched Ford to photograph the fighting once it erupted. When carrier-based Japanese planes roared in to attack the island on the morning of June 4, Ford and cameraman Jack Mackenzie, Jr., were waiting on the roof of a powerhouse, equipped with a pair of 16 mm cameras and color film. Bombs exploded nearby, shaking the cameras, and a piece of concrete struck Ford in the head and briefly knocked him out. Recovering, he continued to shoot despite an ugly, three-inch shrapnel wound in his arm. "It was a merry little hell all around," Mackenzie remembered.

Exciting as it was, the fight for the island was a mere sideshow to an even bigger battle waged far out to sea, where American carrier-based planes pounced on the Japanese fleet and sank four of its aircraft carriers. That Battle of Midway proved to be a turning point in the Pacific war.

Ford took the raw footage from his small portion of the fight and began shaping it into a short film. He enlisted Hollywood friends to lend assistance—Henry Fonda and Jane Darwell from *The Grapes of Wrath* provided voices, Donald Crisp from *How Green Was My Valley* added narration, and Alfred Newman, who oversaw music for Twentieth Century-Fox, wrote the score. Ford insisted that his editors include a brief shot of Major James Roosevelt, the president's son, in the final cut. If he did that to curry favor with Roosevelt, it worked. After screening the 18-minute short at the White House, the president told his chief of staff, "I want every mother in American to see this film." *The Battle of Midway* began appearing in theaters, as a short before the main feature, in September. Critic James Agee called it "a brave attempt to make a record—quick, jerky, vivid, fragmentary, luminous—of a moment of desperate peril to the nation."

"Even now, far removed from Midway and the war, *The Battle of Midway* resonates," wrote Ford biographer Scott Eyman. "It remains one of Ford's great achievements."

Ford continued his work for the Navy for the rest of the war. He ventured into harm's way again in late 1942 when he oversaw shooting in North Africa and later filmed activity in Burma and China. In June 1944 Ford supervised filming of the D-Day landings, work marred when he went on an epic three-day bender in mid-June. Once he sobered up, Ford spent some time aboard a PT boat commanded by John Bulkeley, the centerpiece of William White's book *They Were Expendable*.

Ford went on inactive status to film an adaptation of White's book. *They Were Expendable* turned out to be one of John Ford's best films, but it was released after the war was over and did only mediocre business at the box office.

For the rest of his days Ford remained proud of his navy service and "shameless" in his pursuit of official medals and ribbons. He continued his film career after the war, creating a series of classic westerns with John Wayne, including *Fort Apache*, *She Wore a Yellow Ribbon*, and *The Searchers*. The Maine-born director is now considered one of the great artists of Hollywood's Golden Age. When filmmaker Orson Welles, no slouch behind the camera himself, was asked who his three favorite directors were, he answered "John Ford, John Ford, John Ford."

In 1998 the city of Portland honored its native son by erecting a bronze statue of Ford at Gorham's Corner near the Old Port. Sculpted by New York artist George Kelly, it shows Ford sitting in a director's chair, with a rocky base that suggests the Monument Valley location from so many of his films. The often cantankerous and hard-drinking director, who died in 1973, might have preferred another tribute to him in Portland—an Irish pub on Fore Street named Bull Feeney's.

〜〜

While John Ford was traveling around the world fighting the war, the war came—however briefly—to the shores of his home state.

Anyone gazing across Frenchman Bay near Hancock Point late on the night of November 29, 1944, might have spotted something unusual as a huge object began to emerge from the bay, water streaming down its dark metal sides. It was a German U-boat, the U-1230. The submarine surfaced just enough so the conning tower was above water. Crew members emerged and splashed across the half-submerged deck. They tugged a rubber raft from inside the submarine and silently inflated it. Once that was done, two sailors climbed aboard. They were joined by two other men, both wearing civilian clothes and lugging a heavy suitcase and a smaller briefcase. The two sailors picked up their paddles and the little rubber boat headed toward shore. It was dark and cold and snow began spinning down from the sky.

The boat bumped ashore as the snow picked up in intensity. All four men climbed out, but only the two in civilian dress remained ashore. The two sailors briefly reveled in their invasion of the U.S. homeland, and then they got back into the boat and rowed out to the submarine. The U-1230 slipped beneath the waves as though it had never been there. The two men left on shore began stumbling their way inland through the dark and the snow. They were spies, and they had landed in Maine on a mission to uncover military secrets and transmit them back to Germany.

Only one of the men was German. He was Erich Gimpel, 34. Born in Germany, Gimpel had moved to Peru in 1935 to work as a radio operator. While there, he learned English. When war appeared imminent, the German secret service recruited Gimpel to report on shipping activities. After America entered the war, Gimpel was arrested and sent to the United States, and from there back to Germany. The German secret service sent him to spy school in Hamburg, and he put his knowledge to work on missions in Spain and even made plans to blow up the Panama Canal.

In 1944 Gimpel received the assignment to infiltrate the United States. He had one request. "I need a proper American," he told his supervisor. He wanted someone who knew the latest slang, popular songs, and fashions and was up to date on baseball and Hollywood gossip.

Nazi Germany had just the man. William C. Colepaugh was a Connecticut Yankee who had defected to Germany. His father was an American who died in 1927, but his grandparents on his mother's side were from Germany, and his mother had been born at sea when her parents were returning from a trip to Europe. One Connecticut acquaintance recalled that Colepaugh's mother was "an admirer of all things German, and especially of Hitler, and the family had a large shortwave radio on which could be heard broadcasts from Germany."

Colepaugh attended the Admiral Farragut Academy, a New Jersey prep school with a nautical emphasis, and went to MIT, but did not graduate. He remained strongly pro-German as Adolf Hitler rose to power, although he never learned to speak German. While working at a shipyard in Boston, Colepaugh became friends with German sailors, and one of them introduced him to Nazi officials stationed in town. On April 20, 1941, Colepaugh visited the German consulate to celebrate Hitler's birthday. Such activities attracted the attention of the FBI, which opened an investigation.

121

As a member of the merchant marine, Colepaugh sailed to Scotland at the request of German authorities to report on convoy activity. He was in Buenos Aires when the Japanese attacked Pearl Harbor. When he returned to the United States, he was arrested for avoiding the draft. Told the charges would be dropped if he enlisted, Colepaugh opted to join the Naval Reserve, but he was discharged after only a few months because of his stridently pro-German leanings. Colepaugh became determined to join the German army, so he signed on as a mess boy aboard a Swedish ship in January 1944 and sailed to Portugal, where he offered his services to the German embassy. From there he went to Berlin, and then to the Hague in the Netherlands. Instead of sending this American into the army, the Nazis decided he would be better utilized as a spy.

Colepaugh met Erich Gimpel while training in the Hague. They also trained in Dresden and Berlin before receiving the assignment for an operation called Elster, or Magpie. A U-boat would take them across the Atlantic and put them ashore in Maine. From there they would make their way to New York City and winnow out whatever they could find about the American political situation, shipbuilding, and weapon development, including the atomic bomb program. It was not the first time Germany had attempted to infiltrate America this way. Two U-boats had landed eight other spies in America. One group went ashore on Long Island and the other in Florida. All eight had been captured and six executed.

The U-1230, a 240-foot-long submarine under the command of Lt. Hans Hilbig, departed from a naval base in Norway on October 6 for a claustrophobic journey across the Atlantic. At one point the diesel engines released gases that nearly asphyxiated the crew, but the U-1230 managed to reach the surface and fresh air. It was the only time the U-boat surfaced until it was far out in the Atlantic, and even then it came up only at night. The rest of the time it ran just below the surface so the boat's snorkel could pull in outside air. On two occasions Allied aircraft dropped bombs and depth charges near the submerged vessel, jangling the crew members' nerves but doing no damage. The journey took 46 long, tension-filled days.

Finally the sub spotted the light on Mt. Desert Rock, but two more weeks passed while the crew struggled to repair their depth-finding equipment, weld shut a leaky battery hatch, and wait for the tides and currents they needed to make a hazardous penetration 14 miles into the bay. On November 29, the submarine began the last leg of its surreptitious journey. It passed Bar Harbor and threaded its way between Burnt and Sheep Porcupine Islands. Hilbig rested the submarine on the sea floor and waited for dark. The crew could hear the engines of boats on the surface passing above them.

That night Hilbig cautiously brought the U-boat to periscope depth. "Before us in the periscope the coastline of the country into which I was to slip unnoticed seemed near enough to touch," Gimpel recalled. Their target was Hancock Point, which jutted into the bay north of Bar Harbor. There was a house on shore, but it appeared deserted. Route 1 was just beyond. The headlights of the occasional vehicles on the road were visible. Hilbig brought the sub, its conning tower now visible above the water, a little closer to shore and had the boat's guns trained on the land while the crew prepared the rubber boat.

The plan had been for just the two spies to row ashore and then have the submarine crew pull the rubber boat back with a rope, but the rope broke, so two sailors rowed the boat instead. Gimpel and Colepaugh wore civilian clothes and overcoats, attire that would get them shot as spies if they were captured. Gimpel had a loaded gun in his pocket and another clutched in his hand. The men had also stuffed sausages into their pockets in case they had to placate any watchdogs. After a row of about 300 yards, the boat bumped ashore and the four men climbed out onto Maine soil.

The spies crossed the beach, climbed a small bank, and then ventured into the woods. "The snow was still falling and the branches of the trees brushed into our faces," Gimpel said. "We could not help making some noise." It was about 11:00 at night, with the temperature around 20 degrees. The handle on the suitcase broke, so Colepaugh made a hasty repair and then the men stashed their loaded pistols in the bag. Once they reached Route 1, Gimpel checked his compass to determine the direction toward Bangor and the men began walking, hatless, through the snow. Colepaugh carried the big suitcase, Gimpel the briefcase, which contained $60,000 in American cash, plus 99 diamonds for use in a financial emergency.

Sometime around 11:30, a car drove by, its headlights sweeping over the two men walking through the snow in the opposite direction. Behind the wheel was 17-year-old Harvard Hodgkins, a Boy Scout and the son of the local deputy sheriff. Hodgkins, who was returning home from a dance, didn't recognize the two men and wondered what they were doing. "I was sure neither was anyone who lived around here and I thought it unusual for anyone to be walking around in a snowstorm," he later told a reporter. He became more suspicious when he noted that their footprints in the snow led off the road and onto a trail that led to the beach.

Mary Forni, 29, had been out that night playing cards and was driving home through the snow on Route 1 when her headlights illuminated the strangers. She did not stop.

A third car did stop. The driver rolled down his window and hailed the two men. In an amazing streak of luck, he turned out to be a taxi driver, Forest Polley, who had just dropped off a fare at a nearby Navy radio station. He thought Gimpel and Colepaugh looked like they could use a lift. Gimpel let the American do the talking. They had run their car into a ditch, Colepaugh explained, and needed a ride to the train station in Bangor. Polley was happy to help.

The distance to Bangor was 35 miles and the fare cost $6. They reached the station four minutes before a train departed for Portland. In Portland the two spies checked their bags at the station and wandered the streets while they waited for a train that left for Boston at 7:00 a.m. Portland provided a stark contrast to grim wartime Germany. "Neon lighting was the order of the night," Gimpel recalled. "Everything in the shop windows was still illuminated, gold watches, fountain pens, wallets, food, wines and spirits."

All this time, Gimpel had been mentally rehearsing his cover story. He was supposed to be Edward Green, recently discharged from the navy for health reasons. He almost tripped up at the station cafeteria in Portland when the man behind the counter asked him what kind of bread he wanted with his ham and eggs. Gimpel struggled to come up with an answer. "The fact that in America people ate five different kinds of bread had caught me out," he said. The near slip left him feeling nervous. Colepaugh, operating under the name of William Charles Caldwell of Connecticut, was visibly nervous, too, and Gimpel worried about his dependability.

The men reached Boston at around 10:00 a.m. on November 30, less than 12 hours after they had landed on the beach in Maine. They went to a clothing store and bought winter coats, hats, and suits and then found a hotel. That night they slept in their new clothes so they would look worn, a trick Gimpel had learned, he said, when he read that British foreign secretary Anthony Eden did it to remove "the vulgarity of pristine newness from his suits." From Boston, the spies caught a train south to New York, their ultimate destination.

Back in Maine, Mary Forni told her husband, the local tax collector, about her odd sighting, He just laughed and told her she was being too "nosy." The next day she mentioned the sighting to her next door neighbor. That neighbor was Harvard Hodgkins's mother, and she told Forni about her son's encounter. Hodgkins's father suspected the strangers might have been burglarizing the summer homes around Hancock Point. He found no evidence of break ins, but he called the FBI in Bangor to report the incident.

The FBI might have dismissed the report if it hadn't been for the U-1230. After dropping off his human cargo, commander Hilbig felt he could go hunting. On the morning of December 3, the U-1230 sank the Canadian cargo vessel *Cornwallis*, alerting military authorities that a German U-boat was in the vicinity. Then the U-1230 headed back across the Atlantic.

In New York, Gimpel bought parts to assemble a radio transmitter and arranged to move out of the hotel they had found and into an apartment. Colepaugh, in the meantime, was enjoying life back in his native land with a wallet full of money provided by the Reich. He spent his nights on the town drinking and picking up women. Tensions rose between the two men. On December 21, Gimpel returned to their apartment to discover that Colepaugh had fled, taking their belongings—and their money—with him. Thinking quickly, Gimpel deduced that Colepaugh would probably leave town via Grand Central Station and would check his bags while he waited for a train. He went to the station himself and spotted the checked bags. After waiting fruitlessly for Colepaugh to show up and claim them, Gimpel told the baggage clerk that he had lost his tickets for the bags and talked him into handing them over.

Colepaugh was having second thoughts about his mission. He looked up an old friend, confessed what he was up to, and said he wanted to turn himself in. After a few days of drinking and talking, Colepaugh's friend contacted the FBI on December 26. Colepaugh told everything to the agents who questioned him. "He is a somewhat unstable New Englander but impressed his interrogators as attempting to tell the truth," the agents reported. "He is intelligent, very observant, and has an extraordinary visual memory for details. His attitude toward the interrogators was friendly and cooperative. He was always careful to distinguish between eye witness evidence and hearsay. The interrogators were under the impression that his helpfulness was inspired by the hope of escaping the death penalty."

Colepaugh told his interrogators that Gimpel liked to buy Peruvian newspapers at a Times Square newsstand that specialized in foreign papers, and that he paid for them with small bills he kept in his breast pocket. Agents staked out the newsstand and pounced when a man answering to Gimpel's description showed up on December 30. Operation Elster was over.

Hodgkins's sighting had not led to the spies' capture, but the Bar Harbor Boy Scout received a hero's reception once Gimpel and Colepaugh had been arrested. A New York paper paid to bring him to the city, where he visited the Empire State Building, had breakfast with Babe Ruth, and met boxer Joe Louis and Governor Thomas Dewey. The Maine Maritime Academy offered him a full scholarship. Mary Forni did not get the same level of recognition. She had to be satisfied with a $100 war bond.

Gimpel and Colepaugh were tried by a military tribunal, found guilty, and sentenced to death by hanging. Franklin Roosevelt died before the spies did, and the president's death put all death sentences on hold for four weeks. By then, Harry Truman was president and the war in Europe was over. Truman commuted the death sentences to life terms. Gimpel served his time in Leavenworth, Kansas, on Alcatraz in San Francisco Bay, and in Atlanta. He was released after 10 years and returned to Germany in 1955. He published a sensationalized version of his story in the 1950s (published in the United States in 2003 as *Agent 146*). Gimpel died in 2010.

Colepaugh was paroled in 1960. He married and moved to King of Prussia, Pennsylvania, where no one knew about his past. In fact, in 1990 his Rotary Club selected Colepaugh as the first recipient of its Distinguished Service Award. Friends and neighbors who thought they knew Colepaugh were shocked in 2002 when *USA Today* exposed him as a former Nazi spy. He died in 2005.

Horst Haslau, the U-boat's radio operator, visited Hancock Point in 1984 to see where his submarine had dropped off its human cargo 40 years earlier. "I think the German navy was very familiar with the surrounding Mount Desert area, because sea maps are accurate down to the smallest details," he told a local paper. "They were better maps than what the Park Service gives you today."

1950s

Margaret Chase Smith Takes a Stand

ON THE MORNING OF JUNE 1, 1950, SENATORS MARGARET CHASE SMITH (R-Maine) and Joseph R. McCarthy (R-Wisconsin) crossed paths in the subway tunnel beneath the U.S. Capitol. The two presented a study in contrasts. Smith, the nation's only female senator, represented Maine. Small, neatly dressed, and quiet, Smith maintained a stillness overlaying steely determination. Her sole flamboyance was a red rose she pinned to her dress every day. McCarthy was gregarious, usually disheveled, perpetually active. Of the junior senator from Wisconsin, a reporter wrote, "He is ignorant, crude, boastful, unaware of either intellectual or social refinements."

McCarthy had grabbed the national spotlight in February when, delivering a speech in Wheeling, West Virginia, he brandished what he said was a list of known communists serving in the U.S. State Department. Since then, McCarthy's campaign against subversives in government had gained intensity and notoriety, to Smith's increasing discomfort. She was preparing to take a stand.

"Margaret, you look very serious," McCarthy said. "Are you going to make a speech?"

"Yes," she replied, "and you are not going to like it."

He did not.

Smith was not only the only woman in the Senate, she was also the only woman in American history to have won election to both houses of

Congress. Margaret Madeline Chase was born on December 14, 1897, in Skowhegan. Her father, a barber, had his shop next door to the family home, which he had built. Her mother picked up such work as she could find. "We didn't go hungry, but we didn't have anything," Smith recalled. At 13, Margaret started clerking at Skowhegan's five-and-dime, in time moving on to the town telephone switchboard and tax office. After graduating from high school, she taught at a one-room schoolhouse near home and worked for the Skowhegan *Independent Reporter*. She never attended college. In 1930, Chase married Clyde Smith, a Republican newspaper publisher who had served as a state legislator, Skowhegan selectman, and state senator. She was 33; he was 54. "It was not a great love, not that kind," Smith later said. "It was more a business arrangement."

When Clyde Smith was elected to the U.S. Congress in 1936, Margaret served as his secretary. A syphilitic, Clyde died in April 1940. Running in the special election to fill out his term, Margaret won his seat for the short term and that fall won the regular election. "I had been close to my husband while he was in Congress," she said. "I knew everything he did, and through him I had been close to many of the Congressmen I had to work with now. So I just kept right on doing what I'd *been* doing. The only thing different was the voting." Smith was a Republican moderate, inclined to follow her own course and at times willing to defy party leadership. Before Pearl Harbor, she backed Franklin Roosevelt's Lend-Lease program to aid Britain, and after the war she endorsed the United Nations and the Marshall Plan to rebuild Europe.

She served three full terms in the House, and when Maine's Senator Wallace H. White announced he would not run for reelection, Smith ran to replace him, positioning herself as "The Can-Do Candidate with the Can-Did Record." Her toughest race was in the GOP primary, but she bested three opponents and in November 1948 cruised to victory.

Joe McCarthy, who had two years on Smith as a senator, came from Appleton, Wisconsin, a son of a large Irish-Catholic family with a hardscrabble background. Graduating from Marquette University in 1935, he practiced law in the town of Waupaca. He entered politics as a Democrat committed to Franklin Roosevelt's New Deal. In 1938, McCarthy set his eyes on the position of circuit judge and beat out the elderly incumbent in a race that saw McCarthy campaign hard and resort to the occasional low blow.

When the country went to war, McCarthy, realizing postwar politics would demand that candidates have war records, joined the U.S. Marine Corps as a lieutenant. He served in the Pacific in a non-combat role as an intelligence officer; the only violence he experienced was breaking a leg in an equator-crossing ceremony aboard ship. Returning home in 1945, he created an image of himself as "Tail Gunner Joe" and claimed, falsely, to have been wounded in combat. He also had a nose for an opponent's political weaknesses. "To the public McCarthy, life was a game in which no quarter was asked and none given," wrote David M. Oshinsky in his 1993 book *A Conspiracy So Immense: The World of Joe McCarthy*. "His approach was so primitive, so cynical, so devoid of commitment to any goal but personal success, that few opponents had the will or the stomach to fight him on his own terms." McCarthy was the clear underdog when he challenged incumbent Senator Bob Lafollette, but he beat Lafollette in the Republican primary and made short work of his Democratic foe in the 1946 general election. As a junior senator, McCarthy displayed disdain for Senate decorum with "a restless and compulsive energy, a hunger for power and public notice, and a casual disregard for custom and authority," historian Robert Griffith wrote. The private McCarthy was affable and friendly, with an almost compulsive need to be liked.

McCarthy began reaching for prominence on February 9, 1950, in Wheeling, West Virginia. In an otherwise ordinary address to the Ohio County Women's Republican Club, he held up a sheet of paper and, according to reports—no recording of the speech survives—said that on it appeared the names of 205 State Department employees known to belong to the Communist Party. Americans had long regarded communism with fear and suspicion, even after the Soviet Union became our ally during World War II. Events following the war, though, made the communist threat even more ominous. In 1948, the Soviets blockaded the divided city of Berlin and the Western powers kept the city fed and supplied with an airlift. In 1949, communist forces under Mao Zedong forced Chiang Kai-shek's Nationalists out of China. The threat of communist North Korea was raising tensions on the Korean Peninsula. Domestically, the country was rocked by the trial of Alger Hiss, a State Department official accused of leaking information to his Soviet handlers. Even worse, the Soviet Union exploded an atomic bomb in 1949, raising the specter that information from American spies had helped the Soviets achieve their goal.

In this climate, McCarthy's hazy complaints resonated. His numbers seemed unsettlingly fluid. He said later that he had 207 names, then the identities of "57 card-carrying members of the Communist Party." Before the Senate on February 20, he cited "81 loyalty risks." His examples, taken from a 1948 FBI inquiry, were often distorted, exaggerated, or fabricated. Still, they reverberated. And with Democrat Harry Truman in the White House and his party ruling Congress, red-baiting made for an effective Republican cudgel.

Senator Smith, no less a Cold Warrior than the Wisconsinite, at first took his statements at face value. "It looked as though Joe was onto something disturbing and frightening," she said. But McCarthy's claims began to rankle. "Photostatic copies" that he said supported his charges seemed to have little to do with them. Cases McCarthy tried to make— such as one that China expert Owen Lattimore was "the top Russian agent" in the United States—didn't hold water. But as a senator, McCarthy had immunity, granted by the Constitution, from being prosecuted for anything said on the Senate floor. "Week after week went by with charge after charge by Joe McCarthy which remained unproved," Smith wrote in her 1972 book, *Declaration of Conscience*. "My doubts increased." She concluded that the gentleman from Wisconsin simply could not back up what he was saying.

"To me, in 1950, the Communist threat of 'confuse, divide, and conquer' was real—but the McCarthy blunderbuss-shotgun approach ultimately was helping to help and serve the communist design of conquest," Smith said. The Wisconsin senator was creating "an atmosphere of such political fear that people were not only afraid to talk but they were afraid of whom they might be seen with." Out of partisan fealty, Smith believed it was Democrats' job to confront McCarthy. She also felt constrained by a tradition that freshman senators were "to be seen and not heard, like good children." But as McCarthy rose, colleagues on both sides of the aisle, fearing he might turn on them, kept silent. "Joe had the Senate paralyzed with fear," Smith said.

Unwilling to keep still, Smith decided to draft a brief "declaration of conscience" and circulate it among fellow Senate Republicans, in hopes they would sign on. She enlisted six. Vermont's George D. Aikin agreed first, followed by New Hampshire's Charles W. Tobey, Oregon's Wayne L. Morse, New York's Irving M. Ives, Minnesota's Edward J. Thye, and New Jersey's Robert C. Hendrickson.

Home in Maine over Memorial Day weekend, Smith worked on a speech she would give introducing the declaration. She returned to Washington on May 30, and the next day had 200 copies made of her impending remarks. She held off distribution, lest the party leadership get wind of her plan and stop it.

On the Senate floor, Smith stood to speak, two rows ahead of McCarthy. Her aide, Bill Lewis, handed copies to pages for reporters. McCarthy sat covering his face with his hand. "Mr. President, I would like to speak briefly and simply about a serious national condition," Smith began. "It is a national feeling of fear and frustration that could result in national suicide and the end of everything that we Americans hold dear. It is a condition that comes from the lack of effective leadership either in the legislative branch or the executive branch of our government."

McCarthy was the topic, but Smith never named him. "The American people are sick and tired of being afraid to speak their minds lest they be politically smeared as 'Communists' or 'Fascists' by their opponents," she said. "Freedom of speech is not what it used to be in America. It has been so abused by some that it is not exercised by others."

Smith included partisan jabs as well. "The record of the present Democratic administration has provided us with sufficient campaign issues without the necessity of resorting to political smears," she said. "America is rapidly losing its position as leader of the world simply because the Democratic administration has pitifully failed to provide effective leadership."

Smith wanted to see the GOP prevail in the coming elections. "But I do not want to see the Republican party ride to political victory on the Four Horsemen of Calumny—Fear, Ignorance, Bigotry, and Smear," she said. She finished speaking and sat down. McCarthy left without comment.

Smith's gesture made a bit of a splash. "Sen. Smith Assails Colleagues," bannered the next day's *Portland Press Herald*. "Says People Sick of Seeing Innocent Victims Smeared." The *Bangor Daily News* blared, "Sen. Smith In Blistering Attack On Both Sides For Red Probe Tactics." Smith made the cover of the June 12 *Newsweek*. "What many a bewildered citizen had waited to hear for a long time was said by a woman last week," the magazine reported. "The diminutive lady from Maine struck precisely the right note. She is attractive and self-possessed—but with a man-sized will. She has gone far and wants to go farther, and is in an excellent position to do so."

At a June 1 press conference, President Truman joked that "he wouldn't want to say anything that bad about the Republican Party." But days later over lunch Truman told Smith, "Your Declaration of Conscience was one of the finest things that has happened here in Washington in all my years in the Senate and the White House."

Retribution was slow catching up with McCarthy. The day after Smith's speech he was on the Senate floor vowing to fight against communism "regardless of what any group in this Senate or in the administration might do." He dubbed Smith and the Republicans who signed her declaration "Snow White and the Seven Dwarfs," counting H. Alexander Smith, of New Jersey, who had not signed but did endorse the document. In January 1951, McCarthy removed Smith from his permanent investigations subcommittee and replaced her with Representative Richard Nixon (R-California). Smith learned of the move when McCarthy had a subordinate slip a note under her office door after hours.

Smith's declaration opened no floodgates of criticism, or did much to slow McCarthy's advance. "Politically speaking, the Declaration had no real impact," wrote Oshinsky. Even senators who signed it began to distance themselves. Ives later offered McCarthy his "full cooperation." Tobey said the senator's "objectives are good." H. Alexander Smith decided it was better to "convert" McCarthy rather than reprimand him in public. Smith by herself could do little in that climate, but she continued to signal opposition. On June 14, 1951, McCarthy attacked Secretary of Defense George Marshall and Secretary of State Dean Acheson as patsies for the communists, spurring Smith to reenter her declaration into the Senate record. "What I said then is even more applicable today, particularly in view of the statements made in the past few days," she announced.

Smith got some payback as a member of a subcommittee investigating the 1950 Maryland elections that cost McCarthy foe Senator Millard Tydings (D-Maryland), his seat. Among agitprop brought to bear against Tydings was a brochure featuring a photo of Tydings chatting with Earl Browder, head of the American Communist Party. That meeting never occurred; McCarthy staffers had created a composite image. Smith supported a report sharply critical of McCarthy, but to get the Republican leadership to issue it, she had to push. McCarthy attacked the report, calling it biased. Smith had her Declaration of Conscience entered into the record a third time.

McCarthy also struck back indirectly. Jack Lait and Lee Mortimer, newspapermen and coauthors of the 1952 redbaiting exercise, *U.S.A. Confidential*, cited Smith as "a lesson in why women should not be in politics. When men argue matters of high policy they usually forget their grudges at the door. She takes every opposing speech as a personal affront and lies awake nights scheming how to 'get even.' She is sincere—but a dame—and she reacts to all situations as a woman scorned, not as a representative of the people." The two characterized Smith as a "left-wing apologist" and tried to link her with a State Department employee McCarthy had attacked as a security risk. Smith sued for libel, winning a $15,000 settlement and a stipulation that Lait and Mortimer run apologetic ads in Maine newspapers—a small victory, but victory nonetheless.

McCarthy, who had won reelection to the Senate in 1952, went after Smith when she was up for reelection in 1954 by making public appearances in Maine for her primary opponent. Smith won handily, a setback and an augury for McCarthy. Even with Republican Dwight D. Eisenhower in the White House and the GOP controlling Congress, he continued his attacks, seeing reds everywhere—at the Voice of America, the International Information Agency, the U.S. Signal Corps, even the U.S. Army.

The attack on the army set the stage for McCarthy's public downfall. His subcommittee on investigations began hearings on the army's behavior regarding security risks on April 22, 1954, and they lasted for almost two months of often contentious proceedings. Televised live, the hearings captivated the public. The dramatic high point came on June 9. Joseph Welch, the Boston lawyer representing the army, was questioning McCarthy's aide Roy Cohn, to McCarthy's obvious annoyance and anger. Unable to resist the temptation to strike back, McCarthy interrupted to point out that a young lawyer in Welch's firm, Fred Fisher, had once belonged to the National Lawyers Guild, which the House Un-American Activities Commission later determined to be "subversive." Welch had learned about this before the hearings began and sent Fisher back to Boston, knowing that McCarthy might try to exploit the situation. When the senator did, Welch was ready. "Let us not assassinate this lad further, Senator," he said. "You have done enough. Have you no sense of decency, sir, at long last. Have you left no sense of decency?"

Thanks to the live broadcasts, ordinary Americans had a chance to see McCarthy in action for the first time and, to a large extent, they did not like what they saw. Sensing weakness, in August the Senate began hearings about officially censuring McCarthy for his behavior as a senator.

After winning reelection despite McCarthy's opposition, Smith set off on an international trip, meeting with Winston Churchill, Francisco Franco, and Soviet Foreign Minister V.M. Molotov, among other leaders.

However, she took care to split her itinerary so she could be in Washington on December 2 to join fellow senators voting 67-22 to censure McCarthy for behavior "contrary to senatorial tradition."

McCarthy, a spent force, faded away, dying on May 2, 1957. Smith remained in the Senate and in 1964 had her name entered as a GOP presidential nominee, the first by a woman for a mainstream party. Defeated for reelection in 1972, Margaret Chase Smith retired. She was 97 when she died in 1995, still remembered as the "conscience of the Senate."

1960s

Maine Enters the Space Age

IN 1962, THE 760 PEOPLE WHO LIVED IN THE TINY WESTERN MAINE town of Andover still used hand-cranked telephones and talked on party lines, so it was a surprising place to find revolutionary communications technology. Yet outside of town, a futuristic complex was rising in a clearing carved out of the Maine woods. Its centerpiece was a huge inflatable dome—18 stories tall and supported solely by air pressure—that looked like a gargantuan ping pong ball embedded in the soil. It was an "Earth station" that AT&T had constructed to communicate with the Telstar I satellite.

A true pioneer, Telstar was the privately owned and operated spacecraft that transmitted the first live television between North America and Europe. According to one historian, it "symbolized like nothing else the potential of space technology to unite the world." The gigantic dome outside Andover housed a huge antenna that made Telstar's broadcasts possible, and it presented a strange, otherworldly sight amid the dense woods and rolling hills of the Maine wilderness.

In 1962, the space race between the United States and the Soviet Union was in full swing. The Soviet Union had won the initial round by sending the first manmade satellite, Sputnik, into orbit in October 1957. It won another round by orbiting the first living organism, a dog named Laika, in another Sputnik that November. When Yuri Gagarin became the first human to orbit the Earth on April 12, 1961, it appeared that the United States was doomed to lose the space race to its Soviet rival.

But like the underdog in a Hollywood movie, the United States began to gain ground. The Explorer I satellite reached orbit in January 1958 and discovered the Van Allen radiation belts that surround earth. Alan Shepard made a suborbital flight the month after Gagarin, and John Glenn became the first American to orbit the earth in February 1962. More and more unmanned vehicles followed, including weather satellites, solar observatories, and missions to the moon and beyond Venus. The rockets hurling them into space, though, were modified missiles, underscoring the precarious state of world affairs.

Telstar I established some firsts of its own. It was the world's first "active" satellite, meaning it received signals from the ground, amplified them, and retransmitted them back to earth. (A "reflective" satellite, like the earlier Echo I, was like a big orbital balloon that merely bounced signals back to earth). Telstar looked something like an oversized soccer ball, its aluminum shell dotted by the black panels of solar cells. It was less than 35 inches in diameter and weighed 170 pounds on earth. (In space, of course, it was weightless.) Telstar was crowned by a spiral antenna that received telemetry commands from earth and had a band of glass antennas around its equator for the reception of telecommunications. The satellite derived its power from nickel-cadmium batteries and solar panels. By today's standards it was primitive. For example, it had only one transponder for sending and receiving. (A modern satellite might have 56, with each one capable of handling 200 separate channels.) It functioned like a relay tower in space, a "bent pipe" that sent electronic signals, which travel in straight lines, around the planet's curved surface.

The satellite was also the world's first privately owned and operated spacecraft. It had been designed and constructed by AT&T, which paid the National Aeronautics and Space Administration (NASA) $3 million for the use of a Thor-Delta rocket for the ride into space.

AT&T had chosen Andover for its earth station because its relative isolation in western Maine and the surrounding hills and mountains sheltered it from radio interference. From space, Telstar could relay the signals Andover transmitted to a pair of European ground stations, Goonhilly Downs in England and Pleumeur-Bodou in Brittany. The

French had a radome and antenna like those at Andover while the British relied on a more conventional dish antenna.

The huge dome outside Andover was an engineering triumph itself. "For today's engineer it's hard to believe how bold the venture was," recalled Milton B. Punnet, the project engineer for Birdair Structures, the company in Buffalo, New York, that built the dome. "Our small company was going to build the largest radome ever conceived, using material that didn't exist, requiring joint strengths never achieved, using a new adhesive in a joint design still to be proved. All within a seemingly impossible time period, which left no room for going back."

There were actually two domes erected at Andover. The first was a temporary shelter used to protect the equipment during construction. It looked much like the final radome but had a big, 50-foot "blister" on the side to fit over the fat end of the horn antenna it was sheltering. Even this smaller, temporary dome offered challenges. Since this was Maine, snow began collecting on top of the dome, flattening the rounded top. An engineer suggested shooting holes through the top from inside the dome to allow the snow melt to drain. That worked fine, but when the shelter popped back into shape, the remaining snow and ice slid off the dome and crushed a construction trailer on the ground next to it.

Another crisis arose when the top of the construction shelter began to tear. Engineers needed to hoist someone up to fix it, a contingency for which they had not planned. They tried tying a rope to an arrow, but no archer could shoot it high enough to go over the dome. The Coast Guard attempted to fire a breeches buoy over the top, but that came up short, too. An attempt to use a helicopter almost ended in disaster when the rope got tangled in the skids and the technician holding the other end broke his finger. A bigger Coast Guard helicopter couldn't get the job done either. Finally, the team rented a 240-foot crane from Boston to get the rope over the dome and hoist up a repair crew. (To avoid this problem with the final dome, designers put a trap door at the top of the dome, with a small platform just below it. To reach the platform, a volunteer had to be hoisted 160 feet in a bosun's chair with a rope and pulleys. Punnett found the experience to be "disconcerting.")

Punnett's team constructed the permanent dome from a combination of Dacron and Hypalon after engineers discovered that a garden hose made out of Hypalon weathered better than hoses made from other materials. The almost 300 panels had to be glued together, which required construction of a special machine. Installing the dome over the temporary construction shelter was "a task which had proved sheer agony and almost desperation," Punnett recalled. An April blizzard delayed the work for a week, but on April 20, 1962, huge cranes began hoisting the permanent dome over the construction shelter, which then had to be removed, Punnett said, like a magician taking off someone's shirt without disturbing his coat.

At its base, the 210-foot-tall dome was secured to a 200-foot-diameter concrete ring. The dome had no internal supports and was supported entirely by air pressure. Five blowers maintained the internal pressure, with several backup power sources on hand to make sure they were always running. AT&T engineers devised circuitry that ensure the blowers kept a consistent air pressure under any wind and weather conditions that Maine could offer. Eight heaters were placed around the base of the dome, but they heated the air so quickly that the increased air pressure quickly exceeded the material's limits.

"It has always amazed me that visitors to a Telstar site would seemingly be most impressed with the radome and the fact that it is held up only with air," Punnett wrote. "When I would point out the complexity of the giant 360 ton antenna sitting inside, they would again ask, 'What did you say holds up the radome?'"

Punnett had a point. The radome was striking, but the real technical wonder was the antenna it sheltered, which was designed to capture the faint signals arriving from Telstar. The horn antenna, 94 feet tall and 177 feet long, looked like something made from a gigantic erector set. The receiving end was 68 feet across; it was only two inches wide at the base. Suspended in the metal framework at the antenna's narrow end was a little 28' x 38' structure called the cab, which housed the electronics. "The cab was filled with gray electronic consoles, four green camp chairs, a tomato-red easy chair and the quiet conversation of men who had done everything possible to ready their gear for its first real test," wrote a *New York Times* reporter. The antenna's heart was a maser (Microwave

Amplification by Stimulated Emission of Radiation), which used an artificial ruby cooled to 456 degrees below zero by liquid helium. The maser boosted the weak signals without adding background noise of its own. "Without the maser, nothing usable would come from Telstar," noted Louis Solomon in a 1964 book about the project.

The entire antenna was mounted on a precisely engineered circular rail so it could rotate smoothly and follow the satellite's motion while Telstar circled the earth in its elliptical orbit. As the antenna rotated, a series of brushes swept the rail to ensure that no grit jostled it and interfered with the satellite link.

The earth station was undeniably the biggest thing to hit Andover, especially on July 10, 1962, when a swarm of arrivals passed through town on their way to witness the first contact with Telstar. "No matter how communicating by satellite might turn out, their town, where communicating by telephone requires turning a crank, was forever and unforgettably on the map of the world," wrote Solomon. Newton Minnow, the head of the Federal Communications Commission and the man who once called television "a vast wasteland," was there. So was Fred Kappel, AT&T's chairman. If all went according to plan, he would make a phone call to Vice President Lyndon Johnson in Washington via Telstar.

NASA's hired rocket hurled Telstar into an elliptical orbit around earth in the early hours of the morning. It was now up to the team of engineers and technicians at Andover to establish communications with the tiny satellite as it whirled through space and then use it to make the first live broadcast across the Atlantic.

But it was going to be an agonizing 15 hours after the launch before the technicians in Andover could establish solid contact with the satellite. Telstar was not in a geosynchronous orbit, which would have kept it stationary above a single point on earth. Instead, it was in a lower, elliptical orbit that ranged as high as 3,500 miles and as low as 580. Traveling at 15,000 miles per hour, Telstar circled the earth in a little more than 90 minutes, and the earth station could communicate with it only when the satellite was in a direct line of sight with the antenna. It would take several orbits before Telstar reached the right position, and then it would be within view for only a limited time before dropping behind earth's rim.

In Andover, project director Eugene F. O'Neill waited anxiously in the control room, a flat white building about five blocks from the radome, to receive confirmation that Andover had picked up the satellite. At 7:17 the satellite came into sight. "We've sighted the satellite!" O'Neill announced. "We haven't got it yet, but we've sighted it!" The complex's antennas, including the big horn antenna, locked on the satellite. "We've acquired Telstar!" O'Neill exclaimed. A radio transmission turned Telstar on. With that done, Andover beamed up a test pattern, which Telstar retransmitted successfully.

At 7:28 everything was ready for the historic telephone call with Johnson. "How do you hear me?" Kappel asked the vice president. "You're coming through nicely, Mr. Kappel," replied Johnson. At 7:31 it was time to beam a television signal to the satellite so Telstar could retransmit it back to earth. The image showed an American flag flapping in front of the Andover radome while "The Star Spangled Banner" played. "As though at a given signal, everyone—engineers, scientists, technicians, reporters, public officials—broke into applause," reported Louis Solomon. Following that was a question-and-answer session with officials in Washington and Andover. At 7:47 word came that the French station at Pleumeur-Bodou, which had been rushing to get ready in time, had received pictures from Telstar.

That night the French broadcast their contribution, a seven-minute film uploaded during Telstar's fifteenth orbit. It began with remarks by Jacques M. Marette, France's communications minister; a song ("La Chansonette") by Yves Montand, some other music, and shots of Pleumeur-Bodou. The British uploaded a nine-minute segment at 10:21. "The British made no attempt to entertain," Richard Witkin reported for the *New York Times*. "They put on a few slides and test patterns. They followed with a message of congratulations broadcast by Britain's Deputy Chief Engineer, Capt. Charles Booth, seated at his post at an electronic console." The British had already been embarrassed when a technician hit the wrong button and prevented Goonhilly-Downs from receiving Telstar's audio, and then they had been irritated that the French had broadcast their own program without input from their other European partners. But at least they had the satisfaction of knowing the British transmission was live, not taped like the French contribution.

There were two other, more ambitious programs broadcast on July 20, one from North America transmitted by Telstar to Europe, and a European production that traveled in the opposite direction. Walter Cronkite, the anchor for the CBS *Evening News*, introduced the North American program, which ranged around the United States, broadcasting part of a Cubs-Phillies game from Chicago and a portion of President John F. Kennedy's press conference in Washington, plus scenes from New York, San Francisco, Niagara Falls, Cape Canaveral, and the Rio Grande on the border of Texas and Mexico. A Canadian portion included a peek at a rehearsal of *Macbeth* with Christopher Plummer and Kate Reid from Stratford, Ontario.

"The plain facts of electronic life are that Washington and the Kremlin are now no farther apart than the speed of light, at least technically," said Cronkite, who shared his hosting duties with NBC's Chet Huntley and ABC's Howard K. Smith. The sixteen nations of the Eurovision network responded to its program that night, sending imagery from all over Europe.

Alas, Telstar soon succumbed to the rigors of space. Four months after launch it began showing signs of failure. Engineers determined that radiation from the Van Allen belts was probably the culprit. In February 1963 Telstar failed for good. It was replaced by Telstar 2 in May. The Andover Earth station remained in operation. The radome became a tourist attraction until it was dismantled in 1985. In 1987 AT&T sold the Earth station to MCI.

Telstar's achievements almost seem quaint today, when satellite dishes sprout like mushrooms from the sides of homes, office buildings, and apartment complexes so people can receive television programs directly from space. In the 1960s, though, it put Maine at the forefront of the space race.

—~—

While Maine was part of a revolution in communications, it lagged lamentably behind on other fronts. On July 10, 1962, the same day that

143

Telstar lifted into orbit, the *New York Times* reported a story from Kennebunkport. The owner of the Kennebunkport Playhouse, Robert C. Currier, was staging a production of *Raisin in the Sun* at his theater. When he tried to find a hotel for his lead actress, Claudia McNeil, the first seven hotels he contacted refused to accommodate her because she was African American. "I called one for a reservation and didn't say Miss McNeil was a Negro, and the reservation was immediately accepted," Currier told the *Times*. "Then when I mentioned she was colored, they withdrew the reservation." Currier said McNeil's presence would "embarrass" the other customers. Such discrimination was illegal.

Another story in the paper outlined the controversy that Rachel Carson had stirred up with the upcoming publication of her book *Silent Spring*. Carson, a frequent visitor to Maine who did much of her writing at a summer home in Southport, intended her book to be a warning about the effects of pesticides on the natural world. "Silent Spring Is Now Noisy Summer," the headline read, and the article explained how Carson's thesis that chemicals posed an increasing threat to our ecosystems outraged the pesticides industry. The president of the Montrose Chemical Corporation, which manufactured a chemical called DDT, complained that Carson was "a fanatic defender of the cult of the balance of nature."

Another story in the *New York Times* on July 22 covered another topic that would inflame the United States for the rest of the decade and beyond. "U.S. Heavily Committed in Struggle to Save South Vietnam," read the headline.

By the time the United States ended its role in the conflict in 1975, almost 47,000 Americans had been killed in combat. Another 300,000 had been wounded, and 11,000 more died in non-combat situations. The names of 344 Maine soldiers are engraved on the granite slabs of the Vietnam Memorial in Washington. Donald Sidney Skidgel is one of them.

Skidgel was only 20 years old when he died, leaving behind a wife, two daughters, and a son. Skidgel had been born in Caribou but graduated from high school in Newport, Maine, and enlisted in the army in February 1968. At the time of his death he was a sergeant in command of D Troop in the 9th Cavalry Regiment of the 1st Cavalry Division.

Skidgel received the Medal of Honor posthumously for "conspicuous gallantry and intrepidity in action at the risk of his life above and beyond the call of duty." On September 14, 1969, Skidgel and his men were serving as a screen for a military convoy near the town of Song Be in Binh Long Province. When the enemy attacked the convoy from cover alongside the road, Skidgel launched into action. According to his Medal of Honor citation, "Sgt. Skidgel maneuvered off the road and began placing effective machine gun fire on the enemy automatic weapons and rocket-propelled grenade positions." He managed to shut down one enemy position, and then shifted to focus attention on another source of incoming fire. After running low on ammunition, Skidgel learned that another part of the convoy was under attack. He returned to his vehicle and he and his driver attempted to draw the enemy fire. "Despite the hostile fire concentrated on him, he succeeded in silencing several enemy positions with his machine gun," read his citation. "Moments later Sgt. Skidgel was knocked down onto the rear fender by the explosion of an enemy rocket-propelled grenade. Ignoring his extremely painful wounds, he staggered back to his feet and placed effective fire on several other enemy positions until he was mortally wounded by hostile small arms fire. His selfless actions enabled the command group to withdraw to a better position without casualties and inspired the rest of his fellow soldiers to gain fire superiority and defeat the enemy. Sgt. Skidgel's gallantry at the cost of his life was in keeping with the highest traditions of the military service and reflect great credit upon himself, his unit, and the U.S. Army."

Skidgel's body was returned to the United States and he was buried in Plymouth's Sawyer Cemetery. In 2011 a bridge in Newport that spans the Sebasticook River was renamed the Donald Sidney Skidgel Memorial Bridge in his honor. Skidgel's children, Maine Congressman Mike Michaud, Senator Susan Collins, and other dignitaries attended the ceremony. "The story of his actions is inspiring, but it's difficult to find the words to say how profoundly appreciative we all are as a country for what he did," Michaud said. "His actions are the very definition of bravery."

Two other Maine soldiers received the Medal of Honor for actions in Vietnam and, like Skidgel, they received their medals posthumously.

Sergeant Brian L. Buker was a special forces soldier from Benton who died on April 5, 1970, while displaying "conspicuous gallantry and intrepidity in action at the risk of life above and beyond the call of duty." Buker was serving as an advisor to the South Vietnamese on the day he died. "Sergeant Buker personally led the platoon, cleared a strategically located and well guarded pass, and established the first foothold at the top of what had been an impenetrable mountain fortress," his citation read. "As a direct result of his heroic actions, many casualties were averted, and the assault of the enemy position was successful."

Thomas J. McMahon of Portland was a specialist fourth class in Company A, 2nd Battalion, 1st Infantry, 196th Brigade, American Division. On March 19, 1969, McMahon died while serving as a medic. When his company came under fire, McMahon disregarded his personal danger to help the wounded. "He fell mortally wounded before he could rescue the last man," said his medal citation, which saluted his "undaunted concern for the welfare of his comrades at the cost of his life."

1970s

Maine Holds the Last Log Drive

IN 1976, MAINE MARKED THE END OF AN ERA. THE AGE OF THE LOG drive was over.

The timber industry had fueled Maine's economy for a long time. The historical record is murky, but it's possible that York established North America's first sawmill as early as 1623. South Berwick certainly had one by 1631. At least 24 water-powered mills were converting logs to lumber in Maine by 1682, and the number continued to rise. The heavily forested state offered a bounty for all those mills. Maine's white pine was especially valuable, but trees of all kinds gave their lives to provide humans in North America and around the world with masts, houses, barrels, fences, shingles, furniture, and paper.

Henry David Thoreau noted the scale of the logging industry when he first visited Maine in 1846 and noted 250 sawmills on the Penobscot near Bangor. "To this is to be added the lumber of the Kennebec, Androscoggin, Saco, Passamaquoddy, and other streams," he wrote. "No wonder that we hear so often of vessels which are becalmed off our coast, being surrounded a week at a time by floating lumber from the Maine woods."

The reason lumber endangered ships at sea was that Maine's rivers, especially the Kennebec and the Penobscot, provided ready-made avenues to transport timber to the sawmills. Some of the harvest slipped past the mills and journeyed all the way to the ocean. Bangor, with its prime

147

location on the deep-water Penobscot, became a bustling hub of the lumber industry, with logs harvested from the north woods floating down the river during the spring log drives. "Slab wood, edgings and sawdust choked the river, sometimes leaving only a narrow channel through the thick bars of waste wood," wrote historian Richard W. Judd. Industrious citizens could salvage plenty of waste wood for their own purposes.

Harvesting the timber, getting it into the water, and floating it downstream was hard, dirty, exhausting work. The lumberjacks typically began their season in the fall, living in crude logging camps and eating basic meals that included the legendary bean-hole beans. After felling the trees, the lumbermen hauled them to the side of a stream to wait for the spring, when snowmelt would raise the water and make floating the logs easier. The best time to haul the huge logs to the riverside was in early winter, when snow allowed the use of sleds, but before it became too deep to make transportation impossible.

Loggers had specialized tools of the trade. The "cant dog" was a pole with a hook called a "dog" at the end. Another tool was the peavey, named after its inventor, Stillwater's Joseph Peavey, who introduced it in 1858. The peavey was an improved cant dog, with the hooked end able to pivot in only one direction to make it easier to grasp the logs. The drivers corralled their harvest with booms, barriers made of logs chained end to end. Booms came in all forms. There were plug booms, sheepshank booms, and chain booms, each suited for a specific purpose. Drivers would rig a fin boom, for instance, to herd the logs around a point of land. Sometimes they would string booms between islands, or logging companies might build piers in the river to attach the chains. Loggers stood at the entrance to a boom and sorted the logs as they arrived—keeping an eye out for company markings blazed onto each log so they could send one company's logs in one direction and another company's to a different side of the boom.

As more and more lumber companies began sending their logs down Maine's rivers, the potential for confusion grew. The solution was to form associations, in which different companies pooled their resources to create a centralized authority to oversee the drives. The Kennebec Log Driving Company (KLDC) was incorporated in 1835, initially with authority only over the stretch of the river between Gardiner and the Forks. That was soon changed to cover the entire river, from its origins at Moosehead to the terminus at the Atlantic Ocean.

Under the new company, the task of overseeing the drive became the responsibility of a master driver. The first was William Connor. He was paid $3 a day plus expenses (later reduced to $2.50). It was his responsibility to recruit men for the drive, arrange their boarding, and keep track of expenses.

Log driving meant log jams, and untangling a jam required brute force and no little courage. Sometimes all it took was one log to start a jam. Drivers called that log a "jill-poke." Others started piling up behind, and the resulting jam could extend for acres. Breaking up a jam might require finding the "key log" and extricating it from the pile. Or it might require dynamite. Sometimes it required the intervention of Mother Nature. In 1854 a jam estimated at 25,000 logs stopped the Kennebec River drive at Norridgewock and it didn't break up until heavy rains raised the river in November.

An account from 1838 described how a river crew broke up one jam, when "a hundred men" set out to perform the task. "The place reached, out swarm the red shirts, handspike in hand. They start a log here, lift up a log there, cut this, pull that out, and with a crash the thousand logs start at once. A rush is made for shore; every man looks out for himself first, and his neighbor afterward . . . . Should once false step be taken, a nerve falter, an eye miss its calculation, to powder would be ground the being who fell among the tumbling mass."

"It was easy to see that driving logs must be an exciting as well as arduous and dangerous business," Thoreau wrote. A typical log driver "must be able to navigate a log as if it were a canoe, and be as indifferent to cold and wet as a muskrat. He uses a few efficient tools,—a lever commonly of rock-maple, six or seven feet long, with a stout spike in it, strongly feruled on, and a long spike-pole, with a screw at the end of the spike to make it hold. The boys along shore learn to walk on floating logs as city boys on sidewalks. Sometimes the logs are thrown up on rocks in such positions as to be irrecoverable but by another freshet as high, or they jam together at rapids and falls, and accumulate in vast piles, which the driver must start at the risk of his life."

Theodore Winthrop, a writer who was killed early in the Civil War, described a Maine log drive in one of his final works, and the description fit until the drives ended in 1976. "The marked logs are tumbled into the brimming stream, and so ends their forest-life," he explained.

Now comes 'the great spring drive.' Maine waters in spring flow under an illimitable raft. Every camp contributes its myriads of brown cylinders to the millions that go bobbing down rivers with jaw-breaking names. And when the river broadens to a lake, where these impetuous voyagers might be stranded or miss their way and linger, they are herded into vast rafts, and towed down by boats, or by steam-tugs, if the lake is large as Moosehead. At the lake-foot the rafts break up and the logs travel again dispersedly down stream, or through the 'thoro'fare' connecting the members of a chain of lakes. The hero of this epoch is the head-driver. The head-driver of a timber-drive leads a disorderly army, that will not obey the word of command. Every log acts as an individual, according to certain imperious laws of matter, and every log is therefore at loggerheads with every other log. The marshal must be in the thick of the fight, keeping his forces well in hand, hurrying stragglers, thrusting off the stranded, leading his phalanxes wisely round curves and angles, lest they be jammed and fill the river with a solid mass. As the great sticks come dashing along, turning porpoise-like somersets or leaping up twice their length in the air, he must be everywhere, livelier than a monkey in a mimosa, a wonder of acrobatic agility in biggest boots. He made the proverb, 'As easy as falling off a log.'

The hardships gave the work a shot of romance, and the lumberjacks and river drivers became examples of rugged America. "How did the cowboy get to be the symbol of the hard, sentimental, freewheeling American male who tamed the great spaces?" asked popular Maine newspaper columnist Bill Caldwell. "The Maine lumberjacks, the river drive bosses, the loggers, the timber cruisers, the cant-dog men, the choppers, the sawyers, the filers, the teamsters, the brawling lumber kings—these are the very stuff of the American spirit and the Yankee pioneer."

—◦—

Nothing lasts forever, and so it was with the log drives, which ended with one final exodus of timber down the Kennebec in 1976.

The end came suddenly. As late as 1970 the state issued a report saying that taking action to stop the drives "is not appropriate and would serve no useful service at this time."

Howard Trotzky disagreed with that. A University of Maine graduate student at the time (he later was elected a state representative), Trotzky believed the log drives not only polluted the water, they also prevented ordinary citizens from enjoying the rivers when they were choked with timber. In 1970 Trotzky founded the Kennebec Valley Conservation Association and he began seeking out like-minded citizens. That spring he testified in front of a legislative committee convened to study log drives. "The meeting was packed with pulp and paper industry lawyers," he said, "but even so I hit at log-driving as hard as I could."

The Scott Paper Company said it was "studying alternatives" to the log drives, but Trotzky didn't want to wait. He filed a lawsuit to stop the drives, which he said were illegally interfering with navigation on the Kennebec. (He did not cite environmental concerns, feeling those would be more difficult to prove in court.) In March 1971, the United States Department of Justice filed its own suit to stop the drives. Seeing that the tide was turning against it, the Scott paper company announced it would end Kennebec log drives by 1976, a decision the state legislature reinforced with a law that required ending the drives that year.

Paper companies had largely stopped getting their wood through log drives, anyway. "It was just getting more and more difficult to drive the volume we needed," Arthur Stedman, an assistant woodlands manager for Scott, told the *New York Times*. "It's just more economic to go by truck." Modern equipment could now strip the branches from entire trees, which were then hauled out of the woods by trucks to newer mills equipped to handle the bigger pieces of timber. Dams built along the rivers to generate electricity also blocked those larger sections of timber from going downstream.

River driving had other disadvantages, too. Up to 27 percent of some wood would get lost or damaged on river drives. Some logs became waterlogged and sank. Others were stranded on shore and left behind. Water could also cause logs to split, reducing their value as lumber. Rocks or sand that became embedded in the wood created hazards at the sawmills. Bark fell off and became an environmental hazard. Take the case of Wyman Lake, one of the big holding areas for the Kennebec drive. Located near Moscow, the lake had been created in 1929 when Central Maine Power constructed a dam across the Kennebec to generate electricity. Log drives covered huge sections of the lake with wood waiting to continue its journey through the dam's sluice. When the U.S. Environmental Agency surveyed the lake in 1971, it found that the bottom was covered by around five inches of decomposing bark from the logs, which had a negative impact on water quality.

In other words, the world of timber harvesting was changing, and this new world had no place for river drives. That meant the steamer *Katahdin* would need a new line of work. For years the *Kate* had towed rafts of logs across Moosehead Lake to the dam at the East Branch of the Kennebec. A 110-foot relic from a time when a small fleet of steamships plied Moosehead's waters, the *Kate* was launched in 1914 at Bath Iron Works and hauled by rail in sections to the lake, where she carried passengers for the Coburn Steamship Company. When the Hollingsworth & Whitney Company bought the *Katahdin* in 1942 she began her lumber work. In October 1975 she towed a raft of 180,000 cords to the East Outlet so they could begin their voyage down the river to the Scott Mill in Winslow, 85 miles away, in the spring. It was the start of the last log drive.

Robert Viles had been the master driver for the Kennebec Log Driving Company for 23 years by that time. The largest drive he could remember was in 1954, when 303,000 cords of wood went floating down the Kennebec. By 1976 that number had dropped to no more than 90,000 cords and only one mill, the Scott plant in Winslow, received wood from the drive. Viles blamed environmentalists for ending the drives but admitted there were other factors involved that made the river drives less economical, including the shift to trucks.

Viles was one of the KLDC's three full-time employees on the drive. The second was his foreman, Leonard "Buster" Violett, and the third was Carlton Dawes, the mechanic. Around 55 other men worked on the last drive, which started when the wood the *Katahdin* had delivered was sluiced over the dam at the East Outlet and into the river. Other logs began their journeys after being trucked through the woods to the Chase River sluice, located where the Chase River meets the Kennebec. The sluice was 165 feet long. The trucks dumped their loads into one end of the sluice, and the logs went sliding down it to the end, where they went hurtling through the air and splashed into the rapid waters of the Kennebec Gorge.

At Wyman Lake, the steamer *Kennebec* moved the rafts of logs across the still surface so workers could direct them into the sluice over the dam. By this point motorboats had replaced the traditional bateaux. Mary R. Calvert, author of *The Kennebec Wilderness Awakens*, described how boatmen Romeo St. John and Wilford Sanabas used their boats the way border collies herd sheep, keeping the logs moving so they wouldn't jam. Buster Violette manned a boat, too, and Calvert watched as he helped break up a jam that formed near Norridgewock. "I admired the way they navigated the four-foot sticks with pickpoles their only aid to balance," she wrote.

Once the wood reached the mill in Winslow, two Scott officials posed for a photo with what they said was the last log from the last drive. It was the end of an era.

"When the last log drive started on its way from Moosehead Lake to Winslow, I, like many others, was caught up in a wave of nostalgia, mine rising from the fact that I had seen the drives come down the Kennebec since childhood," Calvert wrote. Many others were sad to see this Maine tradition end. "I think people were a bit angry, they didn't understand why this thing they had been doing for 30 years all of a sudden had to stop," said one log driver. Walter Gary, the captain of the *Katahdin*, didn't see any reason to end the drives. "I don't know if it's going to help or hurt, it's hard to tell," he said, citing the increased number of trucks that would be on the road. Joseph Myerson, the editor of the Somerset *Reporter*, said that almost everyone he talked to said they regretted seeing the drives end, and that they saw this as part of the local culture and a tradition. "Everyone you talk to hates to see the end of the era," said Scott paper's Phil Walker. "This is it, it will never be back, there will never be more log drives. It was a good way, an easy way to get wood to a mill, and a quiet way. It didn't bother many people. It went down the rivers pretty silent there, and you get all these trucks hauling, there's going to be quite a lot more fuel involved and trucks, people on the highway. It's going to be a lot of changes all right."

"I miss the drive," Walker said "I liked that. That was a good job in the spring. You was out in the air and the sun, and away from the flies—a lot of flies in the woods in the summertime, you know. It was a good job."

"I didn't want it to end, because I liked the job," David Calder told a reporter for the *Morning Sentinel* 40 years later. "I liked being outdoors. I liked being on the river. I liked everything about it."

But, like they say, all good things have to come to an end.

1980s

Samantha Smith Seeks World Peace

A CROWD OF AROUND 300 PEOPLE BRAVED A FRIGID MONDAY MORNING in December 1986 to gather outside the State Cultural Building in Augusta. The center of their attention was an object covered by a veil of red satin. Sculptor Glenn Hines and Tiffany Jones, the manager of the Auburn Mall, pulled aside the veil to reveal a life-sized bronze statue. It depicted a young girl holding a dove. A bear cub sat at her feet.

The statue's subject was Samantha Smith of Manchester. She had been only 10 years old back in 1982 when she wrote a letter to Soviet premier Yuri Andropov that catapulted her to international fame. After *Pravda*, the Soviet Union's official newspaper, printed an excerpt, Samantha made headlines all over the world, appeared on television shows from *Today* to *Tonight*, visited the Soviet Union as a guest of the Soviet government, interviewed presidential candidates for a cable television program, and was cast to play Robert Wagner's daughter in a television series. Her future seemed assured.

When she wrote her letter, Samantha was a fifth grader at Manchester Elementary School. She was in many respects a typical American girl. She was a pretty brunette, a little shy, and she liked reading, playing softball, and listening to Prince, Huey Lewis and the News, and Phil Collins. Her mother, Jane, was originally from Virginia, where her father was a minister and her mother a homemaker. When a senior at Roanoke College, Jane met Arthur Smith, a New York City native who had grown up in West Virginia. They married and moved to Pittsburgh so Arthur could teach there, and then relocated to the Houlton area when Arthur got a teaching position at Ricker College. Samantha, their only child, was born in Houlton on June 9, 1972. The family moved to Manchester in 1980 when Arthur began teaching English at the University of Maine at Augusta. Jane, a social worker, worked at the Maine Human Services Department, where she handled cases of children in state custody.

The 1980s were a tense time for relations between the United States and the Soviet Union. Ronald Reagan, a hardline anti-Communist and stalwart Cold Warrior, had been elected president in 1980. In November 1982, Yuri Andropov, a former head of the Soviet secret police—the KGB—became the premier of the Soviet Union. He succeeded Leonid Brezhnev, who had died on November 12.

Samantha, or Sam as she was known, asked her mother if there was going to be a war and suggested that Jane write a letter to Andropov. Jane said Sam should do it instead. So the 10-year-old sat down at her kitchen counter and, using her best penmanship, composed a letter. "My name is Samantha Smith," she wrote. "I am ten years old. Congratulations on your new job. I have been worrying about Russia and the United States getting into a nuclear war. Are you going to vote to have a war or not? If you aren't, please tell me how you are going to help to not have a war. The question you do not have to answer, but I would like to know why you want to conquer the world or at least our country. God made the world for us to live together in peace and not to fight."

Samantha addressed the letter to Andropov at the Kremlin in Moscow and stuck two 20 cent stamps on the envelope. Her father mailed it for her. "It was a nice letter," he said. "She really constructed it well."

The Smiths got their first hint of the impending media maelstrom on April 12, 1983, when the school secretary called Samantha down to the office. A reporter from United Press International was on the phone and wanted to talk to her because *Pravda* had printed some of her letter. Before long, she received another phone call, this one from a man with a heavy accent. He said Samantha could expect to receive a letter from Andropov. It arrived at the Manchester post office on April 25.

Andropov's letter was much longer than Samantha's. In it, the Soviet leader compared the Manchester girl to plucky Becky Thatcher in Mark Twain's *The Adventures of Tom Sawyer* and tried to assuage her fears. "Yes, Samantha," the letter read, "we in the Soviet Union are trying to do everything so that there will not be war between our countries, so that in general there will not be war on earth." Andropov said the Soviets wished to end the production of nuclear weapons and denied any wishes to conquer the United States. And he invited Samantha and her parents to visit the Soviet Union, where "everyone is for peace and friendship among peoples."

The correspondence set off a firestorm of media coverage from television, radio, and newspapers. Two reporters from the Soviet Union's bureau in Washington traveled to Manchester, where they were taken aback by the American media's eagerness to film them filming Samantha. Samantha went to New York to appear on the *Today* show and other media outlets, and to California for an appearance on *The Tonight Show* with Johnny Carson. "Ten-year-old Samantha Smith of Manchester has accomplished what America's politicians and diplomats have failed to do," said an editorial in the *Daily Kennebec Journal*: "she initiated a candid dialogue with the leader of the Soviet Union." Samantha met with Maine Governor Joseph Brennan, and the state legislature praised her in a joint resolution that said she "sparked a glimmer of hope in the coldness of international relations." For her part, Samantha said it was "exciting to be famous," but tiring as well, especially since the members of the media seemed to ask the same questions over and over again.

It had been quite an experience. "Samantha quite likely will never have another month like April 1983," the *Kennebec Journal* predicted, incorrectly. In fact, it was just the beginning.

The Smiths accepted Andropov's invitation and made plans to visit Moscow in July 1983. They packed a suitcase full of American souvenirs they could give to the Soviet citizens they met—tee-shirts from Colby

College, souvenirs from Bowdoin and Bates, and trinkets like pens, lobster pins, decals, postcards, and keyrings. When asked by a reporter what she planned to bring for Andropov, Samantha declined to say. "I don't want him to find out before we give it to him," she explained.

On July 7 the Smiths flew out of Augusta to Boston on Bar Harbor Airlines, and then to Montreal to catch an Aeroflot plane for the nine-hour flight to Moscow. "I wondered if I could be friends with Soviet kids," Samantha wrote later. "Would they think that I was a spy or that I was afraid of them? Would they think I wanted to conquer them? Maybe they would hate me."

She had nothing to fear. The Soviet Union treated Samantha like a celebrity. She and her parents toured Moscow and visited Red Square, the Kremlin, and Lenin's tomb, which Samantha found "kind of scary." In Moscow, Samantha developed a taste for chicken Kiev. After that, the Smiths were flown to the Black Sea so Samantha could spend time with Soviet youngsters at a Pioneer Camp in Artek. Arthur and Jane stayed in a hotel, but Samantha gamely opted to stay at the camp, and she quickly made friends with her new Soviet acquaintances.

"The kids had a lot of questions about America—especially about clothes and music," she said. "They were all interested in how I lived and sometimes at night we talked about peace, but it didn't really seem necessary because none of them hated America, and none of them ever wanted war." On a boat trip on the Black Sea, she and the other campers threw bottles with peace messages into the water. When a Soviet reporter asked her what she would do if she were a magician, she answered, "Get rid of the bombs."

"My stay at sea camp in Artek has been wonderful, very wonderful," she said in her farewell to the camp. "I shall miss my new international friends. But we shall remain friends across the sea. Let our countries be friends, too. I love you, Artek."

The Smiths did not meet Andropov, who arranged for the gift of a samovar and a tea set trimmed with gold. Their gift to Andropov, the surprise Samantha did not want to spoil, was a book of Mark Twain's speeches, selected because the Soviet premier had compared Samantha to Becky Thatcher. The Smiths did meet Valentina Tereshkova, the first woman in space, and were impressed by her willingness to admit to problems in the Soviet Union. "I thought she was very candid," Jane said. They visited a collective farm, toured Leningrad, and attended a ballet at the Kirov Ballet.

Meanwhile, Samantha-mania continued in the United States, especially in Maine. We're all tickled to death over this," said Lloyd Smith (no relation), who owned Daggett's Country Market in Manchester. "Everybody's particularly happy with the way she is. Speaking for the majority, we feel she's a pretty composed girl who handles herself with dignity." Augusta citizen Jim Crawford wrote "Samantha's Song." Jim Terr, a musician in California, wrote a song with the same name and recorded it with backing from the rock band Dr. Hook.

A Bar Harbor Airlines plane brought the Smiths back to Augusta at 3:30 p.m. on Friday, July 22, to a media scrum rare for Augusta. "The onslaught included a herd of media types, who elbowed, slithered and all but bribed their way within earshot of Samantha, who has faced more cameras in the last two weeks than a long-shot political candidate can dream about," wrote the media type who covered the arrival for the *Kennebec Journal*. A Rolls Royce waited to take the Smiths to Manchester, where they found a banner reading "Welcome Home" stretched across the front of their house. The family faced the press one last time before going inside. Samantha, apparently weary of answering the same questions, was silent while her father spoke. "No more letters," he said. "We need a rest." Said Samantha, "There's no place like home."

Not everyone thought Samantha's trip was such a great event. When a reporter from the *Kennebec Journal* interviewed members of the Russian community in Richmond, Maine, he found that most of them believed the Soviets had showed Samantha exactly what they wanted her to see. "They didn't show her the concentration camps, the prison camps, the lines for bread," said one woman. "Samantha got used," said a Russian man.

Another voice of dissent came from Malcolm Toon, a former ambassador to the Soviet Union. "I frankly do not like to see our children exploited, either by their parents or by major powers such as the Soviet Union, for purely political purposes," he said.

Dean Rusk, who had served as secretary of state for presidents Kennedy and Johnson, had a more favorable reaction. "The purpose of this note is simply to say that I was enchanted by the way you handled yourself on that extraordinary visit," he wrote Samantha. "You gave the Russians a chance to see an attractive, natural and unpretentious young American and therefore made a significant contribution toward understanding between the peoples of our two countries."

Samantha returned to the headlines in December, when "Maine's globetrotting schoolgirl" departed on a 10-day trip to Japan to deliver a short speech in Kobe at the Children's International Symposium for the 21st Century. The Smiths spent the holiday in Japan, eating Chinese food on Christmas, receiving a Sony Walkman from Sony's honorary chairman, and attending the symposium with four other American teenagers.

In February 1984, the Disney Channel aired *Samantha Smith Goes to Washington*, a program in which she interviewed candidates in the 1984 presidential campaign. She talked to Fritz Hollings, George McGovern, Reuben Acken (the former governor of Florida), Jesse Jackson, Gary Hart, and Alan Cranston. Walter Mondale and John Glenn turned down her interview requests.

Kennebec Journal columnist Jim Fain defended Samantha's apparent embrace of celebrity. "Is there anything wrong with her becoming a preteen Diane Sawyer or Barbara Walters?" he asked. "Probably, but not because of Samantha, a nice little girl with loving parents who help her handle her celebrityhood carefully." Fain said the real problem stemmed from ordinary people obsessed by fame. "We take these strobe-lit instants of celebrityhood and translate them into some mystical substitute for competence, or even above-average wisdom," he said.

Samantha continued spreading her message for peace. In December 1984 she visited the Soviet compound in Washington, D.C., and met the children of the diplomats there. "We all hope for peace, at least between children," she told them. When a Russian girl asked her how it felt to be famous, Smith replied, "OK, I guess." The visit was arranged by a toy company that wanted to publicize its stuffed animals.

Samantha also continued inching her way into show business. She appeared on an episode of the TV series *Charles in Charge* but got her big break in February 1985 when she was cast in a two-hour ABC pilot called *Lime Street*. Robert Wagner starred as a Virginia-based insurance investigator, with Samantha playing one of his daughters. By this point Arthur Smith had left UMA to oversee his daughter's burgeoning career, and the family started making plans to relocate to California.

Then tragedy struck. On August 25, 1985, Samantha and Arthur were flying home from filming *Lime Street* in London. Their flight from Boston to Augusta was on Bar Harbor Airlines. The Beechcraft 99 added an unscheduled stop in Auburn to accommodate passengers whose flight had been canceled. Shortly after 10:00 that night, Auburn residents heard the airplane flying much too low. It clipped some trees and crashed 4,000 feet short of the runway. All eight people aboard, including two crew members, were killed.

Jane Smith had been waiting at the Augusta airport when she learned the plane had crashed. Smith had told reporters that her husband and daughter were "the articulate ones," but she issued a very articulate statement. "Each generation contributes a building block for the next generation," it read. "As individuals, we are the particles of earth from which the blocks are formed. I hope Samantha and Arthur have helped us realize how important each one of us can be. Samantha couldn't accept man's inhumanity to man. She stood fast in the belief that peace can be achieved and maintained by mankind. With her father supporting her actions, Samantha has contributed to understanding among youth for conservation of our world."

Robert Wagner was in Geneva when he heard the news. "It was as if the breath left my body," he wrote in his memoir. "My own kids and Samantha had played all the time. She had a career and, more importantly, a life ahead of her that would have been wonderful." Columbia Studios wanted to recast the part and keep filming, but Wagner refused. Instead, the production shut down.

Wagner had suffered a stunning personal loss before, when his wife Natalie Wood had drowned. "With the exception of Natalie's death, Samantha's death and its aftermath was the most emotionally upsetting thing I've ever gone through, and it drained a lot of the affection I always had for the business," he wrote. In fact, the tragedy led him to decide to start a "judicious retreat" from acting.

Some 1,500 people packed into St. Mary's Church in Augusta for a memorial service on August 28. Wagner sat "grim-faced" in a pew behind the Smith family members. Vladimir Kulagin, an official from the Soviet embassy, also attended. He said that Samantha "was like a small but very powerful and brilliant beam of sunshine which penetrated the thunderstorm clouds which envelope between our two countries." Kulagin also read a statement from the latest Soviet leader, Mikhail Gorbachev. "Everybody who knew Samantha in the Soviet Union will forever hold in remembrance the image of an American girl, who like millions of Soviet boys and girls, wish for peace and friendship with the peoples of the United States and the Soviet Union," it read.

After a long investigation, the National Transportation Safety Board blamed the crash on pilot error, but said the pilot had received faulty instructions from Air Traffic Control. Jane Smith later sued the airline for $50 million and eventually settled for an undisclosed sum.

In October 1985 she founded the Samantha Smith Foundation in memory of her daughter. The next June Jane accompanied 22 students from Maranacook Community School on a trip to the Soviet Union organized under the auspices of Project SAME (Soviet-American Memorial Exchange). On July 4, the students opened the Goodwill Games in Moscow, the brainchild of CNN founder Ted Turner, who donated $87,700 to send the Maine students to Moscow.

The Soviet Union also saluted Samantha by putting her face on a postage stamp and naming a mountain and an asteroid after her.

The Auburn Mall commissioned Houlton sculptor Glenn Hines to make a small model of a proposed monument and set out to raise money for the full-size statue that was later placed in front of the Cultural Building in Augusta. In Minneapolis, a TV station collaborated on a joint production with the Soviet Union on a program called *Minneapolis-Moscow: A Children's Space Bridge*. Singer John Denver hosted the U.S. portion and called Samantha "a young lady whose sparkling personality lit up both our countries." Young people from both countries sang and danced and performed scenes that stressed the need for world peace.

In August 1987, Jane and the foundation arranged to have Soviet schoolchildren, four girls and four boys, visit the United States, with stops in Washington, D.C., Annapolis, Maryland, Boston, and a stay at Alford Lake Camp in Union, Maine. Accompanied by a media horde in Washington, they ate lunch at McDonald's and toured the Smithsonian's Air & Space Museum. In Augusta, the two groups placed flowers at the statue of Samantha. One of the Soviet girls, Tatyana Nikitina, had met Samantha in the Soviet Union. "I remember Samantha's goal toward peace," she said. "It is absolutely necessary to continue the goal Samantha started. There has to be peace in the world."

At Camp Alford the children played basketball, hiked, and enjoyed a performance by singer Noel Paul Stookey of Peter, Paul and Mary, who sang "Puff, the Magic Dragon" in Russian. A group of Passamaquoddy from Maine put on a fireside performance for them.

Jane Smith had suffered an almost unbearable loss, but she found solace in working to further her daughter's message. "Setting up the foundation and talking about Samantha have been very therapeutic," she told a reporter as she approached the first anniversary of the crash. "Despite the fact that I sometimes look back, I firmly believe in building a new life and going on." She admitted to feeling lonely and even angry at times and said when she saw the school buses on the first day of school, it was "a little hard." Still, she said she had no regrets about the events following her daughter's famous letter. "I've thought about it," she said, "but I'd do the same thing again. It was good for Samantha, and it was good for the world. We had a lot of fun as a family during that time. The only thing I would have asked was that it had lasted longer."

1990s

Maine Ices Over;
Wiscasset Loses its Schooners

THERE'S A SAYING THAT PEOPLE ALWAYS COMPLAIN ABOUT THE weather, but nobody ever does anything about it. In January 1998, hundreds of thousands of Mainers were complaining. A devastating storm swept through the state, coating everything with a translucent layer of ice and wreaking havoc on the state's electrical grid. At one point, as many as 600,000 people—half the state's population—had lost power. Families huddled around fireplaces to keep warm or sought relief from the cold in public shelters; stores conducted business by candlelight; dairy farmers struggled to milk their cows; electrical workers put in long hours to restore power. And practically everyone in Maine, it seemed, emerged from the Great Ice Storm of 1998 with a story.

It started on Tuesday, January 6. Warm air heading north from the Ohio Valley intersected with cold air moving in from the northeast. In the resulting slow-moving storm front, the warmer air rose to higher altitudes and shed its moisture as rain. Passing through the colder air below it, the rain froze and began coating everything—trees, roads, sidewalks—with ice. The thick coating took a toll on trees. Limbs tore off with explosions like gunshots. Sometimes entire trees crashed to the ground. The trees and branches took power lines down with them or snapped utility poles like toothpicks. Huge swathes of the state plunged into darkness. "We have so many people without electricity or heat, and some people in outlying areas are isolated out there because of the ice," announced Bill Libby, the director of Maine's Emergency Management Agency. "And it's not close to being over." Libby called it "a very dangerous situation."

The Augusta area had it the worst. "It sounded like a war with all the popping going on and the flashing blue lights," said one Augusta resident. "It's unbelievable—we've never seen anything like this." Police counted 100 trees down on Thursday. Central Maine Power, which serviced that part of the state, said that 100,000 customers had lost electricity. "I liken this to the kind of damage you see from a major hurricane, a once in 10 years kind of hurricane," said CMP spokesperson Mark Ishkanian. "The unique thing about this storm is it is such a broad area of extreme icing."

On January 8, Governor Angus King declared a state of emergency and contacted the federal government for financial assistance. "This is the worst storm to hit Maine in a generation, and according to Central Maine Power, it is the worst electrical-related problem ever," said King, who had spent nights with his family and others at a neighbor's house in Brunswick. He called up the Maine National Guard, and troops deployed across the state to do what they could, including clearing fallen trees and debris and distributing generators to shelters. King's press secretary, Dennis Bailey, advised people to remain patient as power companies struggled to restore power. "For the first few days it's like going to camp," he said. "It's kind of fun. But another couple of days and people are going to be tired of no showers and no heat."

As more and more people lost power, they sought shelter at schools, churches, and other buildings that were pressed into service. About 235 people used the Augusta Civic Center for shelter. "This place has been a godsend, I'm telling you," said Gardiner's Lila Waugh. "The staff has been great. They've worked around the clock to keep people warm and comfortable." Her 13-year-old son, though, had one complaint. "Many people snore a lot," he said.

In Pittsfield, nursing homes had to evacuate their residents and send them to the local hospital. Police in Waterville drove some residents to emergency shelters at the Mount Merci Academy and Convent and also the fieldhouse at Colby College. Fairfield citizens went to the junior high school, but then had to be sent to another school when the first one lost power. The American Red Cross opened shelters in the Portland area. "I'm just glad these people are here," said one woman her took refuge in a shelter in Windham with three grandchildren, two suffering from the flu.

In Waterville, the Kimberly-Clark Corporation offered its soon-to-be-closed paper mill, which had its own power supply, as a shelter. Litchfield used its middle school, with residents donating food, the National Guard providing cots, and volunteers offering their time. Litchfield's Lillian Murphy, 72, didn't want to go to a shelter, but she eventually relented. "Thursday morning I didn't have any heat, any power," she said. "I tried to cover myself with blankets to keep warm. Then trees started to come down all around my house, and I got scared."

Some shelters in Cumberland and Kennebec counties ran out of cots and resorted to using strips of bubble wrap provided by the National Guard for cushioning. In Lewiston, 224 people used the shelter at the high school on Friday night. "We were getting overwhelmed with people who needed medical attention," said Cecile Doyen, who managed the facility, "and I had one nurse."

Some 115 people found shelter at the Air National Guard base in Bangor. In Ellsworth, seniors from the Meadowview Apartments were sent to the middle school to wait out the power outage. "I'm 93 years old and I've lived in Maine my whole life and this is the first time I've had to be evacuated," said Emily Kane. Pat's Pizza in Orono, which had a generator, remained packed and sent pizzas to the people taking shelter in Orono's municipal building.

"A lot of people want help," said one Machias firefighter. "But Down East Maine people are real independent. They don't want help unless it's absolutely necessary." Many Mainers opted to wait it out at home, like Carleton and Connie Robbins in Franklin. "We've been here for 40 years," said Carleton, 82. "If we can't tough it out here, we might as well quit altogether."

Rufus Merrill exemplified the toughness of many Mainers. Merrill, an 88-year-old retired welder, lived alone in a cabin on Beech Hill Pond outside Otis. He spent more than a week without power, keeping warm with his cast-iron stove and venturing onto the ice of the pond to get fresh water. In between, he did crossword puzzles and read *Cold Mountain*.

The governor recognized the problems that Maine stubbornness could create. "This is the moment of maximum danger," he said on Saturday, when temperatures started to plunge. "Being independent and crusty and staying home can be all well and good, but let's put it aside for a night because I just don't want to wake up and find we have lost somebody."

As the crisis dragged on, huge lines formed in grocery stores and at Wal-Marts, with generators and batteries in great demand. In stores without power, employees worked by candles or flashlights and added up tallies with calculators. Hotels and motels were booked to capacity. "Most people are talking about the war zone they've gone through—trees everywhere down and tops of trees down," said Mike Callahan, who owned the Cobbossee Cash Market in East Winthrop. "Everybody thinks they've seen the worst until they hear from the next guy."

By Friday, Steve Watson, director of the Emergency Management Agency in Penobscot County, rated the situation as a 10 on a scale of one to 10 and said it was "absolutely the worst situation this state has dealt with in decades." Bangor Hydro estimated that up to 25,000 of its customers were without power. By the weekend, the *Bangor Daily News* was reporting that 300,000 homes had lost power. "ICE WON'T LET UP" screamed the headline. "This is an absolutely major storm," said Watson, who added that it could be days before some homes got their power back. "We're finding that people in Maine have become very accustomed to power and have forgotten what to do in this kind of situation. The average maximum length in time for a power outage in Maine is three hours. This is not an average situation."

Without electricity, people couldn't pump water from their wells. Darlene Simpson of South China had an artesian well and word got out that people could get water there. At one point nearly 200 were lined up in Simpson's yard for their turn for water. Some waited in line for two hours. In Monroe, David and Bernys Doak had to dump 3,600 gallons of milk from their dairy farm. "Still considering how some others have it, we're doing pretty good," said Bernys. "It could be a lot worse."

On Monday, a crowd formed at Portland's Home Depot, waiting for a shipment of generators to arrive. As the customers waited, employees provided folding chairs and coffee.

Hospitals, which often had to rely on generators for power, began treating people for carbon monoxide poisoning, caused by poorly ventilated generators and heaters. In Bangor, a mobile home burned in a fire caused by a camp stove. In Portland a woman and her two young daughters were treated for smoke inhalation after a knocked-over candle started a fire in their home. A fireplace ignited the ceiling of another house in Portland.

Things had improved by Sunday night, but at least 200,000 people still lacked power. In Washington County, the heavy ice took out 100 poles and eight miles of transmission lines that brought power to 10,000 people in Eastport, Jonesport, Lubec, and Machias. Bangor Hydro-Electric scrambled to find alternate ways of providing power. Even with the help of crews from Rhode Island and Massachusetts, Central Maine Power reported it still had 185,000 powerless households, a modest improvement over the 273,000 without power on Thursday and Friday. "Every time crews would restore a section of line, we would get a report of another one being out somewhere else," said a spokesperson. The workers struggling to cope with the storm's aftermath began suffering what was called "ice fatigue" after long days with little rest.

Many Mainers saluted the selflessness they witnessed, as people volunteered their time, food, and other resources to help others. "I have never seen such a sense of community," said Dana Sweet, the fire chief in Fairfield. "People are opening their homes to strangers who need to get warm. People are working 12 and 18 hours without rest and without a complaint, ready to do more. It is absolutely fantastic."

In the town of Burnham, Stuart and Susan Huff kept their S&S Variety open despite the lack of power, closing only after dark. Even then, they said, neighbors would stop by their house, which was next to the store, to ask if they could open up so they could purchase an item. The Huffs even took in a couple and their baby girl from down the street. "We didn't even really know them before the storm," said Mark Huff. "It's a helluva way to make friends with someone."

In Fairfield, town manager Terry York seemed a living embodiment of what Mainers had gone through. She had a black eye from falling on the ice, suffered burst pipes in her home, and ended up staying in a hotel room with her husband and their two dogs. She had cooked spaghetti for Fairfield workers and spent a night in the town's community center. "We're exhausted, and we've heard a lot of sad cases come through here today," she said on January 15, "but at the same time, I can't say enough about the town workers. There was none of 'this isn't my job' stuff."

Mac Gillet, 70, lost his power around 3:00 a.m. Thursday. His phone went out on Friday. Gillet lived outside Bridgton, a mile down a dirt road off Route 107, and fallen trees blocked him from the outside world. "There was no way I could have gotten out," Gillet said. "It was all ice. It looked like a war zone." Using a plow and multiple chainsaws, a trio of volunteers spent three hours clearing a path to Gillet's isolated cabin.

Not everyone was so selfless. Bangor Hydro dropped plans to use a wood-fired plant in Jonesboro to provide electricity to Washington County because the out-of-state owners were asking for "an outrageous price," according to a Bangor Hydro spokesperson. The company began exploring alternatives. There were stories about people posing as electrical repairman and offering to restore electricity—for a fee. Another duo pretended to be repairmen. While one asked to see the fuse box, the other snuck off to ransack the house.

On Monday, January 12, western Maine received some much-needed assistance from crews and equipment sent from Baltimore. On Thursday, utility workers from North Carolina flew into the Brunswick Naval Air Station on military airplanes. They arrived as Maine braced for another winter storm, this one bringing powdery snow instead of ice. L.L. Bean and the Maine National Guard donated winter clothing for the workers from the south. Vice President Al Gore also flew into Brunswick on Thursday. Accompanied by Governor King, Gore made a helicopter tour to survey some of the damage and visited a neighborhood outside Auburn to get a close-up look at the devastation. He promised more federal financial assistance.

The electric companies continued the demanding work of restoring power, but people still without electricity after more than a week were losing patience, especially if they could see that their neighbors' lights were back on. "I'm at the end of my rope," said Sylvia Hodgdon of Otis. On Sunday, January 19, work crews told her she probably wouldn't get power until the next day, and "it was all I could do to keep from crying," she said. Central Maine Power was receiving an influx of angry phone calls and the utility even hired off-duty police officers as security in response to various threats they had received. "Obviously, it's a small minority of people, but we've got to take prudent steps in response to it," said a spokesperson. For those without power, frustration was reaching a boiling point. "CMP keeps saying they're working so hard, and I'd just like to know where," said one woman from Westbrook who lacked power after more than a week.

It took almost a month to get power back to the last holdouts and by the time the Great Ice Storm of 1998 began receding into memory, the costs of dealing with it had reached an estimated $320 million. There were four fatalities blamed on the storm—two from carbon monoxide poisoning, one killed by a falling tree limb, and one man who fell down his basement stairs in the dark. It had been an experience that tested the resilience of Maine's citizens, and, for the most part, they came through with flying colors. "It was an extraordinary coming together," said King, looking back ten years later. "It really was the best of Maine in the sense of people reaching out to one another. I always tell people in Washington that Maine is a big small town with long streets. This was the best example of that."

If nothing else, the storm gave many Mainers a renewed appreciation for electricity and all it provides. When their power came on after 12 days, Bob and Betty O'Keefe of Otis looked forward to one thing most of all—hot water. "She soaks in the bathtub and I love hot showers," Bob told a reporter from the *Bangor Daily News*. "So we'll be doing that."

For decades the *Hesper* and the *Luther Little* rested on the mud flats of the Sheepscot River in Wiscasset, a vision from the past for the people driving by on busy Route 1. They were the world's last surviving four-masted schooners and thousands of people stopped by the waterfront of

"Maine's prettiest village" to photograph, draw, and paint the deteriorating ships, even as time attacked the wooden hulks. They caught on fire, shed pieces into the mud, and slowly collapsed, as the weight of years took its toll. Finally, in 1998, the remains of the *Hesper* and the *Luther Little* were hauled off to a landfill. One of Maine's most recognizable sights had become just a memory.

"The world has moved on and we will never see their kind again," wrote M. Chris Roy in a pamphlet he wrote about the schooners. "Perhaps, just perhaps, that is the saddest part of all."

They became Maine landmarks, but the two schooners hailed from out of state, having been built in Massachusetts. Named after an American naval officer from the Revolutionary War, the *Luther Little* was actually the second vessel to bear that name. The first one never reached the water, as she burned during construction when a fire destroyed the Read Brothers shipyard in Somerset, Massachusetts, in December 1917. A vessel at the nearby Crowninshield Shipbuilding Company inherited the name, and on December 20, 1918, she slid down the ways into the Taunton River, "riding gracefully as a swan," noted the *Fall River Evening News*. "There were people present who have seen many launchings, and all agreed that never had one been accomplished in a smoother manner." Nearby ships blew their whistles and a tug sounded its siren.

The new vessel was 204 feet long, had a 41-foot beam, and weighed 1,234 tons. Even when brand new, the ship was already out of date. Steam-powered vessels had made sailing ships like the *Luther Little* obsolete. The big four-masted schooner did boast some modern amenities, including a winch and capstan powered by steam, which also provided heat to the cabins. She made her first voyage to Hampton Roads, Virginia, and then she was off to Buenos Aires with a cargo of coal, returning with linseed oil.

From the beginning, it seems that the fates of the *Luther Little* and *Hesper* were yoked together. "Now that the Luther Little has been launched," said the *Fall River Evening News*, "all energies of the Crowninshield Shipping Company will be bent on completing the Hesper, the sister ship of the Little, which, however, is a trifle larger than the ship just launched." The *Hesper* took her name from the evening star in Greek

171

mythology, but it echoed the name of the doomed vessel in "The Wreck of the Hesperus," a famous poem by Maine native Henry Wadsworth Longfellow.

The *Hesper*'s launch did not proceed as smoothly as the *Luther Little*'s. She was supposed to slide into the water on July 4, 1918, but the ship got stuck on the ways, disappointing the people who had come to see the launch. "The vessel started nobly, amid the blare of the whistle at the works, and the cheers of the throng, but after sliding swiftly, perhaps 40 feet, toward the water, lost speed and stopped, and all hope of getting her into the water that day had to be abandoned," noted the *Evening News*. The ship did not finish her short trip into the river until August, when a flood tide finished what the shipbuilders failed to accomplish.

The two ships were not sleek and fleet like the square-rigged clipper ships that set speed records in the 1800s. There was nothing glamorous about them. They were working-class vessels, built to transport things like lumber, manure, and coal, although on one occasion in 1918 the *Luther Little* rescued balloonists who had taken off from Cape May, New Jersey, and made an unscheduled stop in the Atlantic Ocean. In 1920 it was the *Luther Little* that needed rescuing when, carrying a shipment of lumber, she went aground in Haiti. It took two weeks of effort to drag her loose. The *Hesper* endured a similar indignity when she went aground in Boston in March 1925. It required the services of nine tugboats to haul her off the bottom.

Even then, the vessels looked like museum pieces, two relics from the age of sail making their way in the steam era. Demand for their services waned, and for several years they sat, unwanted, in Portland harbor. Auburn businessman Arthur W. Winter bought the two vessels at auction in 1932, paying $525 for the *Luther Little* and $600 for the *Hesper*. Winter planned to bring Maine lumber to Wiscasset on a narrow-gauge railroad he owned and use the schooners to haul the wood south. However, Winter's plan never reached fruition. The *Hesper* and *Luther Little* made it to Wiscasset, but they never left town. Instead, they became its most famous residents. In 1940 the two ships were hauled closer to shore, where they remained stuck in the river mud.

The *Hesper* was shorn of its masts by a salvager and sat outside the *Luther Little*, heeled slightly up on its port side. For years the *Luther Little* kept remnants of her four masts, even after fire damaged her in 1948. In the 1960s there was talk of restoring the *Luther Little* and destroying what remained of the *Hesper*, but nothing came of those plans. Instead, the ships were left to the contending forces of flame and rot. On July 4, 1978, the schooners caught fire after someone threw a sparkler onboard. A few days later, 17-year-old Jay Siegers of nearby Westport Island found what he identified as a part of the *Hesper*'s bow drifting in the Sheepscot River. He brought it to shore and turned it over to the town of Wiscasset.

After the fire, Wiscasset held a town meeting to determine the fate of the ships, which resulted in the formation of a group called the Friends of the Wiscasset Schooners. The Friends hoped to preserve and document the now-historic vessels "and to keep the physical evidence of the four-masted schooner in America from slipping into obscurity." Nothing came of those efforts and the ships were left to rot. In 1979 an earthquake caused even more damage to the deteriorating vessels and toppled the *Luther Little*'s rear mast. A portion of the stern fell away, part of the bow fell off in 1990, and the ships caught fire again on July 4, 1990. That was a bad year for the schooners—in November the *Hesper*'s entire hull collapsed into itself.

In 1998 the town's board of selectmen decided it was time to break up what remained of the ships and get rid of them. Town selectman Bob Blagden helped haul the remains to the landfill in a dump truck, a task that required more than 300 loads. "It wasn't like a pile of lumber," he told a reporter in 2017. "It was more like a pile of mud with wood sticking out of it." The cost to the town was $70,000. The town retained some pieces, but the rest went to the landfill, where it formed a pile that was as long as a football field and 20 feet high in spots.

"I remember watching them being broken up and thinking of the times my friends and I spent playing onboard them as kids," said Ben Rines, Jr., who went on to become chairman of the town board. "Many, many homes have some sort of knickknack from the tall ships," Rines said. "When they were dismantled, many people got brass spikes and copper nails and stuff like that."

That wasn't quite the end of the story of the *Hesper* and the *Luther Little*. Their remains remained moldering in the landfill until 2001, when the state's Department of Environmental Protection ruled that the pile of rotting wood had to be disposed of properly. Wiscasset put out word that the general public would have a chance to pluck out items from the pile. Hundreds of people did. A clockmaker obtained pieces of the *Luther Little*'s masts. The Maine Table Company in Brunswick salvaged enough wood to make a dining room table. A cabinet maker in Auburn used pieces of the schooners to fashion kitchen cabinets for a Wiscasset home. Woodturner Peter Asselyn of Durham carved some bowls from the pieces he salvaged, but it wasn't a pleasant task with the sodden, hard, and smelly wood. "It was like trying to turn a piece of cement," he told a *Portland Press Herald* reporter in 2017. "They were almost petrified, and the whole shop would just stink of clams and clam flats. It was really nasty work."

The schooners are gone, but they live on in fragments of wood, like the frame around a mural of the *Hesper* and *Luther Little* in Sarah's Café in Wiscasset or the pieces on display in the Somerset Historical Society. They live on in the slew of photographs and paintings they inspired over the years. And they will live on in memory, as long as people remember seeing the world's last four-masted schooners deteriorating in the Sheepscot River mud.

2000s

Terror Strikes Home;
New Mainers Reach Lewiston;
Red Sox End a Curse

No one knows why Mohamed Atta and Abdulaziz al-Omari decided to fly from Portland on the morning of September 11, 2001. They had been in Boston the day before, but for some reason they rented a car and drove north to Portland, where they checked into a Comfort Inn near the Portland International Jetport. Security cameras in the area captured their images at a gas station, a Wal-Mart, and a Key Bank ATM. The two men had dinner at a nearby Pizza Hut.

The next morning, they planned to take a United Airlines flight from Portland back to Boston to connect with American Airlines Flight 11, scheduled for a nonstop flight to Los Angeles.

Atta and al-Omari had no intention of flying to California. A 33-year-old Egyptian, Atta was the leader of a group of fanatical Islamists who had been recruited by Osama Bin Laden, the Saudi-born leader of the al-Qaeda terrorist group. Fueled by an unremitting hatred of the West, Bin Laden had hatched a plan to have his followers hijack American airliners and crash them into prominent targets, in effect using them as huge fuel-filled missiles to strike at the heart of the United States. The plan called for two planes to hit the twin towers of the World

Trade Center in New York City, and a third to aim for the Pentagon in Arlington, Virginia, just across the Potomac River from Washington. The target for the fourth was Washington, but it's not known whether its target was the White House or the U.S. Capitol.

Mike Tuohey arrived for his job at the ticket counter for United Airlines at the Portland Jetport at 4:30 a.m. on September 11. He was about to step outside for a cigarette at 5:40 when he saw the two men approaching. They had $2,400 first-class tickets for a 6:00 departure for Boston. They had a couple of bags to check and one each to carry on. There was something about the two men, especially Atta, that struck Tuohey as suspicious. Atta seemed especially angry when Tuohey told him he would have to check in again for the connecting flight in Boston. "They told me one-step check in," Atta insisted.

"I said to myself, 'If this guy doesn't look like an Arab terrorist, then nothing does,'" Tuohey later told a reporter from the *Portland Press Herald*. "Then I gave myself a mental slap, because in this day and age, it's not nice to say things like this. 'You've checked in hundreds of Arabs and Hindus and Sikhs, and you've never done that.' I felt kind of embarrassed." Despite Tuohey's misgivings, Atta and Omari had done nothing that would require him to keep them from the flight. He simply told Atta he had better hurry or he would miss the plane.

Jackie and Robert Norton of Lubec were on their way to attend the wedding of one of Jackie's children from her first marriage. Their flight out of Bangor departed early the next morning, so they decided they would stay the night of September 10 near the airport. Robert, 85, was a Lubec native, although he had earned his engineering degree in Massachusetts and worked there before returning to his hometown with his wife in the 1970s. Widowed in the 1980s, Norton managed to pull out of his depression and marry Jackie McGuire. Jackie, 61, was a native Californian who had moved to Lubec in the 1990s after she fell in love with the place during a vacation. Her first marriage had ended in divorce, and she met Robert through the Lubec Congregational Christian Church, where he served as a deacon and she worked as a clerk. On September 10 the Nortons drove from Lubec to Bangor and parked their green Dodge

Caravan at the airport. They flew out the next morning to Boston's Logan Airport, where they caught American's Flight 11.

Jim Roux, 42, was the grandson of former Maine governor James Longley. He had graduated from Lewiston High School and Bowdoin College and then joined the army and became a paratrooper. Later Roux had established Roux & Ghimire, a law practice in Portland. It wasn't your typical practice, but Roux wasn't your typical lawyer. The *New York Times* later described him as "a spirited litigator, outdoorsman and windmill-tilter" who had "made impracticality an art form." Roux's law partner was in Nepal and his clients were no longer corporations fighting lawsuits over lead paint and asbestos, but were instead "artists, the homeless, and the Sherpas." But by 2001 Roux had reached some kind of a crossroads. Divorced twice and with two sons, he closed his practice and planned a vacation in Thailand while he considered what to do next. He stayed for a while at the Portland home of his sister, Mary Train, who made the travel arrangements for him. "It was sort of an interesting time," Train told a reporter for the Lewiston *Sun Journal*. "I would ask him, 'So, what's next?' He would say, very nonchalant, 'I don't know. I can't see the next chapter.' That's always been very eerie. Just that he was so content to be wrapping things up with no plan."

On Monday, September 10, Train drove her brother to the bus station in Portland. Roux took the bus to Boston to spend the night with a friend before proceeding to Logan to pick up United Flight 175, a nonstop to Los Angeles.

Gorham native Stephen Ward, 33, had started his new job as a certified public accountant for the equity firm Cantor Fitzgerald three weeks earlier. His office was on the 101st floor of the World Trade Center's North Tower. At 8:18 on the morning of September 11, he sent an email to his sister Katie, saying that he had found a new apartment in New York and had put down the security deposit. Before that he had been forced to "couch surf" with friends in New York. Ward was friendly and outgoing, someone described as "the social president of the neighborhood," the person who organized games and events. "He was an airplane-rides-around-the-living-room-until-you-want-to-throw-up kind of an uncle," his sister, Susan Moore, told the *New York Times*. "I called him a devil boy, one of those little devilish, impish-looking people, blond-haired, blue-eyed. He looked like an angel, but then he'd give you that grin and uh-oh!"

On the morning of September 11, Commander Robert Allan Schlegel was in the Pentagon at work with the chief of naval operations, where he was deputy current operations and plans branch head, which meant he was responsible for scheduling Navy ships. Schlegel was working out of a temporary location on the second floor of the building's outer ring because his regular space was being renovated.

Schlegel, 38, was a native of Gray, where he had enjoyed a fairly bucolic childhood. His next door neighbor there recalled games of flashlight tag and the way Schlegel stuck up for him when he was being bullied on the school bus. Another remembered that Schlegel was "wicked smart, wicked funny, and was wild about Ozzy Osbourne." He also liked sports, especially football and hockey. In 1981 Schlegel graduated from Gray-New Gloucester High School, which was also where he met the woman he married. Schlegel got his degree from Washington and Lee University in Lexington, Virginia, where he majored in journalism and minored in French, and graduated magna cum laude. After school he worked for a time as a reporter for the Lewiston *Sun Journal* before joining the navy, like his father and his two brothers had. He went to officer candidate school in Newport, Rhode Island, and served aboard the USS *Spartanburg County*, the USS *Henry E. Yarnell*, and the USS *Scott*. On shore, he was a cruise missile instructor and commanded the Atlantic Tomahawk Afloat Planning System before returning to sea as the executive officer aboard the destroyer USS *Arthur W. Radford*. He also found time to get his master's degree in international affairs from Old Dominion University. Schlegel had just been promoted to commander in August. People who served with him in the navy said he was one of the best officers they had known. Another recalled that in Navy meetings, "You could always count on him to whip up a quick one-liner that would make everyone laugh."

In Boston, Atta and Omari made it onto Flight 11 with plenty of time. Three other members of their team were also aboard, as were Robert and Jackie Norton. Shortly after the Boeing 767 lifted off the runway, flight controllers on the ground lost communication with the aircraft. They became more worried when Flight 11 deviated from its flight path and someone in the cockpit turned off the transponder, the device that transmits flight information to air traffic controllers. At 8:46, American Flight 11 crashed into the North Tower of the World Trade Center, tearing a hole that extended from the 93rd to the 99th floors, its fuel burning white hot and igniting flammable materials in the building. Elevators and stairways were severed, meaning the people on the floors above had no means to exit. Cantor Fitzgerald occupied floors 101 to 105. None of the 658 employees at work that morning, including Stephen Ward, made it out of the building alive. Some were killed when the plane struck, some were overcome by the flames and the smoke, and others jumped or fell to their deaths from windows. Any who were still alive died when the North Tower, its support structure weakened by the heat and the damage, collapsed onto itself until all that was left was rubble and dust.

United Flight 175, with Jim Roux aboard, departed Logan at 8:14. Notified about the troublesome behavior of Flight 11, the pilots scanned the sky for the American airplane and spotted it flying below them. Shortly afterward, Flight 175 also broke off contact with flight controllers and changed course toward New York City. It slammed into the South Tower of the World Trade Center at 9:03. Everyone aboard the airplane died instantly. Although hit 17 minutes after the American flight struck the North Tower, the South Tower collapsed first.

American Airlines Flight 77 was a Boeing 757 that flew out of Dulles Airport in Virginia at 8:20 on a nonstop to Los Angeles. Hijackers took over the airplane shortly after takeoff and guided it toward the Pentagon. At 9:37 the fuel-filled aircraft hit the ground and bounced into the west side of the huge building. Robert Schlegel's temporary office on the second floor was either at or very near the spot where the airplane hit. "At the moment of impact, the jet was traveling at roughly 530 miles per hour, or 708 feet per second, loaded with 5,300 gallons of fuel," noted Mitchell Zuckoff in his book *Fall and Rise: The Story of 9/11*. Schlegel, the quietly wise-cracking commander from Gray, was one of 125 people inside the building who died that day.

A fourth flight, United Flight 93, departed at 8:42 that morning from Newark with a destination of San Francisco. As on the other airplanes, hijackers aboard attacked passengers and crew and took over the cockpit. This time, though, passengers had learned about the fate of the other hijacked flights and fought back. Several of them worked together to subdue some of the hijackers and were attempting to force their way into the cockpit when the plane plunged into the ground outside Shanksville, Pennsylvania. All aboard were killed, but the crash saved the lives of untold people at the hijackers' target, which was either the White House or the Capitol in Washington.

The terrorists murdered almost 3,000 people that terrible day. That included more than 2,000 who died in the twin towers of the World Trade Center, 421 first responders in New York, 246 people aboard the four planes, and the 125 people at the Pentagon. It was a day of terror, shock and unspeakable grief, to be sure, but also a day that demonstrated, time and time again, America's great capacity for resilience and heroism.

Mike Tuohey, who retired from his job with United in 2004, was another kind of victim. His encounter with the hijackers at the ticket counter in Portland haunted him for years. "Why didn't I recognize the devil?" he asked Mel Allen of *Yankee* magazine. "I did recognize him. But I didn't stop him." Tuohey was traumatized by the encounter and the resulting feelings of guilt that he could have done something, anything. At one point he became convinced he saw Atta at the Maine Mall, and another time he thought he spotted him driving down the street.

In May 2011, when Tuohey heard that American Navy Seals had tracked down al Qaeda leader Osama Bin Laden and killed him at his compound in Pakistan, he reacted with "great joy," he told CNN. "I suffered anguish, and I still do," he said. "But maybe, even just in a fleeting moment, I wanted him to feel that he was losing something precious to him, like a son, a life, like all the lives we lost that day."

It was the best of Maine, it was the worst of Maine. Starting in 2001, thousands of refugees from the African nation of Somalia began relocating to Lewiston, attracted by the plentiful housing, low cost of living, and low crime rate. Lewiston, already teetering economically following the closure of the mills and factories that had once provided jobs for the city's Franco-Americans, struggled to adjust. So did the Somalis. Some Mainers rose to the occasion and did their best to help the new arrivals. Others, for various reasons, did not.

Somalia, a poor African nation on the horn of Africa that juts into the Indian Ocean, had slid into brutal civil war in 1991 after dictator Siad Barre had been toppled. The ensuing power struggle pitted Somali against Somali and was marked by murder, kidnapping, rape, and terror. Hundreds of thousands fled the country and many of them ended up in hellish refugee camps in neighboring Kenya. "It was so horrible that it is undiscussable," said a man who spent time in one of the camps and eventually ended up in Lewiston.

In 2001, the United States offered refugee status to nearly 12,000 Somalis. They arrived in cities ranging from Portland, Oregon, to Hartford, Connecticut. Most of them were woefully unprepared for life in the United States, lacking the ability to speak English and without any prospects for employment or knowledge of the technologies they would encounter in their adopted homes. They faced new lives mired in poverty while living in substandard housing. They were strangers in a strange land.

The first to reach Lewiston was Awil Bile, who arrived in January 2001. Back in Somalia, Bile had held a post in the country's finance ministry under Barre, but he fled to a Kenyan refugee camp with his family. After receiving refugee status from the United States, Bile and his family had first settled in Pittsburgh and then moved to Portland. Hearing good reports about Lewiston, Bile and a couple of other families decided to try their fortunes there.

They were the first, but they were far from the last. By 2011, estimates of the Somali population in Lewiston ranged from 3,000 to 6,000. Whatever the number, it made up a large segment of the city's 36,000 people.

As Lewiston's Somali population increased, so, too, did tensions with Lewiston's largely white population. Locals complained that the new arrivals were overwhelming the city's schools and social services and were receiving assistance that should have gone to native-born Mainers.

"Their arrival provoked furious debates about the cost of poor immigrants to Lewiston's precarious economy and the impact of cultural and racial difference on the city's proud Franco-American identity," wrote Catherine Besteman in her book *Making Refuge: Somali Bantu Refugees and Lewiston, Maine.* "Before the 2001 arrival of Somalis, Lewiston was 96 percent white and 'the most Franco city in the U.S.' By the end of the decade, Somalis had become about 15 percent of the population, and the changes they brought to the city were everywhere in evidence, from the school hallways to the city's main street."

About a thousand Somalis moved to Lewiston within a year, straining the city's ability to help them with housing, jobs, education, financial assistance, and whatever else they needed. And it wasn't like Lewiston was experienced in dealing with refugees. "We didn't know what we were doing and yet we had to tell everyone else what to do," remembered Sue Charron, the director of the city's General Assistance office. The schools, too, were forced to deal with an unprecedented situation, as hundreds of Somali children entered the system with little or no education or knowledge of English. It was not just a culture gap—it was a chasm.

Some Mainers resented these people of color who were making up an ever larger part of the population. (It didn't help that two of the soldiers killed in the 1991 "Black Hawk Down" incident, when an American helicopter was shot down in Somalia's capital of Mogadishu, were from Maine.) The "New Mainers" dressed differently, spoke a different language, and—as Moslems—practiced a different religion. People yelled at them on the streets, telling them to "Go home" or "Dress like an American." In one 2006 incident, a man rolled a frozen pig's head into a Somali mosque; in 2006 a teenager threw leftover Easter ham at a group of Somalis. (As Moslems, the Somalis do not eat pork.) "If somebody says 'I'm happy in Lewiston,' they're lying," Haaruan Sheekhey told a reporter in 2007. "We're having a hard time in this city. We're struggling. We're trying so hard to be part of this community, trying so hard to find a job, but nobody gives us a chance."

One native Mainer who wrote to the Lewiston *Sun Journal* in 2002 worried that the new arrivals "are going to change the Maine I know and love." Among other things, she worried that the classic Maine accent would disappear. For their part, Somalis worried that their children would lose their heritage as they became assimilated into American culture, seduced by values radically different from those in Africa.

Residents expressed their concerns at a public meeting in May 2002. "Lots of angry people came," remembered Charron. "People stood at the microphone and said terrible things. My music teacher said terrible things. I sat there watching my town break my heart." The situation prompted Mayor Larry Raymond to write an open letter to Somali residents requesting that they discourage any more of their countrymen from moving to Lewiston. "The Somali community must exercise some discipline and reduce the stress on our limited finances and our generosity," he wrote. "Our city is maxed out financially, physically, and emotionally." Reaction to the letter, said the Lewiston *Sun Journal* "was largely scathing" and put the city under a spotlight. Tensions between white residents and Somalis increased. "Those days, it was really tough," said Hussein Ahmed, who had moved to Lewiston from Georgia in 2002. "It was everywhere."

Ironically, Lewiston owed a good deal of its identity to an influx of immigrants, the French-Canadians who had flocked to the city in the mid-to-late 1800s to work in the textile mills and shoe factories. The locals back then regarded those new arrivals with suspicion. For one thing, the Franco-Americans were largely Catholic, which many in Protestant Maine saw as foreign and threatening. In 1871, when Pierre Hevey reached Lewiston to take on his new responsibilities as pastor of St. Peter's parish, no one would rent him a room. Much as the Somalis would later do, Franco-Americans established their own communities within Yankee New England. Also like the Somalis, many of the Franco-Americans were forced to live in grinding poverty in the city's worst neighborhoods. In 1888 the city's board of health said the Lewiston neighborhood known as "Little Canada" was "the worst and most dangerous place in the city."

In 1901, a resident of Biddeford who was upset about the French and Irish who were moving into town, wrote, "We are not French, neither Irish. We are true born Americans and we don't want to read any more about the exploits of the French in Biddeford, nor of the Irish neither, for one is no better than the other." That complaint was being echoed in Lewiston a century later.

Many French residents of Lewiston bristled when people drew parallels to the Somali experience, though. "As a Franco, I find the comparison insulting!" said one in a letter to a local paper. "The people from Quebec came here to work—not to live off welfare!" Said another, "The only comparison between the French-Canadians and the Somali is that neither is native to this country. Don't try to excuse one by down-grading the other."

In February 2003 a white supremacist group, inspired by the turmoil, held a rally in Lewiston. However, a counter rally, held at Bates College, attracted 4,000 people, compared to the racist group's 40. "We had such a big, big, big community support that showed up at Bates," Ahmed told the *Sun Journal*. "It made me realize there was big support that we were not aware of. It motivated a lot of Somalis, gave them hope that they can stay here."

There were other bright spots, too. The public library began offering Somali students help with homework—on some days a hundred kids might show up. The Trinity Jubilee Center, a downtown shelter in an Episcopal church, provided food, clothing, services, and translators. Somali businesses began springing up on Lisbon Street, often filling formerly vacant storefronts. An Islamic center opened downtown. For her book, Besteman talked with Marc Robitaille, a police lieutenant who headed the "substation" in downtown Lewiston. He told her he once heard an older Franco-American woman complaining about the Somalis, so he personally took her to several Somali businesses so she could meet some of the immigrants. Larry Gilbert, a former police chief who served as mayor from 2007-2011, also provided a positive voice for the New Mainers. "I see so many similarities to Franco-Americans and people get upset with me for saying that," he told Besteman. "Francos came here to work. Somalis came here out of necessity and to feel safe. They are both good family people."

In January 2009, eight years after Awil Bile reached town, *Newsweek* published an article claiming that the Somali immigrants had been responsible for reviving the dying city. Income had risen, the crime rate had dropped, and in 2004 the National Civic League named Lewiston an "All-American City," a designation no Maine town had received in four decades. "Practically everyone in Lewiston credits the Somalis' discovery of their town with its newfound success," said the magazine. "It's been an absolute blessing in many ways," said Paul Badeau of the Lewiston-Auburn Economic Growth Council. "Just to have an infusion of diversity, an infusion of culture and of youth."

Not everyone agreed with the magazine's assessment and some voiced their opinions in comments on the magazine's website. "Revived my ass!" read one. "They have done nothing good for our city! We have lost jobs. People who actually need state assistance can't get it because them and their ten kids have used up what little there was to begin with. Areas that used to be decent to live in are now infested with them. Seriously, find twenty people in Lewiston who are glad they are here. I know I can't."

"Yes, there is some friction every once in a while, but that often gets blown out of proportion," Pierrot Rugaba, program director for refugee and immigration services of Catholic Charities Maine, told a reporter for the Lewiston *Sun Journal* in 2007. "Things have improved, but like everything else it takes time."

———

Maine, and all of New England, received a reason to cheer in 2004, when the Boston Red Sox placed the Curse of the Bambino in the dustbin of history by winning their first World Series since 1918.

Maine has long provided heart and soul for Red Sox Nation. The ties were strengthened even more in 2003, when the Portland Sea Dogs, formerly the AA franchise for the Miami Marlins, became an affiliate of the Red Sox. That meant Maine would help grow talent for Boston. (And the Sea Dogs did nurture some quality future Sox, including Dustin Pedroia, Jon Lester, Josh Beckett, Kevin Millar, Jonathan Papelbon, Xander Bogaerts, and Mookie Betts.)

Even without the Sea Dogs, Maine was Red Sox country. Generations of Mainers had grown up rooting for the team, listening to the radio on hot summer nights as the voices of Curt Gowdy, Ned Martin,

Ken Coleman, or Joe Castiglione drifted through the ether. They listened or watched as the Red Sox came distressingly close to winning it all. In 1946 the St. Louis Cardinals beat them in the World Series, with shortstop Johnny Pesky emerging as the scapegoat for allegedly holding the ball too long as Enos Slaughter scored from first. The Cardinals beat them again over seven games in 1967, the "Impossible Dream" year that saw Carl Yastrzemski win the triple crown and young Tony Conigliaro nearly get killed when a pitch struck him in the face. In 1975 the Red Sox forced a game seven against the Cincinnati Reds in dramatic fashion, as catcher Carlton Fisk waved the ball fair for a walk-off home run in game six, but they lost game seven. They lost in seven games to the New York Mets in 1986, a series that will always be remembered for the Bill Buckner error that led to a Mets victory in game six.

Eighty-six years had passed since the last Red Sox World Series championship. The gap led *Boston Globe* writer Dan Shaughnessy to speculate about a "Curse of the Bambino" that doomed the team to lose because they sold Babe Ruth to the hated New York Yankees in January 1920. (The curse, however, did not explain why Ruth and the Sox did not win a World Series in 1919.)

All of that angst was swept away in October 2004. First, the Red Sox came back from an 0-3 deficit in the best of seven American League Championship Series to beat the hated Yankees and advance to the World Series against the Cardinals. Then, on October 27, 2004, Red Sox closer Keith Foulke grabbed the ball and tossed it to first baseman Doug Mientkiewicz to make the final out of game four and sweep the Cardinals.

"At last!" screamed the banner headline in the next day's *Kennebec Journal*. "FINALLY!!" blared the *Portland Press Herald*. ""BELIEVE IT!" demanded the *Bangor Daily News*.

It had been a time coming—generations had come and gone without ever seeing the Red Sox make it all the way—and the celebrations in Maine exorcized 86 years of gloom and disappointment. Maine native Fred Hale, 113 years old and recognized as the oldest man in the world, lived just long enough to see it. He died less than a month later. Even the dead became part of the celebration—families decorated the tombstones of deceased Red Sox fans with hats, pennants, and other Sox paraphernalia.

The Loose Moose Saloon in Gray emailed the team. "Your first round of drinks is free," it said. At the Liberal Cup in Hallowell, owner Geoff Houghton bought a round for everyone in his crowded bar as they watched game four. Pandemonium erupted once the Sox made it official, with group hugs and beers lifted in triumphant toasts. "I have been waiting for this my whole life," said China's Maxine Whiteside, who told the *Kennebec Journal*'s reporter that she had not changed her Red Sox shirt since game seven of the Yankees series. "I almost gave up on them for a long time," she said. "They'd get right up there, and they'd get down. I almost gave up, until this year."

At the University of Maine in Orono, 4,000 people gathered for a bonfire and a celebration. In Bangor, Sherly Collyer nervously watched the game on the television at the Sports Arena Bar and Grill. When Mientkiewicz touched first base to make the final out, she celebrated with the other patrons. "This is my dream come true," she said, adding, "You wake up and it's still real, that's the beauty of it."

In Portland, 96-year-old Rosella Lovett celebrated the win. A retired history teacher, she remembered celebrating the 1918 championship in South Portland when she was 10. In the years since, she had attended plenty of Red Sox games at Fenway Park. She had seen Ted Williams and Dom DiMaggio play, and was there when pitcher Lefty Grove notched his 200th win on July 25, 1941. But she had not seen another World Series victory. Until 2004. "It's about time that they won, isn't it?" she asked.

Portland's David Fillinger remembered being 11 when the Red Sox lost the series in 1967. On the night of October 27, 2004, he was in Boston's Kenmore Square celebrating the victory with his 12-year-old son. Jessica Lyons, who had grown up in Dover-Foxcroft, was there, too. She told a *Boston Globe* reporter that she remembered seeing her father cry when the Sox lost in 1986. Now, she said, it felt like a "great sigh of relief."

The rallying cry of the persistently disappointed Red Sox fan used to be, "Wait 'til next year." Now, some wondered how the end of the curse would affect Red Sox Nation. "I think people are really, really happy,"

Colby College historian Richard Moss said. "But somewhere in the back of their minds they're asking, 'Aren't we supposed to lose?'"

Maine author and life-long Red Sox fan Stephen King had a different take on things. The day after he Red Sox victory over the Cardinals he wrote, "This morning's sense of splendid unreality will surely rub away, but the feeling of lightness that comes with finally shedding a burden that has been carried far too long will linger for months or even years."

2010s

Maine Gets Elephants and Goes into Space

ROSIE AND OPAL WERE DEFINITELY "FROM AWAY." THAILAND, TO BE precise. They were both former circus workers who had moved to Maine from Oklahoma in late 2012 to settle into the small town of Hope, about eight miles from Camden. The hope was that Rosie and Opal would find peace and comfort as they spent their twilight years in the Pine Tree State.

What makes this story unusual is that Rosie and Opal were elephants. In Maine they were the four-ton centerpieces of Hope Elephants, a nonprofit that cared for them while teaching visitors about the big animals and their increasingly threatened place in the modern world.

Jim Laurita, who co-founded Hope Elephants with his brother Tom, called Rosie and Opal "the girls." "Rosie is the sweetheart, sort of, she's the one who's definitely more human-socialized, happier to be around people," he told an interviewer in 2014. "Opal's mischievous. I wouldn't say dangerous, but she's always looking for ways to pick your pocket, steal something from somewhere." Laurita first met the girls when he and his brother worked as jugglers for the Carson & Barnes circus in the 1970s. Jim also cared for the circus's elephants, Rosie and Opal among them, and he later worked with elephants at the Bronx Zoo, Wildlife Safari in Winston, Oregon, in India and in Florida. After becoming a veterinarian, he opened a practice in Camden. All the time, he and his brother dreamed that one day they could do something for the elephants they had known.

Rosie and Opal were calves when they arrived in the United States. They were in their 40s when they reached Maine, with Rosie the elder by two years. She was an orphan and had been bottle raised by humans. "It's like a kid being raised by wolves," Laurita said. As a result, Rosie never learned how to properly interact with other elephants, which have a complex social structure. "She's been bossed around and pushed around a lot in her life," Laurita explained. Another elephant once shoved Rosie against a truck, inflicting a shoulder injury that continued to plague her. She had partial paralysis of her trunk, which may have been the result of an elephant herpes virus, and both animals also suffered from arthritis.

Laurita kept tabs on Rosie, who was living out her retirement at the Endangered Ark Foundation in Hugo, Oklahoma, a nonprofit that houses ex-circus animals. Laurita considered bringing her to Maine with another elephant named Sis. When Sis died, Laurita decided to see if Rosie could get along with Opal, another resident at Endangered Ark. Getting the two pachyderms to Maine, though, required wading through thickets of certifications and permits, starting with the town of Hope.

"In a small town you wear many hats," said Jonathan Duke, who was Hope's administrator and code officer at the time. "There are no hats that prepare you for pachyderms." The approval process intensified when animal rights groups questioned the wisdom of keeping elephants in Maine or opposed the idea of captive animals in general. Duke was bombarded with protests from all over the country, to the point where the town office had to shut off its fax machine. Even actress/comedian Lily Tomlin weighed in. "I wholeheartedly agree that Rosie deserves a better home," Tomlin wrote to Maine governor Paul LePage. "But the best course of action is to send her to an established sanctuary, where she would receive specialized care from a staff of highly trained caretakers and would live with other elephants in a spacious, natural habitat situated in a far more moderate climate."

Laurita admitted that having elephants in Maine did appear odd, but he pointed out that other cold-weather cities—Syracuse, New York, and

Denver among them—had elephant programs, and that the best breeding program for Asian elephants was in Ontario.

One authority who expressed reservations about keeping older elephants in Maine was Dr. Chatchote Thitaram of the Elephant Research and Education Center at Chiang Mai University in Thailand. "In my opinion and experience, I don't think it is proper to put the aged elephants in the extremely cold climate," he said. He agreed that Asian elephants can adjust to cold and said healthy elephants live in cool climates at London and Canadian facilities. But he pointed out that those were younger animals. Older animals like Rosie and Opal could experience more difficulty, especially with their arthritis.

Despite the protests and the paperwork, Laurita forged ahead. In July 2011 the town held a meeting to consider his proposal. "It was the largest turnout of any town meeting I had been to in the town of Hope, in the eight years that I've been here," said Duke, who estimated that around 100 people showed up (in a town with a population of only around 1,600). The reactions were largely positive, Duke said, and the town voted its approval.

Laurita built a barn for the animals and received permits from the state and the U.S. Department of Agriculture. The elephants (still owned by Endangered Ark, which charged Hope Elephants a "minimal fee" for them) made the 44-hour truck journey from Oklahoma to take up residence in a 52' x 60' structure that had a sand floor warmed by radiant heat. (Elephants produce up to 30 gallons of urine a day, so concrete floors are the norm at most facilities, but Laurita wanted a sand floor because it is easier on the elephants' feet.) Outside the barn, Rosie and Opal had an acre of fenced-in land.

"We haven't had any real opposition since they arrived," Laurita told his interviewer in 2014. "Perhaps people see the treatment they're getting and they see the care they're getting and it's sort of changed their perception a little." Rosie received acupuncture for her shoulder and both elephants were treated with therapeutic ultrasound (sound waves sent deep into the tissue), shortwave diathermy (the same thing, but with radio waves), and hydrotherapy for their feet. For their arthritis they received glucosamine, a dietary supplement made from sea cucumbers and donated by the local manufacturer. The girls apparently adjusted to the Down East weather as well and liked playing in the snow. Rosie scooped up snowballs with her damaged trunk and Opal liked to ignore the plowed paths to plunge through the deep stuff. The community pitched in to help their new neighbors. Local companies and farmers donated food, and residents turned in empty bottles and cans so Hope Elephants could use the deposit refunds.

Hope Elephants had big hopes. With its centerpieces in place, the organization aimed to evolve from "a nonprofit that has elephants and does some education to an educational nonprofit that has elephants," said Andrew Stewart, the executive director. Stewart, who studied animal biology in his native Scotland and reached Hope after stints as a raft guide in Wyoming and at a safari camp in Botswana, oversaw development of an educational curriculum that he planned to test in schools in 2014.

In one year, some 17,000 people visited the elephants in their new home. The visitors paid a donation to see Rosie and Opal and learned about the girls and about the threats elephants faced around the world. Poachers kill African elephants at unsustainable rates for their tusks, while the loss of habitat has reduced the world population of Asian elephants to no more than 50,000. "The groups that we bring here and all the school groups that we reach, we're trying to teach them how wonderful and complicated elephants are," Laurita said. "We try to interest them in the fact that the elephants are in trouble right now and they're in need of conservation."

Eliot Elementary School in Eliot, Maine, was one school that used Rosie and Opal as the foundation for a reading program without even getting a chance to visit. The students created a book about the girls, skyped with "Dr. Jim," and learned about the plight of elephants in the world today. "They were really motivated after that," said Joanne Hoerth, the school's reading specialist. The school even raised $2,200 for Hope Elephants.

And then it all suddenly ended. On the morning of September 9, 2014, Jim Laurita was found dead in the barn he had built to house the elephants he loved so much. Maine's medical examiner's office said Laurita's death was accidental and caused by "asphyxiation and multiple fractures because of the compression of his chest." The autopsy report indicated that Laurita had apparently fallen and struck his head while tending to the animals and that one of the animals had then stepped on him. It was a tragic end to a story that, to many, had seemed like a dream come true.

"Hope Elephants is deeply saddened by the loss of our founder, Dr. Jim Laurita," said a statement by the organization. "Jim's passion for all animals, but especially elephants, was boundless. It was Jim's ability to share that passion with all around him that not only helped to make our organization a reality, but also enriched and enhanced the lives of all those who had a chance to know Jim. It was through education that Jim passed on his passion and the importance of wildlife conservation."

"It's not any easier to take today than yesterday," Jon Duke told a reporter for the *Bangor Daily News* a day after Laurita's death. "It's a small, tight-knit community. Everyone knows everyone. Obviously, 24 hours afterward, we're still in shock."

Laurita's death removed the hope from Hope Elephants. Rosie and Opal returned to the Endangered Ark Foundation, where Opal died on January 9, 2017, after injuring her leg. She was 48 years old. "Her dear companion Rosie along with all of the elephants are feeling the loss of Opal," Endangered Ark said in a statement. "Regardless of what species, it is always difficult to lose a member of the family." That was something that Rosie and Opal—and the community of Hope—knew too well.

Dusk was shadowing Kazakhstan on the evening of September 25, 2019. It was almost 7:00 p.m. local time. At the Baikonur Cosmodrome, a 162-foot-tall Soyuz rocket stood isolated on its launch pad, the flat steppes beyond it stretching to the horizon. Steam from the condensation caused by the super-cold liquid oxygen inside the booster streamed down the rocket's sides.

Suddenly the rocket's five engines burst into life, turning dusk into a temporary dawn. The rocket slowly lifted off the pad, accelerating steadily as the engines' 930,000 pounds of thrust pushed it into the clouds. The Soyuz climbed higher and higher into the darkening sky, moving faster and faster. A little more than two minutes after liftoff, four strap-on boosters separated from the main rocket, which was now traveling 3,300 miles per hour. After five minutes, the fifth, core engine separated. The upper stage's engine ignited and propelled the capsule sitting at the top of the rocket into orbit. Six hours later, after making four circuits of the planet, the capsule docked with the International Space Station. The three people inside the Soyuz climbed through a hatch and joined the six people already aboard the ISS.

Jessica Meir of Caribou, Maine, had finally made it into space.

Meir, 42, was part of a truly international mission. Commanding the flight was Russia's Oleg Skiripochka, his third mission into space. Hazzaa Ali Almansoori was a "space flight participant" from the United Arab Emirates. Like Meir, it was his first space mission and also the first flight for an astronaut from the UAE. Meir provided an international background all by herself. Her father, Josef, was born in Iraq but emigrated to Israel when he was young. After fighting in Israel's war for independence in 1948, he studied medicine and eventually began practicing in Sweden. There he married Jessica's mother, a nurse, and they eventually relocated to Caribou, where they raised their five children.

As a student in Maine, Jessica earned a reputation for her ambition and drive—character traits that would come in handy as an astronaut candidate. Her sports included soccer, skiing, and track, and she also played saxophone and flute. "She's driven, but she always did it with a smile on her face," her band director told a reporter from the *Portland Press Herald*. While in high school, Meir met astronaut Charles Duke, who had walked on the moon during the Apollo 16 mission, when he was speaking in Presque Isle. The encounter sparked her interest in becoming an astronaut. When Meir graduated as the valedictorian of her high school class, her yearbook entry said her dream was to walk in space.

Meir attributes her Maine upbringing with her desire to venture into space. Growing up in Caribou, a remote part of the state surrounded by woods, she said, "really ignited in me this passion for exploration and this appreciation for nature, and really this scientific curiosity and trying to learn more and understand more about the natural world around us. That was the thing that got me interested in my previous career as a physiologist and a biologist and of course the same is true in this role as an astronaut now."

"More than anything, Caribou was home," she said when inducted into her high school hall of fame in 2016. "Home was full of family, friends and teachers who provided me with countless memories and the foundations of an education that was truly paramount in getting me where I am today." After high school she graduated from Brown University and then went to France to get a master's degree from the International Space University, followed by a Ph.D. from the Scripps Institution of Oceanography in San Diego.

During her career as a physiologist, Meir studied seals and penguins in Antarctica, which required scuba diving beneath the sea ice where the water temperature is always a mere 28 degrees Fahrenheit. She conducted ground-breaking experiments with bar-headed geese, which can fly high enough to cross over the Himalayas, conditions that require the birds to adapt to an oxygen-deprived environment. During her experiments, Meir studied a group of geese that had "imprinted" on her as goslings and accepted her as one of their own. "Meir spent almost all of her waking hours with the goslings at the bird park," said the *Washington Post*. "They chirped and cried at the sound of her voice as she approached their pens each morning. She took baby birds for walks. When she sat on a blanket to read, they smothered her in a fluffy, gray goose-pile. 'They would just nap and snuggle and cuddle up inside,' she said." At the University of British Columbia in Vancouver, Meir helped the birds learn how to fly. Once they took to the air, the geese would fly alongside Meir as she drove a motor scooter. She later studied the geese as they flew inside a wind tunnel while wearing special masks so the scientists could control the air they breathed and observe how their bodies reacted when deprived of oxygen.

Meir was an assistant professor at Harvard when she was selected to become an astronaut in 2013, one of eight chosen out of 6,000 who applied. Her astronaut training included a trip to Sardinia, where she had to squirm through tight passages in caves deep beneath the earth, and more than a year at Star City, the Russian facility where cosmonauts have trained since the 1960s. (The Russian partnership is essential because the

United States has lacked the capacity to send humans into space since the end of the U.S. space shuttle program. Astronauts have to use Russian Soyuz spacecraft to reach the space station.)

Meir remained aware of the somewhat ironic circumstances that she had been studying the physiology of animals who live in extreme environments, and now she would be the animal in the most extreme environment of all. Humans who have spent long periods in the microgravity of space have undergone some physical changes. Their vision degrades, perhaps due to changes in the retina, and ceratoid arteries harden, much as they do for older people. "Unfortunately, unlike these animals, we are not very well adapted to survive in space, and that's why we have all these scientific studies to understand what happens to our bodies and how they change," Meir said in a NASA video. For the six months she spends in space, Meir would be the test subject. "I guess it's only fair," she said.

On 7:49 on October 18, 2019, Meir made her yearbook dream a reality when she exited the space station on her first spacewalk. She spent more than seven hours outside the station while she helped replace a battery charger and performed other maintenance tasks. She also made history on that day. Her partner on the walk was astronaut Christina Koch, making it the first time two women had done a spacewalk together.

Meir was the third person from Maine to reach space. The first was Charles Hobaugh from Bar Harbor, who flew into orbit aboard the American space shuttle *Atlantis* in 2001. The second was Chris Cassidy. Although born in Massachusetts, Cassidy grew up in York, Maine, and considers it his home. He had been a member of three space missions and once served as NASA's head astronaut. Plans call for Cassidy to return to the space station in 2020, meaning that two astronauts from Maine will be in orbit when the state celebrates its bicentennial.

Maine has come a long way in 200 years. In the 1820s two men in a boat fought a bear. In 2020 two people from the state orbited the planet on a space station. Who knows what we can expect in another two centuries?

Acknowledgments

I wish my friend Richard Sassaman was around to accept my thanks. Richard, who died suddenly in 2019, wrote a fine article about the Aroostook War for *American History* magazine when I was the editor. He also wrote about the Nazi spies who landed in Maine for *America in WWII* magazine, and it was Richard who suggested that the Stanley twins would make a good subject for this book. I think he would have enjoyed it.

Melanie May, a onetime classmate of mine at Bowdoin College, suggested that the Somali immigration of Lewiston was worth covering, and I agreed. Thanks, Melanie! And thanks to Daniel E. Blaney, the authority on Old Orchard Beach's history, for providing me with lots of information about Arthur Schreiber and his flight across the Atlantic.

Thanks also to the various libraries and institutions I used for my research. The Cumberland County Library System here in Pennsylvania was very helpful in filing all my interlibrary loan requests, and I also found lots of good stuff at the Pennsylvania State Library. I spent many hours at the Maine State Library in Augusta, too. It's a wonderful facility.

I'd like to express my thanks to Michael Dolan, the editor of *American History* magazine, who assigned me to write an article about Margaret Chase Smith and arranged to publish it online in time so I would reuse it in this book. The material about Hope Elephants began as an article for *National Geographic Online*, but circumstances prevented it from being used.

Weird as it may seem, I'd also like to say thank you to the state of Maine. Although I have now been living outside the state longer than

I lived in it, I always have been and always will be a native Mainer. It's embedded in my DNA. With some of the later chapters of this book, I often found personal connections to the history I was researching, whether it was my recollections of a visit to Telstar's earth station in Andover with my family in the 1960s, or memories of watching the steamer *Katahdin* doing her log driving work on Moosehead Lake. When I was a student at Bowdoin, I knew Jim Roux, who was on one of the planes that crashed into the World Trade Centers on that horrible September day in 2001. In 2014 I traveled to Hope, Maine, to talk with Jim Laurita about the elephants he was caring for there. All these pieces of history became part of my life. I guess history has a way of doing that, if you live long enough.

Finally, my most heart-felt thanks go to my lovely wife, Beth Ann, who provided support, listened to my complaints, and soothed my spirits when necessary. She was also a great travel companion for many of my research expeditions to Maine. She's terrific—and she's not even from Maine!

Sources

1820s—Maine Achieves Statehood; Peter Brawn Fights a Bear

Banks, Ronald F. *Maine Becomes a State: The Movement to Separate Maine from Massachusetts, 1785-1820.* Middletown, CT: Wesleyan University Press, 1970.

Hatch, Louis Clinton. *Maine: A History,* Vol. 1. New York: The American Historical Society, 1919.

Judd, Richard W., Edwin A. Churchill, and Joel W. Eastman. *Maine: The Pine Tree State from Prehistory to the Present.* Orono: University of Maine Press, 1995.

Smith, Edgar Crosby. "Peter Brawn and His Celebrated Bear Fight on Sebec Lake." In *Collections of the Piscataquis County Historical Society,* Vol. 1. Dover, Me: Observer Press, 1910.

Willis, William. *The History of Portland, from 1632 to 1864: With a Notice of Previous Settlements, Colonial Grants, and Changes of Government in Maine.* Portland, ME: Bailey & Noyes, 1865.

1830s—Jonathan Cilley Fights a Duel; Maine (Almost) Goes to War

Abbot, John S. C. *The History of Maine,* 2nd ed. Augusta, ME: E.E. Knowles & Co., 1892.

Aroostook War: Historical Sketch and Roster of Commissioned Officers and Enlisted Men Called Into Service for the Protection of the Northeastern Frontier of Maine from February to May, 1839. Augusta, ME: *Kennebec Journal,* 1904.

Cleveland, Nehemiah. *History of Bowdoin College, with Biographical Sketches of its Graduates.* Boston: James Ripley Osgood & Co., 1882.

Ginn, Roger. *New England Must Not Be Trampled On: The Tragic Death of Jonathan Cilley.* Lanham, MD: Down East Books, 2016.

Hatch, Louis Clinton. *Maine: A History,* Vol. 1. New York: The American Historical Society, 1919.

Hawthorne, Nathaniel. "Jonathan Cilley." In *Hawthorne's Works,* Vol. 22. Boston: Houghton, Mifflin, & Co. 1899.

James, George Payne Rainsford. *A Brief History of the United States Boundary Question, Drawn Up from Official Papers.* London: Saunders and Otley, 1839.

Levine, Robert S. "The Honor of New England: Nathaniel Hawthorne and the Cilley-Graves Duel of 1838." From *Field of Honor: Essays on Southern Character and American Tradition*, edited by John Mayfield and Todd Hagstette. Columbia: University of South Carolina Press, 2007.

Mansfield, Edward Deering. *Life and Services of General Winfield Scott: Including the Siege of Vera Cruz, the Battle of Cerro Gordo, and the Battles in the Valley of Mexico, to the Conclusion of Peace, and His Return to the United States*. Auburn, NY: A.S. Barnes & Co., 1852.

Piscataquis County Historical Society. *Collections of the Piscataquis County Historical Society*, Vol. 1. Dover, ME: Observer Press, 1910.

Sassaman, Richard. "A Borderline War." *American History*, February 2001.

Simpson, Craig M. *A Good Southerner: The Life of Henry A. Wise of Virginia*. Chapel Hill: University of North Carolina Press, 1985.

Stanley, R. H. and George O. Hall. *Eastern Maine and the Rebellion*. Bangor, ME: R.H. Stanley & Co., 1887.

Wise, Barton Haxall. *The Life of Henry A. Wise of Virginia, 1806-1876*. New York: The MacMillan Company, 1899.

1840s—Thoreau Goes Wild

Gibson, John. *In High Places with Henry David Thoreau: A Hiker's Guide with Routes & Maps*. Woodstock, VT: Countryman Press, 2013.

Hamlin, Charles E. *Routes to Ktaadn*. Reprinted from *The Appalachia*, Vol. II. No. 4, 1881.

Moldenhauer, Joseph J., ed. *The Illustrated Maine Woods*. Princeton, NJ: Princeton University Press, 1972.

Sims, Michael. *The Adventures of Henry Thoreau*. New York: Bloomsbury, 2012.

Slayton, Tom. *Searching for Thoreau: On the Trails and Shores of Wild New England*. Bennington, VT: Images from the Past, 2003.

Thoreau, Henry David. *The Maine Woods*. New York: Thomas Y. Crowell Company, 1909.

Walls, Laura Dassow. *Henry David Thoreau: A Life*. Chicago: University of Chicago Press, 2017.

The 1850s—Portland Riots Over Rum; Harriet Beecher Stowe Writes a Book

Burns, Eric. *The Spirits of America: A Social History of Alcohol*. Philadelphia: Temple University Press, 2004.

Calhoun, Charles C. *A Small College in Maine: Two Hundred Years of Bowdoin*. Brunswick, ME: Bowdoin College, 1993.

Cleveland, Nehemiah. *History of Bowdoin College, with Biographical Sketches of its Graduates*. Boston: James Ripley Osgood & Co., 1882.

Clubb, Henry Stephen. *The Maine Liquor Law: Its Origin, History, and Results, Including a Life of Hon. Neal Dow*. New York: Fowler and Wells: Maine Law Statistical Society, 1856.

Dow, Neal. *The Reminiscences of Neal Dow: Recollections of Eighty Years.* Portland, ME: Evening Express Publishing Company, 1898.

Hedrick, Joan D. *Harriet Beecher Stowe: A Life.* New York: Oxford University Press, 1995.

Judd, Richard W., Edwin A. Churchill, and Joel W. Eastman. *Maine: The Pine Tree State from Prehistory to the Present.* Orono: University of Maine Press, 1995.

Portland, Maine, Coroner's Jury. *The Death of John Robbins, of Deer Isle, Who Was Shot in the Streets of Portland by Order of Neal Dow, Mayor, June 2d, 1855: A Full Report of the Testimony Taken Before the Coroner's Inquest, as Published in the "State of Maine" Newspaper.* Portland, ME: Bearce, Starbird, Rich & Co., 1855.

Stowe, Harriet Beecher. *The Annotated Uncle Tom's Cabin.* Edited with an introduction and notes by Henry Louis Gates, Jr. New York: W.W. Norton & Co., 2007.

1860s—Maine Defends the Union

Civil War pension records, National Archives, Washington, D.C.

"Comrade Leroy H. Tobie's Military Career." Author unknown. In the *First Maine Bugle.* Campaign III, Call 4, October 1893.

Dingley, Edward Nelson. *The Life and Times of Nelson Dingley, Jr.* Kalamazoo, MI: Ihling Bros. & Everard, 1902.

Eaton, Harriet. *This Birth Place of Souls: The Civil War Nursing Diary of Harriet Eaton.* Edited by Jane E. Schulz. New York: Oxford University Press, 2011.

Gould, John Mead. *The Civil War Journals of John Meade Gould, 1861–1866.* Edited by William B. Jordan. Baltimore, MD: Butternut and Blue, 1997.

Hale, Clarence. "The Capture of the Caleb Cushing." In *Collections of the Maine Historical Society,* Third Series, Vol. 1, 1904.

Hatch, Louis Clinton. *Maine: A History,* Vol. II. New York: The American Historical Society, 1919. Volume II.

Kenniston, William B. "The Capture of the *Caleb Cushing.*" In Donald W. Beattie, Rodney M. Cole, and Charles G. Waugh, eds. *A Distant War Comes Home: Maine in the Civil War Era.* Camden, ME: Down East Books, 1996. (Originally printed in *Lewiston Journal Illustrated Magazine,* May 30, 1908.)

Maine Adjutant General. *Annual Report of the Adjutant General of the State of Maine for the Year Ending December 31, 1863.* Augusta, ME: Stevens & Sayward, 1863.

Maine Adjutant General. *Annual Report of the Adjutant General of the State of Maine for the Years 1864 and 1865.* Augusta, ME: Stevens & Sayward, 1866.

Maine State Archives:
    http://www.maine.gov/tools/whatsnew/index.php?topic=arcsesq&id=147045&v=article.
    http://www.maine.gov/tools/whatsnew/index.php?topic=arcsesq&id=147479&v=article.
    https://www.maine.gov/tools/whatsnew/index.php?topic=arcsesq&id=186601&v=article.

Portland Daily Press, June 29, 1863.

Schultz, Jane E. *Women at the Front: Hospital Workers in Civil War America.* Chapel Hill: University of North Carolina Press, 2004.

Shaw, Horace H., and Charles J. House. *The First Maine Heavy Artillery, 1861-1865: A History of Its Part and Place in the War for the Union, with an Outline of Causes of War and Its Results to Our Country.* Portland, ME: Publisher unknown, 1903.

Stanley, F. E. "The Kingfield Rebellion as I Recall it." From Donald W. Beattie, Rodney M. Cole, and Charles G. Waugh, eds. *A Distant War Comes Home: Maine in the Civil War Era.* Camden, ME: Down East Books, 1996. (Originally published in the *Lewiston Journal Illustrated Magazine*, April 27, 1918.)

Stanley, R. H., and George O. Hall. *Eastern Maine and the Rebellion.* Bangor, ME: R.H. Stanley & Co., 1887.

Swartz, Brian. "Some Mainers broke racial barriers in 'white' state regiments." *Bangor Daily News*, December 11, 2013.

United States Navy Department. *Official Records of the Union and Confederate Navies in the War of the Rebellion.* Series 1, Vol. 2. Washington, DC: U.S. Government Printing Office, 1895.

Warner, Ezra J. *Generals in Gray: Lives of the Confederate Commanders.* Baton Rouge: Louisiana State University Press, 2006.

Whitman, William E. S., and Charles H. True. *Maine in the War for the Union: A History of the Part Borne by Maine Troops in the Suppression of the American Rebellion.* Lewiston, ME: Nelson Dingley Jr. & Co., 1865.

1870s—Maine Teeters on the Precipice

Articles from the *Kennebec Journal*, November 1879-January 1880.

Barker, Lewis A. "The Great Maine Conspiracy." *The New England Magazine*, Vol. 37, September 1907–February 1908.

Chamberlain, Joshua Lawrence. *The Grand Old Man of Maine: Selected Letters of Joshua Lawrence Chamberlain, 1865-1914.* Edited by Jeremiah E. Goulka. Chapel Hill: The University of North Carolina Press, 2004.

———. *The Twelve Days at Augusta, 1880.* Portland, ME: Smith & Sale, 1906.

Dingley, Edward Nelson. *The Life and Times of Nelson Dingley, Jr.* Kalamazoo, MI: Ihling Bros. & Everard, 1902.

Graham, John. Month of Madness: Maine's Brush with Civil War. Master's thesis, University of New Hampshire, December 1981.

Hatch, Louis Clinton. *Maine: A History.* Vol. 2. New York: The American Historical Society, 1919.

Maine State Legislature. *Report of the Joint Select Committee to Inquire Into the Condition of the Election Returns of September 8th, 1879, and the Expenditure of Public Moneys Under the Direction of Gov. Garcelon and Council, Together with the Evidence Taken Before the Committee, Made to the 59th Legislature of Maine.* Augusta, ME: Sprague & Sons, 1880.

Pullen, John J. *Joshua Chamberlain: A Hero's Life and Legacy.* Mechanicsburg, PA: Stackpole Books, 1999.

1880s—James G. Blaine Runs for President

Blaine, Harriet S. *Letters of Mrs. James G. Blaine*, Vol. 1. New York: Duffield and Company, 1908.

Daily Kennebec Journal, June 14, 1920.

Hamilton, Gail. *Biography of James G. Blaine*. Norwich, CT: The Henry Bill Publishing Co., 1895.

Hatch, Louis Clinton. *Maine: A History*, Vol. 2. New York: The American Historical Society, 1919.

Howard, Oliver Otis. *Autobiography of Oliver Otis Howard, Major General, United States Army*, Vol. 1. New York: The Baker & Taylor Company, 1907.

Russell, Charles Edward. *Blaine of Maine*. New York: Cosmopolitan Book Corporation, 1931.

Stanwood, Edward. *James Gillespie Blaine*. Boston, MA: Houghton Mifflin Company, 1905.

———. *A History of Presidential Elections*. Cambridge, MA: The Riverside Press, 1892.

Summers, Mark Wahlgren. *Rum, Romanism & Rebellion: The Making of a President, 1884*. Chapel Hill: University of North Carolina Press, 2000.

1890s—Louis Sockalexis Socks It to Them

Barr, Daniel P. "'Looking Backward': The Life and Legend of Louis Francis Sockalexis. In Richard C. King. *Native Americans in Sport and Society: A Reader*. Lincoln: University of Nebraska Press, 2005.

Eastman, Charles A. *The Indian To-day: The Past and Future of the First American*. New York: Doubleday, Page & Company, 1915.

Felber, Bill. *A Game of Brawl: The Orioles, the Beaneaters, and the Battle for the 1897 Pennant*. Lincoln: University of Nebraska Press, 2007.

Fleitz, David L. *Louis Sockalexis: The First Cleveland Indian*. Jefferson, NC: McFarland & Company, Inc., 2002.

McDonald, Brian. *Indian Summer: The Forgotten Story of Louis Sockalexis, the First Native American in Major League Baseball*. New York: Rodale, 2003.

Powers-Beck, J. P. *The American Indian Integration of Baseball*. Lincoln: University of Nebraska Press, 2004.

Rice, Ed. *Baseball's First Indian, Louis Sockalexis: Penobscot Legend, Cleveland Indian*. Windsor, CT: Tide-Mark Press, Ltd., 2003

1900s—The Stanleys Get Steamed

Beahm, George. *The Stephen King Companion: 40 Years of Fear from the Master of Horror*. New York: Thomas Dunn Books, 2015.

Bentley, John. *Oldtime Steam Cars*. New York: Arco Publishing Company, Inc., 1953.

Davis, Susan S. *The Stanleys: Renaissance Yankees*. New York: The Newcomen Society of the United States, 1997.

Derr, Thomas S. *The Modern Steam Car: A Background*. Los Angeles, CA: Floyd Clymer, 1934.

Displays at the Stanley Museum, Kingfield, Maine.

Hatch, Louis Clinton. *Maine: A History*, Vol. 4. New York: The American Historical Society, 1919.

Jessen, Kenneth. "The Inventive Freelan O. Stanley Made His Mark on Estes Park." *Loveland Reporter-Herald*, August 18, 2018.

Lord Montagu of Beaulieu and Anthony Bird. *Steam Cars, 1770-1970*. New York: St. Martin's Press, 1971.

Pickering, James H. *Mr. Stanley of Estes Park*. Kingfield, ME: Stanley Museum, 2000.

Punnet, Dick. *Beach Racers: Daytona Before NASCAR*. Gainesville: University Press of Florida, 2008.

Woodbury, George. *The Story of a Stanley Steamer*. New York: W.W. Norton & Co., 1950.

1910s—Hiram Maxim Invents Modern War

Bratten, Jonathan D. "Some in Maine Indian Tribe Joined 103rd Infantry for War." *Army*, April 2017.

Callandar, Bruce. "Five Smart Men Who Did Not Invent the Airplane." *Air Force Magazine*, January 1990.

"Case of the William P. Frye." *The American Journal of International Law*, Vol. 9, No. 3, Supplement: Diplomatic Correspondence Between the United States and Belligerent Governments Relating to Neutral Rights and Commerce (June 1915).

Chivers, C. J. *The Gun*. New York: Simon & Schuster, 2010.

Damrosch, Walter. *My Musical Life*. New York: Charles Scribner's Sons, 1924.

Goldsmith, Dolf L. *The Devil's Paintbrush: Sir Hiram Maxim's Gun*. Cobourg, Ontario: Collector Grade Publications, Inc., 2002.

Hawkey, Arthur. *The Amazing Hiram Maxim: An Intimate Biography*. Staplehurst, UK: Spellmount, Ltd., 2001.

Libby, Jason C., and Earle G. Shettleworth, Jr. *Maine in World War I*. Charleston, SC: Arcadia Publishing, 2017.

Maxim, Sir Hiram. *My Life*. London: Methuen & Co., Ltd., 1915.

Maxim, Hiram Percy. *A Genius in the Family*. New York: Dover Publications, 1962. (Originally published in 1962.)

McCallum, Iain. *Blood Brothers: Hiram and Hudson Maxim: Pioneers of Modern Warfare*. London: Chatham Publishing, 1999.

Sangerville, Maine, 1814-1914: Proceedings of the Centennial Celebration. Dover, ME: Publisher unknown, 1914.

Sprague, John Francis. "Sir Hiram Maxim." In *Sprague's Journal of Maine History*, Vol. 4, No. 5, April 1917.

Ticknor, Caroline. *New England Aviators 1914-1918: Their Portraits and Their Records*, Vol. 1. New York: Houghton Mifflin Company, 1919.

1920s—Lindbergh Comes to Town
Articles from the *Portland Press Herald*, July 22-26, 1927.
Articles from the *Biddeford Daily Journal*, June 20, 1929, June 26, 1929, and June 27, 1929.
Berg, A. Scott. *Lindbergh*. New York: G.P. Putnam's Sons, 1998.
Blaney, Daniel E. *Old Orchard Beach*. Charleston, SC: Acadia Publishing, 2007.
Hale John. "Stowaway, Co-Pilot Relive Flight Across Atlantic 45 Years Ago." *Portland Press Herald*, June 13, 1974.
Hamlen, Frederick R. "Old Orchard Beach: Beginnings to Old Glory." *Dirigo Flyer,* September 2000.
Jackson, Joe. *Atlantic Fever: Lindbergh, His Competitors, and the Race to Cross the Atlantic.* New York: Farrar, Straus, and Giroux, 2012.
Kanes, Candace. "We Saw Lindbergh!" On the Maine Memory Network, https://www.mainememory.net/sitebuilder/site/748/page/1157/display.
Kehoe, Donald. *Flying with Lindbergh*. Pickle Partners Publishing, 2017, ebook (reprint edition).
"Paris Crowds Cheer and Mock Schreiber, 'Yellow Bird' Stowaway. *Jewish Daily Bulletin,* June 18, 1927.
Pyle, Encaracion. "Dare Brings Fame." *Oxnard Press Courier*, July 31, 1993.
"The first aviation stowaway or how to make throw overboard champagne by a Frenchman." Avialogs, November 25, 2015. http://www.avialogs.com/index.php/avialogs/the-first-aviation-stowaway-or-how-to-make-throw-overboard-champagne-by-a-frenchman.html.

1930s—Al Brady Meets His End
Articles from the *Bangor Daily News*, October 13-16, 1937.
Author unknown. "Marker dedication for Al Brady's grave Sept. 12 in Bangor," *Bangor Daily News*, September 7, 2007.
Burnham, Emily. "Col. Walter R. Walsh, expert marksman who shot Al Brady in Bangor, dies at age 106." *Bangor Daily News*, May 1, 2014.
Federal Bureau of Investigation. "The Brady Gang." FBI Famous Cases. https://www.fbi.gov/history/famous-cases/the-brady-gang. "Ex-Agent Recalls Role in Gangster Era" (video). https://www.fbi.gov/video-repository/newss-ex-agent-recalls-role-in-gangster-era/view.
Gagnon, Dawn. "Bangor ready to re-enact Brady Gang shootout." *Bangor Daily News,* October 6, 2007.
Hickok, Lorena. *One Third of a Nation: Lorena Hickok Reports on the Great Depression.* Urbana: University of Illinois Press, 1981.
Scee, Trudy Irene. *Public Enemy Number One: The True Story of the Brady Gang.* Camden, ME: Down East Books, 2015.

1940s—John Ford Films Midway; German Spies Come Ashore
Brechlin, Earl. "Torpedoed ship is forgotten victim." The *Ellsworth American*, January 20, 2012.

Buffa, Denise. "Niantic Boy Became Nazi Spy." *The Hartford Courant,* April 23, 2014.

Cohen, Stan, Don DeNevi, and Richard Gay. *They Came to Destroy America: The FBI goes to War Against Nazi Spies Before and During World War II.* Missoula, MT: Pictorial Histories Publishing Company, 2003.

Dixon, Mark E. "One Lower Merion Man's Secret Double Life." *Main Line Today,* July 2018.

Eyman, Scott. *Print the Legend: The Life and Times of John Ford.* New York: Simon & Schuster, 1999.

Gimpel, Erich. *Agent 146: The True Story of a Nazi Spy in America.* New York: St. Martin's Press, 2003.

Harris, Mark. *Five Came Back: The Story of Hollywood and the Second World War.* New York: The Penguin Press, 2014.

Levitt, Jonathan. "Nazi Spies at Hancock Point Recalled Anew by Local Author." The *Ellsworth American,* date unknown.

Miller, Richard A. *A True Story of an American Nazi Spy: William Curtis Colepaugh.* Bloomington, IN: Trafford Publishing, 2003 (Kindle edition).

Navy Department. REPORT OF THE INTERROGATION OF GERMAN AGENTS, GIMPEL AND COLEPAUGH, LANDED ON THE COAST OF MAINE FROM *U-1230.* http://www.ibiblio.org/hyperwar/USN/rep/U-1230/index.html.

Sassaman, Richard. "Nazi Spies Come Ashore." *America in WWII,* November 2005.

Weaver, Jacqueline. "Story of Two World War II Spooks Lives On." The *Ellsworth American,* June 2, 2014.

1950s—Margaret Chase Smith Takes a Stand

Author Unknown. "Sen. Smith in Blistering Attack on Both Sides for Red Probe Tactics." *Bangor Daily News,* June 2, 1950.

Author Unknown. "The Lady from Maine." *Newsweek,* June 12, 1950.

Bangor Daily News, June 2, 1950.

Cook, Fred R. *The Nightmare Decade: The Life and Times of Senator Joe McCarthy.* New York: Random House, 1971.

Craig, May. "Sen. Smith Assails Colleagues." *Portland Press Herald,* June 2, 1950.

Crouse, Eric R. *An American Stand: Margaret Chase Smith and the Communist Menace, 1848-1972.* Lanham, MD: Lexington Books, 2013.

Fitzpatrick, Ellen. "The Unfavored Daughter: When Margaret Chase Smith Ran in the New Hampshire Primary." *The New Yorker,* February 6, 2016.

Graham, Frank Jr. *Margaret Chase Smith: Woman of Courage.* New York: The John Day Co., 1964.

Griffith, Robert. *The Politics of Fear: Joseph R. McCarthy and the Senate.* Lexington: The University Press of Kentucky, 1970.

Newsweek, June 12, 1950.

Oshinsky, David M. *A Conspiracy So Immense: The World of Joe McCarthy.* New York: The Free Press, 1983.

Portland Press Herald, June 2, 1950.

Smith, Margaret Chase. *Declaration of Conscience*. New York: Doubleday, 1972.

1960s—Maine Enters the Space Age

Articles from the *New York Times*, July 10, 11, 12, 20, 24, 1962.

Collins, Martin. "Telstar and the World of 1962." Smithsonian National Air and Space Museum, July 23, 2012.

Lewis, Peter H. "The Night the Satellite Flew." *New York Times*, July 5, 1987.

McDougall, Walter, A. *The Heavens and the Earth: A Political History of the Space Age*. New York: Basic Books, 1985.

"Observed in Maine." Space.com, July 11, 2002.

Punnett, Milton B. "First-Hand: Telstar . . . and Some Personal Recollections. https://ethw.org/First-Hand:Telstar..._and_some_personal_recollections.

Solomon, Louis. *Telstar: Communication Break-through by Satellite*. New York: McGraw Hill, 1962.

Zimmerman, Robert. "Telstar." *Invention & Technology*, Fall 2000.

1970s—Maine Holds the Last Log Drive

Author Unknown. "Lawsuits May Terminate Annual Log Drive Down the Kennebec." *New York Times*, April 17, 1971.

Bryant, Ralph Clement. *Logging: The Principles and General Methods of Operation in the United States*. New York: John Wiley & Sons, 1914.

Calder, David. "The Last Log Drive: When a Maine Way of Life Came to an End." *Portland Press Herald*, February 20, 2016.

Caldwell, Bill. *Enjoying Maine*. Portland, ME: Guy Gannett Publishing Co., 1977.

Calvert, Mary R. *The Kennebec Wilderness Awakens*. Lewiston, ME: Twin City Printery, 1986.

Harlow, Doug. "When a Way of Life Ended with the Last Log Drive, a New Kennebec River Emerged." *Lewiston Morning Sentinel*, February 20, 2016.

Judd, Richard W., Edwin A. Churchill and Joel W. Eastman. *Maine: The Pine Tree State from Prehistory to the Present*. Orono: University of Maine Press, 1995.

Kifner, John. "Last Log Drive in U.S. Floating to End in Maine." *New York Times*, September 8, 1976.

Northeast Historic Film. *The Last Log Drive Down the Kennebec* (DVD), 1976.

Osborn, William C. *The Paper Plantation: Ralph Nader's Study Group Report on the Pulp and Paper Industry in Maine*. New York: Viking Press, 1974.

Thoreau, Henry David. *The Maine Woods*. New York: Thomas Y. Crowell Company, 1909.

Winthrop, Theodore. *Life in the Open Air and Other Papers*. New York: John W. Lovell Co., 1862.

Wood, Richard G. *A History of Lumbering in Maine, 1820-1865*. Orono: University of Maine, 1935.

1980s—Samantha Smith Seeks World Peace

Meyers, Tracy Lynn. *Samantha Smith: The Girl Who Dreamed of Peace.* Middletown, DE: Publisher unknown, 2017.

Samantha Smith: Newspaper Stories from the Kennebec Journal. Compiled by the Maine State Library, 1988.

Smith, Samantha. *Journey to the Soviet Union.* Boston, MA: Little, Brown and Company, 1985.

Wagner, Robert J., and Scott Eyman. *Pieces of My Heart: A Life.* New York: HarperCollins, 2008.

1990s—Maine Ices Over; Wiscasset Loses its Schooners

Adams, Abigail. "Ownership of Iconic Wiscasset Shipwreck Artifact Remains in Question after Nearly Four Decades." *Bangor Daily News,* November 18, 2015.

Associated Press. "Scuttled and Dumped, Schooners up for Grabs." *Los Angeles Times,* September 23, 2001.

Author unknown. "Wiscasset Legal Owners of Hesper and Luther Little Remains." *The Lincoln County News,* December 21, 2015.

Di Vece, Phil. "More than just memories remain of schooners *Hesper* and *Luther Little*." *Wiscasset Newspaper,* July 14, 2015.

"Story retold of Wiscasset's *Hesper* and *Luther Little*." *Wiscasset Newspaper,* December 12, 2015.

Goad, Meredith. "Taking wood from derelict schooners becomes the ultimate recycling project." *Portland Press Herald,* June 4, 2017.

Graham, Gillian. "Maine's Historic Ice Storm of 1998 Brought Extraordinary Destruction—and Cooperation." *Portland Press Herald,* January 4, 2018.

Grenon, Ingrid. *Lost Maine Coastal Schooners: From Glory Days to Ghost Ships.* Charleston, SC: The History Press, 2010.

Newspaper articles from the *Daily Kennebec Journal, Bangor Daily News,* and *Portland Press Herald* from January 1998.

Roy, M. Chris. *The Wiscasset Ships: A Remembrance.* Westport Island, ME: Pumpkin Press, 1994.

2000s—Terror Strikes Home; New Mainers Reach Lewiston; Red Sox End a Curse

"Agent who checked in 9/11 hijackers: Bin Laden death brought 'great joy'." CNN, May 3, 2011.

Allen, Mel. "9/11 Started Here." *Yankee,* 2006.

Associated Press. "Fred Hale Sr., world's oldest man at 113." November 21, 2004. http://archive.boston.com/news/globe/obituaries/articles/2004/11/21/fred_hale _sr_worlds_oldest_man_at_113/.

Averett, Nany, Mike Frassinelli, and Christine Schiavo. "Bright Morning, Dark Day." *The Morning Call,* September 10, 2002.

Besteman, Catherine. *Making Refuge: Somali Bantu Refugees and Lewiston, Maine.* Durham, NC: Duke University Press, 2016.

"CDR Robert A. Schlegel, USN." *The National 9/11 Pentagon Memorial.* https://pentagonmemorial.org/explore/biographies/cdr-robert-schlegel-usn.

"Cmdr. Robert Allan Schlegel 9/11/01." *American Infidel.* http://kjw-today.blogspot.com/2009/09/91101_2494.html.

Cullen, Andrew. "Struggle and Promise: 10 Years of Somalis in Lewiston." *Lewiston Sun Journal,* December 18, 2011.

Ellison, Jesse. "Lewiston, Maine, Revived by Somali Immigrants." *Newsweek,* January 16, 2009.

Graettinger, Diana. "A pocketbook full of memories. Friends, family recall Lubec couple who died on Flight 11." *Bangor Daily News,* September 7, 2002.

Harkavy, Jerry. "Encounter haunts ex-ticket agent." *Portland Press Herald,* September 11, 2006.

Harkavy, Jerry. "Somalis find new lives, adjustments in Lewiston." *Lewiston Sun Journal,* May 12, 2007.

Hench, David. "Ticket Agent Haunted by Brush with 9/11 Hijackers." *Portland Press Herald,* March 6, 2005.

Judd, Richard W., Edwin A. Churchill, and Joel W. Eastman. *Maine: The Pine Tree State from Prehistory to the Present.* Orono: University of Maine Press, 1995.

Newspaper articles from the *Bangor Daily News, Daily Kennebec Journal, Boston Globe,* and *Portland Press Herald,* October 2004.

New York Times. "Portraits of Grief." https://archive.nytimes.com/www.nytimes.com/interactive/us/sept-11-reckoning/portraits-of-grief.html.

"9-11 Heroes. In Memory of Stephen Gordon Ward." http://www.9-11heroes.us/v/Stephen_Gordon_Ward.php.

O'Nan, Stewart, and Stephen King. *Faithful: Two Diehard Boston Red Sox Fans Chronicle the Historic 2004 Season.* New York: Scribner, 2004.

"Remembering 9/11 in Maine." *Lewiston Sun Journal,* September 11, 2015.

"Robert Allan Schlegel." Obituary, accessed through Pennlive.com. https://obits.pennlive.com/obituaries/pennlive/obituary.aspx?n=robert-allan-schlegel&pid=93624.

Routhier, Ray. "A Maine Family Reaches for 'Something Positive.'" *Portland Press Herald,* September 9, 2011.

Schulkind, Andy. "Portland Maine, Where 9-11 Began." *The Good Men Project,* September 11, 2015.

Sharp, David. "On eve of 9/11 10th anniversary, Maine airport working to move past notorious notoriety." Associated Press, September 10, 2011.

Skelton, Kathryn. "A Brother Leaving for His Next Adventure: Jim Roux's Sisters Look Back." *Lewiston Sun Journal,* September 4, 2011.

Walsh, Barbara. "Gorham Family Fears for Loved One." *Portland Press Herald,* September 13, 2001.

Zuckoff, Mitchell. *Fall and Rise: The Story of 9/11.* New York: HarperCollins, 2019.

2010s—Maine Gets Elephants and Goes into Space

"An Interview with Both Maine Astronauts" https://www.newscentermaine.com/
   article/entertainment/television/bill-greens-maine/an-intI erview-with-both
   -maine-astronauts/97-b5be5e52-7835-481e-9ef6-f6ef1cb930ff.

Bell, Tom. "Prospective Astronaut from Maine Always on a Mission." *Portland Press
   Herald,* June 19, 2013.

Bettcher, Lewis. "Hope Elephants' Opal Dies in Oklahoma." *Village Soup* (Knox), January 23, 2017. https://knox.villagesoup.com/p/hope-elephants-opal-dies-in
   -oklahoma/1617182.

Curtis, Abigail. "After Hope Elephants Founder's Death, Rosie and Opal going back to
   Oklahoma." *Bangor Daily News,* September 10, 2014.

Davenport, Christian, and Lateshia Beachum. "NASA's All-Female Spacewalk Makes
   History: 'One Giant Leap for WOMANkind!' *Washington Post,* October 18, 2019.

Email from Dr. Chatchote Thitaram.

Graham, Gillian. "Astronaut from Maine Prepares for Takeoff." *Portland Press Herald,*
   September 8, 2019.

Guarino, Ben. "This Astronaut Raised Geese to Study Their Hearts. The Birds Stole
   Hers." *Washington Post,* September 4, 2019.

Interviews with Jim Laurita, Andrew Scott, and Jonathan Duke.

NASA Videos:
   https://blogs.nasa.gov/spacestation/2019/10/18/nasa-astronauts-wrap-up-historic
   -all-woman-spacewalk/.
   https://www.youtube.com/watch?v=t934Df26xIE.
   https://www.youtube.com/watch?v=2UP-Gyk_5dU.
   https://www.facebook.com/watch/?v=890872021295585.